Vocal Vibrance

The Complete Technique for Singers and Speakers

Revised Edition

Suzann Kale

Copyright © 2011 by Suzann Kale

All rights reserved. No part of this publication may be reproduced or transmitted in any form or by any means, electronic or mechanical, including photocopy, recording, or any information storage and retrieval system, without the prior written permission of the author.

ISBN 13: 978-1463566265
ISBN 10: 1463566263

Cover photo Copyright © 2011 James Juhasz. All rights reserved. International copyright laws apply. This photo may not be reproduced or transmitted in any form or by any means.

To Megan, Ian, Aidan, Maddie, and Jesse

To Jamie, Michelle, Emilie and Kip

To my dog Caesar, who could bark in chest tones and howl in head tones.

And to Mary Feinsinger, my awesome New York City voice teacher.

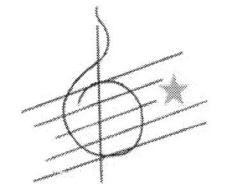

Vocal Vibrance – Revised Edition
The Complete Technique for Singers and Speakers

TABLE OF CONTENTS

Chapter	Page
Introduction: In Search of the Magic Gig	8
The Articulators	13
Breathing	
Why Breathe?	18
Your Body, The Wind Instrument	20
Basic Breathing Technique: The Inhale	21
Basic Breathing Technique: The Exhale	23
Modified Breathing Technique	25
Breathing Exercises: Greatest Hits	26
Breathing: The Terminology Controversy	30
The Diaphragm: Where Is This Thing?	33
Care of the Instrument: The Voice - A Precious Instrument	34
Dynamics	
Energy and Emotion	38
Loud and Soft	46
Ear Training: What Key Is Your Refrigerator In?	54
Elements of Voice Study: What Do You Study When You Study Voice?	64
Ensemble Singing	
Ensemble Singing	66
Anatomy of a Jazz Ensemble	80
Expanding Your Range: Singing - Its Highs and Lows	83
Eye Contact: When to Go Eyeball to Eyeball	90
Finding a Voice Teacher: How to Find the Perfect Voice Teacher	92

Glass Breaking: How to Break Glass	97
Glossary: What Do You Actually *Mean* When You Say I'm Singing Flat?	100
The Glottal Stop	110
The Larynx	112
Legato Singing: Smooth Moves	115
Memorizing: The Challenge of Storage and Retrieval	119
Modes: How to Develop a Bionic Ear	125
Phlegm: Can't Live With It, Can't Live Without It	131
Pop, Rock and Belt: Belting	135
Reading Music: Where to Begin	138
Registers: The "Breaking Point" - The Story of Registers, Ranges, and Bridging the Gap	142
Rehearsal Tapes	150
Resonance: Resonance, Placement, and Tone	152
The "R" Sound	160
Scat Singing: A Scat for All Genres	162
Singer's Formant	174
Song Singing: Repertoire, Upkeep, and Automatic Pilot	177
Speaking: Elements of a Good Speaking Voice	184
Stage Fright: Stage Fright and Bubonic Plague - A Comparative Study	188
Toning: It Just Feels Good	193
Vibrato: If You're Calm, You Will Oscillate	196
Vocal Cords	202

<u>V</u>ocalizing: How to Vocalize	203
<u>V</u>oice and Age	212
<u>V</u>owel Sounds: Their Importance, Their Pronunciations	216
<u>W</u>arm-ups	
Warm-up I	225
Warm-up II	230
Warm-up III	236

**The Complete Technique
for Singers and Speakers**

Overview
Beautiful, effective, *dependable* vocal production that is uniquely tailored to an individual's specific needs, is a reachable goal for almost everyone. How? Through technical learning and training the muscles, and through practice and repetition. You practice until the techniques become automatic. After that you can concentrate on the meaning of the song.

This book can help you in many ways. You can use it to study voice on your own. You can use it as an adjunct to your voice lessons or classes. If you're a teacher, you can use it as a reference or text book. Those who are already musically accomplished can use **Vocal Vibrance** to refresh learning, practice new skills, or look up specific trouble spots. **All the subjects are alphabetical, so you can easily find whatever you need.**

Set Your Own Pace: Design Your Own Course
There is a logical order to studying voice, and I would suggest you begin with breathing. After that, go to the chapter on vowel sounds followed by the chapter on resonance. The warm-up chapters can be studied concurrently with all the material. But aside from this general sequence, it's really up to you. There cannot be one way to learn voice that is suitable for everyone.

Therefore, **Vocal Vibrance** requires you to tune in to yourself. You must know your voice, know your strengths and weaknesses, and especially know your goals.

And because you are designing your own program, you can be creative with it. Design your own vocal exercises, based on the examples I give in the different chapters. Play with the material; test different placements within your own body to see which placements produce what kinds of sounds. Then zero in on the sounds you want to keep. Work with the breathing techniques I describe, and then develop your own mental imagery that best brings these techniques to life.

Chaos to Order: We Take It Apart, Then We Put It Back Together

The different aspects of vocal production are taken apart for you in this book, so you can work on them individually; so you can concentrate on just your problem areas, or focus on your strong areas. You can see from the Table of Contents, there are chapters on Inhaling, Exhaling, How to Pronounce the "A" Sound, Stage Fright, Vibrato, and just about anything you can think of.

But at some point we must put it all back together again and make it one smooth, fluid whole. Singing or speaking is not inhalation, *then* muscle pushing out air, *then* articulator definition, *then* decisions about loud and soft. It's a totality of expression. It's one unit. The goal in learning the technical aspects of singing and speaking is to become so proficient in them that they become automatic.

Once your breathing, vowel sounds, tone production, and all the other elements become automatic - so automatic you don't have to think about them but they happen correctly anyway - then you can put the magic into your voice. Then you can let the emotion of the song carry you away.

The Magic Circle

Singing rides on the breath, glides over the vocal cords and articulators, resonates off the well-toned body's internal surfaces, and projects tones, overtones, ideas, and feelings that then resonate with a listener. It begins and ends with the breath - with taking in and giving out. It's a circle.

And for the listener, it begins and ends with taking in and giving back as well - for the listener is part of the circle, and the listener gives back information to the singer who then responds in kind to the listener. Thus even between singer and audience there is a constant dynamic of change; a continual flow of energy and information; a seeking of harmonic resonance and matching vibration.

I hope this book will help you on your path to many magic gigs.

The Articulators

The Articulators. It sounds like some sort of terminator squad. And indeed, untrained, unflexed, stiff articulators can ruin your sound. The articulators (lips, tongue, teeth, and jaw) are the shapers, if you will, of the tone that is produced by the supported breath. These "instrument parts" have the final say as to what your voice will sound like.

The worst enemy of the articulators is tension. Give in to facial tension and you'll be hearing yourself produce mangled words and pinched sounds.
Flexible, agile articulators are what we're after here. In general, try to let the tongue and lips do most of the work - not the jaw. The tongue and lips can move quickly and adeptly to handle most vowels and consonants with a minimum of disruption to the fluidity of tone and sound. But let's look at these potential terminators one by one.

Jaw - The Hinged Articulator
The jaw needs to be especially relaxed. You will never hear singing teachers say, "Open your mouth." They will say, "Drop your jaw." If you hear "open your mouth" you've ended up at the dentist's by mistake.
But think about it - at the dentist's, you open your mouth, you sit there with it open like a crocodile for eons, and while you're doing this you're carrying on some kind of gnarled conversation. It's physically stressful, right? In singing, we need to avoid stress and produce coherent sounds. Therefore, we use the image of the jaw being on swings which then allow for the free flowing movement.

You can actually feel these swings, or hinges. Place a finger on either side of your head, just in front of the lower part of your ear, above the bottom of the earlobe. Now talk or sing. Do you feel that?

The other problem with crocodile mouth is the implication that the upper lip and roof of the mouth open upwards while the jaw opens downward. This is incorrect. The only part of the head that actually moves is the lower jaw. The upper part of the head stays put.

As loose and hinged as the lower jaw is, there is one direction it must not swing. That is forward. The jaw drops <u>downward.</u> It does not jut out. Sing in front of a mirror to see what's going on.

Jaw Check

Say the word "dah," dropping your jaw on the "ah". As you drop your jaw, make sure it is relaxed and that it does not jut forward. Feel it just fall. Don't force it open or down. (Have you ever sat in the front of the airplane on a red-eye flight and after an hour or so looked back at the rows of people behind you? Chances are, you've seen a sea of dropped jaws as people have fallen asleep sitting up. This is the kind of dropped jaw - rather than opened mouth - we're going for.)

Teeth

As the jaw drops, so of course do the lower teeth. It is possible, and I have seen singers do it, to drop the jaw (or attempt to) and keep the teeth somewhat clenched. The resulting sound is stiff and stifled. Again, the mirror is a quick way to check for this habit. And while you're at the mirror, check that you don't see too much of your lower teeth during singing or speaking. Lower teeth that are too visible would indicate tension in the lips.

Tongue

That most unruly of muscles, the tongue has a mind of its own. Sometimes it seems like the more you try to get it to lie flat in your mouth, the more rambunctious and out of control it gets. It's a mental thing. But the tongue should indeed lie flat, though relaxed, during much of your singing, with the tip of the tongue gently touching the back of the bottom teeth. When the tongue moves to articulate consonants, it then goes back to its place, resting gently on the bottom of your mouth.

Be careful, though - if the tongue is too flat, and becomes tense, you will choke your sound. When we talk about a "flat" tongue, we mean a relaxed tongue rather than a stiff slab.

Lips

The lips must be flexible and loose. When the jaw drops, the lips must follow - although you don't want them to exaggerate or anticipate the jaw motion.

Articulator Exercises

Any vocal exercises you can think up that will loosen the articulators and relax your face is probably a good exercise. Here are some examples:

Rubber Lips (from Warm-Up I)

Sing (on one note in your midrange) or speak the syllables "may mee mah moh moo", making sure each vowel sound is pronounced perfectly and clearly. Gradually build to a faster and faster tempo, still keeping the vowel sounds pure and the articulators relaxed. The minute you hit tension or slack off on enunciation, go back to a slightly slower pace. If singing, change pitch with each repetition, going up chromatically. Don't go higher or lower than is comfortable. Change consonants when you feel like it (lay lee lah loh loo, bay bee bah boh boo, etc.).

Yeow

In slow motion, quietly say the word "yeow," exaggerating each sound. You should feel like a cat yawning. Start with "yee", then drop the jaw as you expand to "ah", then round out the mouth as you continue through to "ow" and finally round the lips (but don't clench the teeth) as you finish with the "oo" sound of "yeow."

Lip Relaxer

Slowly say the sound "buh", with air under the upper lip. It's like an exaggeratedly loose lip motion, while keeping the whole face very relaxed. Repeat it for a minute or so. Go up and down 5-note scales in your midrange with this sound.

Tongue Twisters

Drag out all the old tongue twisters you knew as a kid. Say them and then sing them all on one note.

Tongue and Jaw Relaxer

Sing or say "lah" 10 times in a row, *keeping your jaw dropped the whole time.* The only thing that moves in this exercise is the tongue. Check in the mirror to make sure the rest of your face is still.

Neck Rolls

If your health practitioner gives you the OK, gently do your neck rolls while keeping your shoulders down, relaxed, and still.

Tongue Trill and Lip Trills

Do these exercises as described in Warm-up I. Then repeat the Lip or Tongue Trill, except this time, do it on one note. Begin softly and crescendo. Repeat a half step up - start mezzo piano and crescendo to mezzo forte. Make sure the crescendo is even. (This is not only a great articulator exercise, it also assures you of singing with a supported breath. It's almost impossible to do these exercises without a correct breathing technique.)

Tongue Release

Contract and release the tongue, to get to know the sensation of the release.

Isolations

Sing "nah" on one note in your midrange. Keep the sound in place (keep your tone even throughout the exercise) and one by one release the tongue, release tension in the lips, let the jaw feel released, if it doesn't already. Breathe when you have to. Then continue releasing one by one, the neck, shoulders, elbows, knees.

Fluid Articulators

Looking into your mirror, sing "nah, nay, nee, noh, noo" up a five note scale beginning at a point in your midrange. Make sure that as you change pitch your head does not move. Keep doing this exercise, going up a half step with each repetition, making sure, too, that your facial expression does not change as the music changes. Keep your head up and posture erect.

Some bad habits that many singers get into are:
- ♪ Looking down, instead of up and out
- ♪ Furrowing the brow or forehead in concentration
- ♪ Making a nodding motion with the head on pitch changes -looking worried as the high notes approach
- ♪ Tensing the articulators as the high notes approach - letting the tongue pull back
- ♪ Jutting the jaw forward.

Nah nay nee noh   noo,   Nah nay nee noh noo

"Ee" Up. "Ah" Down
Do this exercise as described in the chapter on resonance, but this time do it in front of a mirror. The tongue should be relaxed and flat during the entire exercise. Though the jaw may move ever so slightly as you change from "ee" to "ah," the tongue should stay still.

The Long and Short of It
In articulation in general, you want to make sure your vowel sounds are elongated (remember, tone carries on vowel sounds) and your consonants are short. Practice this on the following phrases. Remember, too, that when you start each note, the beginning consonant must be exactly on pitch. If you don't think of consonants as being on the same pitch as the following vowel, you risk singing flat - or worse, swooping up to the note.

moderately slow

Bring back the mu- sic let's bring back the dance

Bring back the mMu- sisic let's bring back the dance

Bring back the mmu- sic let's bring back the dance

Notes:

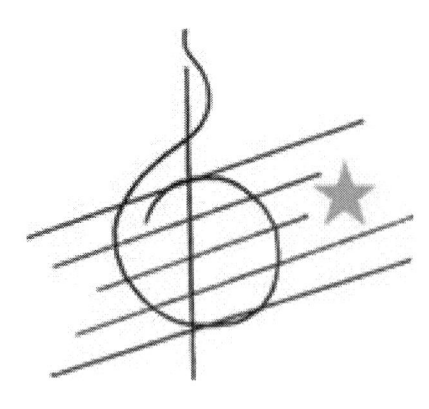

Breathing: Why Breathe?

Why do anything? To sing, of course.

But breathing to sing is a learned technique - it's not the daily shallow breathing we tend to do. It involves developing the diaphragm and the muscles supporting the lower ribcage. Some people master it easily - and for others it takes longer. But once learned, it becomes automatic - meaning that it will come naturally to you without your having to think about it. Still, even after the technique is learned and becomes automatic, it should be practiced daily, just as an athlete would work out daily, to keep the muscles in shape.

Choose Your Own Technique

Since each person's instrument is different, each person will need to make their breathing technique their own. For some that means simplifying - for others it means getting the diaphragm muscle so strong you can lie on your back on the floor and let your three-year old stand on it.

I've got two breathing techniques for you to try. You may already use slightly different versions. Whatever works for you (gives you the control you need, allows beautiful tone to come out, and keeps your voice healthy) is what you should do.

The first technique is a basic, classical breathing technique (page 21-24). It's suitable for any style of singing, and will allow you to go places with your voice you may never have dreamed possible. I love it. It's magic. It takes a great deal of practice to master, and then more practice for it to become automatic. I think it's worth it.

The second technique is a modified version of this basic, classical breathing (page 25). It's almost the same, will be just as magical, but is a little easier to learn. If you use a microphone a lot, the modified technique is perfect.

The Perks
Whatever technique you choose, the important actions are:
- ✓ learn it,
- ✓ let it become automatic,
- ✓ use it whenever you sing.

Use it when you vocalize, warm-up, use it when you're doodling at the piano learning a new song. Never sing without it.

Good breathing is essential to the health of your voice over a lifetime. It will expand your range dramatically. It is basic to tone, pitch precision, and fluidity. It will allow you to sing and speak for hours without becoming fatigue or hoarse. A breathing technique will solve a myriad of problems that manifest themselves as glitches or impurities in the sound of the voice. **I guarantee, singers who sound good in their later years are singers who have learned to breathe. That's their secret.**

Notes:

Breathing:
Your Body, the Wind Instrument

The "Basic" breathing technique is based on a controlled expansion and contraction of the diaphragm and lower ribcage. **On the inhale**, the lower ribs (never the upper chest) gently and evenly expand out to the sides (not up), as the diaphragm is expanding. **On the exhale**, the lower ribs stay stationary in their expanded state while the diaphragm contracts. Upon contraction of the diaphragm, the ribs then slowly and evenly contract.

All this is done in one graceful, fluid motion.

(If you're using the "Modified" version, your inhale will be the same - but on the exhale the ribs and diaphragm will contract at the same time, rather than separately.)

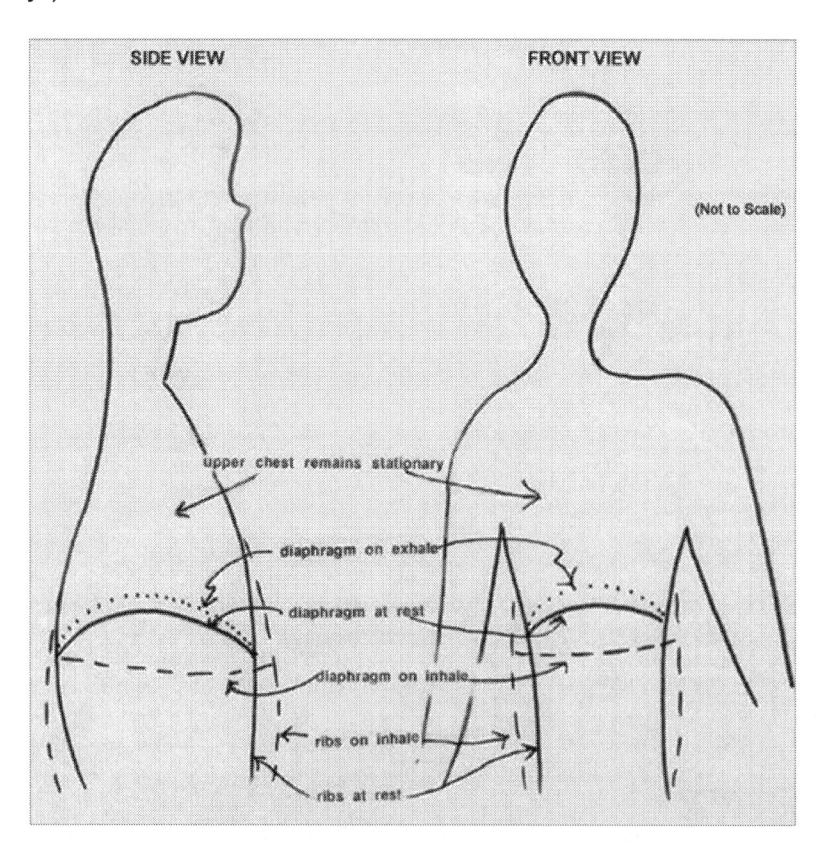

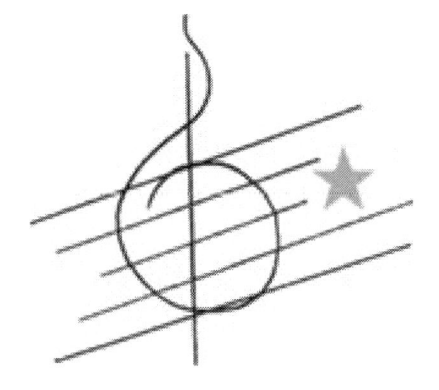

Breathing

**Basic Breathing Technique:
The Inhale**

1. Posture
♪ If sitting, sit with feet flat on the floor in a relaxed way, back straight, and head up but not tilted back. Shoulders relaxed but not rounded.
♪ Standing is preferable.
- Stand with one foot slightly in front of the other to prevent knees locking.
- Back straight.
- Shoulders down and back. Relaxed. Not rolled forward.
- Head up but not tilted back or rolled forward.
- Arms gently at sides, elbows slightly bent to prevent locking.
- Neck and jaw consciously relaxed.

♪ Imagine a string pulling you up from a point in the center of your chest (not the top of your head).

Note: Breathe in through the nose when possible
♪ Mouth inhalation can tighten and dry out the throat, but is handy to use in an emergency (an emergency being a cold or allergies, or a song where you have a 16th of a beat in which to take in enough air to last you for the next 20 beats!).
♪ Keep the throat "opened." (This is the same sensation you get in the back of your throat when you yawn with your mouth closed.)

2. In one smooth motion, your lower ribs expand outward to all sides, and your diaphragm and lower abdomen expand to the front
♪ The expansion of the ribs and diaphragm will <u>naturally</u> draw the air into your lungs.
♪ You're not pulling air in - you're letting it fall in.
♪ There should be no tension in the neck.
♪ The inhale is slow and gentle.
♪ The shoulders and upper chest remain stationery throughout. Check this in a mirror.
♪ Some singers used the mental image of your lower abdomen being like a

balloon that's filling up.
♪ Another mental image used by many singers is that the lower ribs expand around the entire body, even the back.

3. Don't overstuff
♪ Too much air can cause tension.
♪ You only need to take in enough air for the upcoming phrase. If you need more air - you can always breathe again.
♪ For learning and practicing purposes, a 5 second inhale works well.
♪ When you are comfortable with the technique, however, you'll want to practice inhaling more quickly, and more slowly - to accommodate the variables that will come up when singing a song. Practice the inhale on 3 seconds. Practice it on 7 seconds.

4. Inhale with a minimum of noise
♪ Gasping is not aesthetic.
♪ If you're on mike in a studio, every little gurgle will be picked up and amplified - even a rumbling stomach.

5. At the "top" of the inhale, turn smoothly around into your exhale
♪ The big rule here is: **DON'T STOP AT THE TOP.** That means, don't hold your breath between inhaling and exhaling - not even for a second.

♪ Think of breathing as one continuous circle of inhale/exhale.

Notes:

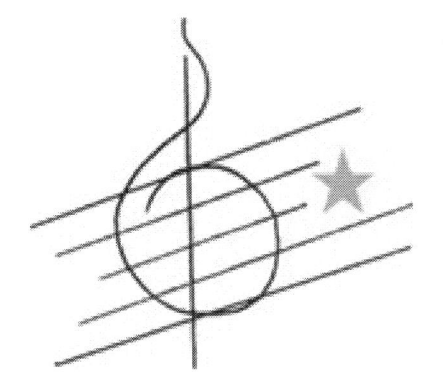

Breathing

**Basic Breathing Technique:
The Exhale**

1. From the top of the inhale, begin the exhale
> ♪ It's one smooth circle of inhaling and exhaling. There is no stop or pause before exhaling. Don't hold your breath, even for a moment, between the inhale and the exhale.

2. To begin the exhale, the diaphragm firmly and slowly contracts
> ♪ This diaphragmatic contraction pushes the air from the lungs, through the larynx, over the vocal cords, and out the mouth.
> ♪ The pressure exerted by the diaphragm is gradual and controlled.

3. As the diaphragm begins its contraction, the lower ribs stay stationary in their expanded position
> ♪ It takes practice for the muscles surrounding the lower ribs to become strong enough to support them in this position without fatigue or stress.
> ♪ Your goal here is *strength without stress*.

4. As the diaphragm finishes its contraction, the lower ribs then begin to contract, keeping the airflow smooth, slow, and even
> ♪ The diaphragm finishes its contraction before it becomes stressed. We're not doing yoga here, or martial arts. There's no need to push out every ounce of air.
> ♪ There is no break or pause as the diaphragm ends its contraction and the muscles surrounding the ribs take over. The change is controlled and flowing.
> ♪ A continuous, even airflow will produce an even, controlled sound.

5. The abdominal muscles help support the diaphragm and ribcage

♪ It's OK to let the "stomach" muscles help out. We don't need to isolate the muscles to the degree that a dancer might need to. Besides, making the diaphragm do all the work can produce tension in the neck.

6. The exhale can take 10 seconds, more or less

♪ For the purposes of learning the technique, 10 seconds is a good goal.
♪ But you will want to expand your practice to include inhales and exhales at slower and faster rates. That's because when you sing, you will need to breathe to accommodate the song's tempo, the phrasing within the song, and other variables.
♪ Although these instructions are divided into steps, the entire process, when mastered, is really one, smooth step.
♪ There is no tension in the body, except for the muscle tension needed to contract the diaphragm and then the ribcage.
♪ To monitor how smooth and even your exhale is, you can exhale on a soft hissing sound. This will give you immediate feedback. Keep the hissing sound perfectly even, and this will tell you your muscles are contracting evenly.

7. Stop gracefully BEFORE you're out of air

♪ Oddly enough, many singers, when practicing, squeeze out every last little bit of oxygen. Don't do that. If you force air out, you'll get a forced sound.

Notes:

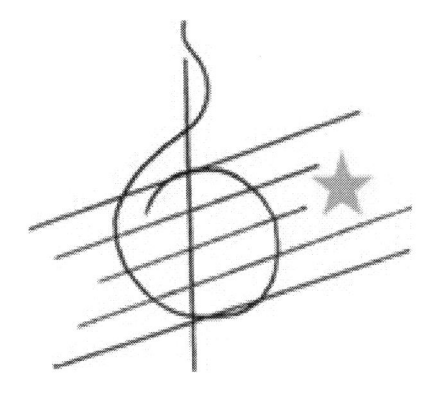

Breathing

Modified Breathing Technique

1. The Inhale
♪ Is the same as "The Basic Technique."

♪ Or, to modify it further, some people think in terms of "expanding the abdomen" on the inhale, rather than targeting specifically the diaphragm and lower ribs.

2. The Exhale
♪ Is the same as "The Basic Technique" <u>except</u> that your lower ribs will contract <u>as you contract the diaphragm,</u> rather than after the diaphragm has contracted.

♪ This contraction of the diaphragm/lower ribs/abdomen is one smooth, even, motion - producing a smooth, even sound.

♪ All the other details of "The Basic Technique" remain the same: strength without stress, ending phrases gracefully, and the production of a controlled, continuous stream of air.

Notes:

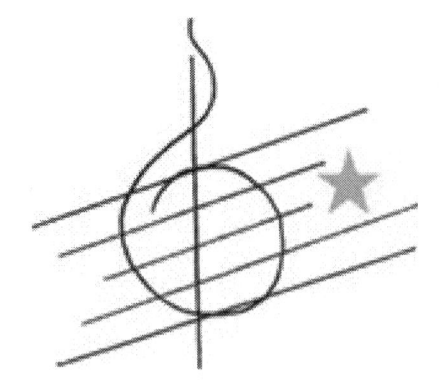

Breathing

Breathing Exercises: Greatest Hits

Following is a potpourri of breathing exercises. Choose the ones you like, vary your exercises, do 5 to 20 minutes every day. Consistency of practice is more important than the length of your practice session.

In addition to the exercises here, check out the three **Warm-up** sections for more.

Levitation
This is an exercise to isolate and strengthen the diaphragm and its surrounding muscles.

1) Lie on your back on the couch.
2) Place a book on your abdomen just below the "V" of your ribcage, and above your naval. (To find this spot exactly, see the chapter called "The Diaphragm: Where Is This Thing?").
3) Place your hands gently by your side.
4) Now use your muscles to raise and lower this book.
5) With time, you should be able to use heavier and heavier books.

Dog Pant
This exercise will also isolate and strengthen the diaphragm and surrounding muscles.

- ♪ Sit straight up in a chair. Don't lean back.
- ♪ Place your hands gently on the diaphragm area of your lower abdomen, to monitor its movement.
- ♪ Expand your diaphragm/lower abdomen and then contract it, quickly and sharply. On the expansion (inhale) the diaphragm pushes your hands outward. On the contraction (exhale), you feel the diaphragm move in.
- ♪ On the contraction, there is also a feeling of the diaphragm moving sharply up, as if you were expelling something that went down the wrong way.
- ♪ Use mouth breathing for this exercise.

Smelling the Roses
    a) Stand, and place your hands gently on the sides of your ribs to monitor the movement. If you place your hands with your thumbs pointing toward your back, your fingers can then extend toward the front of your abdomen and you'll be able to monitor both the ribs and the abdominal activity.
    b) Breathing in through your nose, pretend you are revelling in the scent of a beautiful rose. You are relaxed as you inhale gently but fully (although not overstuffed). Your upper chest is motionless, and your ribs expand slowly and evenly out to the sides as you diaphragm expands slowly and evenly out toward the front. (If you feel tension in your neck, you have taken in too much air.)
    c) At the top of the inhale, without any stop of any kind, turn around and begin a slow, even contraction of the diaphragm. *
    d) Let the air come out of your mouth.
    e) As the diaphragm nears its stopping point, allow the ribs to continue the contraction, seamlessly taking over where the diaphragm left off.*

    *-If you are using the "Modified Breathing Method," let the diaphragm and ribs contract evenly *at the same time,* rather than keeping the ribs expanded during the diaphragm's contraction.

Upside Down Inhale
- ♪ Sit on a chair, and bend over at the waist.
- ♪ Now inhale.
- ♪ Hold the inhale and sit up. You should find that you have naturally inhaled from the lower abdominal area, with the upper chest and neck completely uninvolved.
- ♪ Exhale gently through the mouth.

Rib Expansion
- ✓ Stand with your hands at your sides, palms facing outward. Raise your arms out to your sides, palms up, inhaling through the nose as you do so. You should feel your lower ribs moving up and out to the sides as you inhale.
- ✓ Lower your arms, keeping your ribs expanded. Feel the sensation of the expanded lower ribs! This is a fabulous exercise.
- ✓ Now exhale through the mouth, allowing the ribs to gently contract.

Count Breathing
You'll find this in "Warm-up III." It's a staple for many singers.

Staccato Diaphragm
It's in "Warm-up II," and it's called "Diaphragm Debriefer." It's a fabulous

strengthening exercise.

Related Strengtheners
Physical exercise, playing a wind instrument, and yoga are all helpful. Some singers report beneficial effects from practicing martial arts.

The Swoop
You never want to swoop up to notes when you sing. So do this exercise and then deny deny deny.
   1. In a standing position, inhale from the lower ribs / diaphragm.
   2. Without stopping or holding your breath, turn at the top for your exhale.
   3. On the exhale, sing "oo" and consciously push the "oo" sound from a medium low pitch in your range, up to a medium high pitch. Do this on a glide, or swoop. As you swoop up, feel the inward and upward push of your diaphragm.
   4. The feeling is that the muscular contraction of the diaphragm causes the sound to be pushed out and up.

The Short and Long of It
When you sing, you will be taking in and releasing different amounts of air, depending on the demands of the song and the phrasing. For a short, quick phrase, you don't need to inhale to full capacity. For a long or difficult passage, you will need more breath. Therefore it is helpful in your vocalizing to include breathing exercises that teach your body smooth, even, and "fluid" breathing on both long and short phrases.

   -Choose a song that you sing, and separate out phrases of different lengths. Use these phrases as exercises, and practice singing them with just the right amount of breath - not too much, not too little.

   -You can do the same exercise over scales and arpeggios. Coordinate your muscles in such a way that you have enough breath to complete phrases of varied length with comfort and an even, consistent tone.

Mental Telepathy
So much of singing comes not from the diaphragm and ribs at all, but from the mind! Here are some images many singers use to make their breathing more effective.
   → You don't pull air in when you inhale. Instead, you expand your lower abdominal muscles, and create a vacuum, allowing the air to then fall into your lungs. To quote Frederick H. Haywood from his book ***Universal Song***, "*Expand to breathe. Do not breathe to expand.*"

- Some singers imagine the air coming in from their feet. This is a grounding and strengthening image. There is a wide variety of bodily images that singers use as inhalation points.
- Imagining your body as a wind instrument, feel as if your neck, throat, and upper chest are merely <u>conduits</u> between your nose and your abdominal muscles. Nothing happens in your neck except that it allows the air to flow freely through it. It's completely passive.
- The back of the throat is thought of as being "opened." It's an unobstructed passageway through which air freely flows. This is the feeling you get when you yawn with your mouth closed.
- Imagine that there is an immediate and direct connecting link between your lower abdominal muscles/diaphragm, and your sound. I call it "the connection."
- There should be a <u>circular</u> feeling or sensation during breathing. Some singers, when they vocalize, place a hand in front of them and draw slow circles in the air to reinforce that seamless, fluid, consistent, even feeling. The breath comes in and goes out as one natural movement, never as a series of stressful events. Of course, to get to this point of seamlessness you need to practice every day - which brings us to the top of the circle of this chapter.

Notes:

**Breathing:
The Terminology Controversy**

There exists in the world of music great emotion surrounding terminology. Of course, there exists in the world of music great emotion, period. But I have seen heated, crisis- level "exchanges" between singers on subjects that leave the layperson dumbfounded - such as vibrato, whistle register, and fach. Singers' Internet threads go on in astonishing detail for weeks on such subjects as chapped lips, nasal douching, and formant. But I have never seen quite the level of volatility as I have seen surrounding the subject of breathing.

If you want to get a singer's attention, start a controversy about breathing. If you're out on a first date with a singer and you don't know how to get the conversation going - ask a question, any question, about breathing.

And the funny thing is, aside from different basic breathing techniques, most of all the brouhaha centers not around breathing per se - no one doubts that we all need to breathe. We will begrudgingly admit that even non-singers breathe. The controversies usually revolve around simple terminology.

How to Get Your Heart Rate Up

Terms like "contract" and "expand" can cause raised heartbeats and sweating palms in musical circles. Especially when talking about the diaphragm action during inhalation and exhalation. Some excellent singers describe their diaphragm as expanding on the inhale and contracting on the exhale. Other equally competent singers will adamantly say that the diaphragm contracts on the inhale and relaxes on the exhale.

What's happening is that we each perceive close to the same phenomena, but we define them differently. Much of what we describe in singing is not described in scientific terms, but rather in terms that elicit certain mental images that singers find helpful. Singing is an incredibly mental, emotional, and spiritual thing. The act of producing specific sounds and hitting specific pitches with certain timbres is much more mental than scientific. You can measure, describe, label, and quantify sound production in the lab - but you can't quantify how a certain singer gets that "certain something" into his or her voice - that certain nuance that is unique to them; that particular, recognizable uniqueness; that tone that conveys an attitude or experience that is particular to that one singer.

So OK. Back to defining things differently. When a singer inhales, the diaphragm, which is a muscle, moves downward. This downward motion creates a vacuum which is quickly filled by air falling into the lungs. Now. When singers vocalize, they often place a hand gently on the spot on the abdomen where the diaphragm connects - because that's where they can feel some of its action and check to make sure it's moving correctly.

In fact, however, the diaphragm cuts across the entire cavity, and what we feel or see in the abdomen is a small part of what's going on in there. A scientist might describe the movement of the diaphragm during inhalation as "downward." I personally define it as "expansion" because that's what I feel, that's what I see in the mirror, and that's what works for me as a singer - it brings me the results I want.

However if you look at a picture of the diaphragm on the inhale, it actually looks like it's "flattening." At rest it's curved upwards. So some people describe the diaphragmatic action on the inhale as "flattening." It is flattening, but for me that term doesn't work because flattening makes me think of "pulling in my stomach" as in "it's bikini season again." So I use "expand." (Not that "expand" has helped the bikini thing either, but hey.)

On the exhale, someone might define the diaphragmatic activity as "relaxation." I like to define it as "contraction," because it feels as if the muscle is contracting. The more smoothly and evenly it "contracts," the more smoothly and evenly singers will be producing their sound. Also, the word "contraction" connotes some action on the singer's part; some control over the muscle. Thus the "contraction" pushes the air - hopefully smoothly and evenly - out of the lungs. For me, "relaxation" of the diaphragm during exhalation doesn't work because it's too passive.

Why It's OK to Write in Book Margins

Here's what to do: Find what's right for <u>YOU.</u> Discover what mental images and terms give you the breath and the voice that you want. Each singer is different in how they learn and how they work. Embrace all the knowledge you can get hold of, try it, discard what doesn't work for you and keep what works. Make notes in the margins of this book.

Within the context of treating your voice with respect, go ahead and try different things. Don't be afraid of things that are called something other than what you are used to calling them. Try them anyway - and call them whatever you need to call them to make sense of things.

Notes:

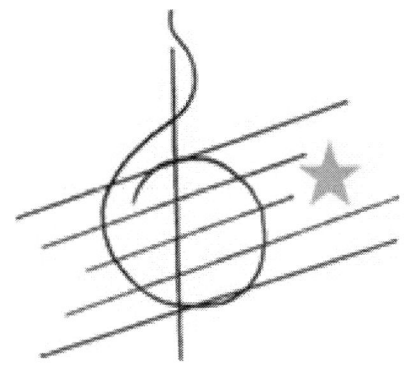

The Diaphragm:
Where Is This Thing?

In many breathing exercises you are asked to place a hand gently on the diaphragm in order to monitor its action. Here's how to find it:

Place your hand on your solar plexus at a spot above your naval, and just below the "v" where your ribs come together in the middle. Now cough. You should feel one small area that moves with more strength or force than the rest of the abdominal area. If coughing doesn't do it for you, try laughing. (What you will feel is only a few small square inches, even though the actual diaphragm is much larger.) When singing teachers say to place a hand on your diaphragm in order to monitor its movement, this is where the hand goes.

Still haven't found it? OK. Place the palm of your hand on your solar plexus again. Using a low, booming voice, try yelling "Hey!", pretending that your sound must quickly reach a parking lot attendant far far away who is revving the engine of your new Porsche. Yes, that's the spot.

This is the point where the diaphragm seems to "join" the solar plexus. Here's what it would look like if life were simple:

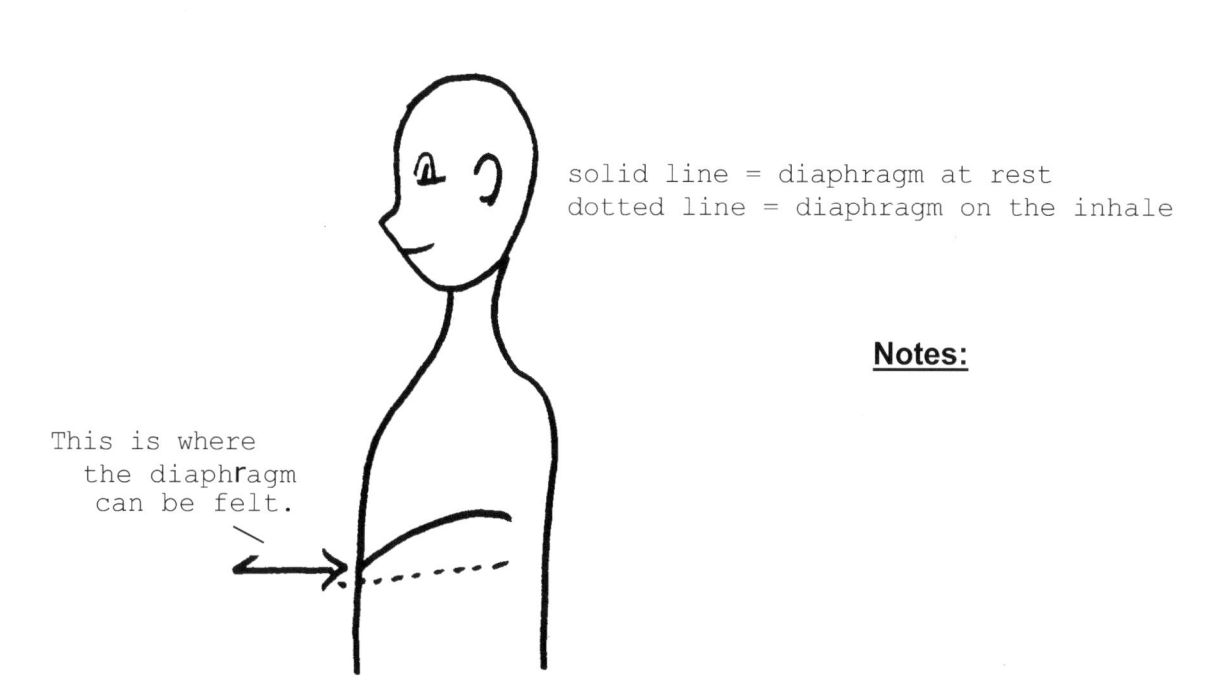

```
solid line = diaphragm at rest
dotted line = diaphragm on the inhale
```

Notes:

This is where the diaphragm can be felt.

Care of the Instrument

The Voice - A Precious Instrument

The care given to Stradivari violins is legendary. Shouldn't singers and speakers take the same care of the voice? An exquisite violinist can make people cry, just by the way the instrument is played - and so can the tone of the voice. The voice can soothe, it can encourage, it can, through nuances that can't even be defined, project the deepest of ideas. Part of singing and speaking is taking care of this priceless instrument, so it can serve you to its fullest capacity. Here are some ideas:

The big warning sign: a pain in the neck

♪ If you feel pain in the throat area, it's time to stop and assess how you're using your voice. In voice lessons, singing, and vocalizing, there should never be pain, sore throats, or hoarseness.

♪ Are you breathing properly? Often a pain in the neck means that the breath is too shallow and is not coming from the right place. Check out the chapter on breathing, and see if you need work in this area.

♪ Is there tension in your body? Physical tension can leave you hoarse or sore. Check specifically your jaw and neck. (Is your jaw tight, or locked? Are veins sticking out of your neck when you inhale, or when you sing? Watch yourself in the mirror or on videotape.) Other common stress-holders are the shoulders, chest, arms (specifically elbows), and knees.

♪ Are you rested? If you're pushing yourself when you're exhausted, you're hurting yourself. That's one thing about being a singer - you simply have no choice but to take care of yourself.

♪ How's your placement? If you are straining to hit high notes in your chest register when you could hit them more easily in your head register, you can hurt your voice. Conversely, if you sing too low in your head register, this can hurt. (Check out the chapter on "Resonance, Placement, and Tone.")

♪ If you smoke or are around a lot of smoke... but you knew that.

♪ If you can't hear yourself on the bandstand (poor monitors, too loud a club, improper balance through the sound system, too loud a drummer), you may find yourself yelling instead of singing, or "pushing," just to be heard. Doing this chronically is dangerous to the longevity of your voice, and many say can contribute to nodes. Tell the drummer to use brushes, and have a talk with the club manager about the sound system. Get the food servers to put that loud espresso machine in another part of the restaurant.

♪ Other causes of a sore throat, like allergies, should be checked out with your health practitioner.

Remember that your voice will naturally be different every day.

♪ Like an athlete, get to know your voice and its "moods." Work with these changes, and gage your daily practice so you are "in tune with" how your voice feels that day.

♪ Never strain your voice (i.e. Don't sing higher or lower than is comfortable, don't sing louder than is comfortable, don't vocalize longer than is comfortable).

♪ Begin your practice in the <u>middle</u> of your range for that day. Extend upward and downward as your voice warms up.

♪ If your voice is strained from mis-use (such as yelling at a sports event the night before, or singing too loudly in choir practice), you cannot do a full workout.

-Stop using your voice for a few days in order to let it heal.

-If you're resting your voice, you can still practice breathing and relaxation exercises that are pitchless. That way you will stay in shape while healing your cords.

Keep the instrument hydrated with lots of water. (Many singers avoid ice.)

Begin your daily practice with warm-ups and your easiest exercises.

♪You can even start your practice by swinging your arms or shaking out your legs, to warm up and loosen up the body.

♪Work up to the more difficult exercises as your practice time goes on.

♪Take one to two minute breaks every ten minutes or so of practice time.

Always avoid:
♪Yelling.

♪Trying to carry on an involved conversation in a noisy environment. So much for discussing Nietzsche at Ringling Brothers Circus.

♪Violent throat clearing; coughing just out of habit.

♪Doing your daily speaking in the wrong "range."

-Yikes. "Range" for speaking? Yes, this is the new thing to worry about. If your speaking voice is constantly too high or too low for what is natural to the way your instrument is built, you can experience chronic sore throats. Your voice instructor will help you find your correct range. If the problem is serious, a speech pathologist might help.

-How do you know if you're speaking in the correct range? For one thing, you won't experience sore throats. If you get a lot of sore throats and all the other variables mentioned in this chapter check out for the positive, you may be speaking daily in the wrong range. Or you might be doing it on purpose - are you trying to force your voice to sound lower than it normally does, for some kind of sexy effect? Or higher, for some kind of feminine effect?

♪Drafts, or cold air on your neck.

♪Most singers wear scarves at the first sign of cool weather. And don't forget a scarf when you go to the movies in the middle of summer. Sitting there with a won't-quit, industrial-strength air conditioner hurling drafty arrows directly at your neck for two hours is dangerous business. I know it might look a little strange going into the movies when it's 95 degrees out, carrying an overcoat and wool scarf, but hey - in your heart of hearts, didn't you always want to be eccentric anyway?

See also the chapters on:
"Voice and Age"
"Phlegm"
"Resonance, Placement, and Tone"
"Breathing"

Notes:

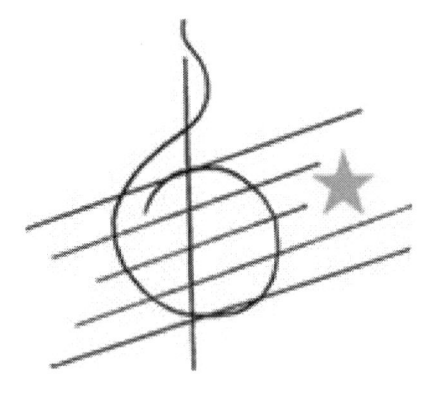

Dynamics: Energy and Emotion

What are dynamics?

♪ In singing, the term "dynamics" usually refers to loud and soft, crescendo and decrescendo.

♪ How one interprets a song dynamically, however, can also mean how the artist uses energies and emotions to project certain ideas, moods, and feelings to the listeners.

♪ "Dynamic" means vibrant, alive, moving, flowing, changing.

♪ A static interpretation of a song or speech is one that doesn't change from beginning to end; that doesn't go anywhere; that doesn't take the listener anywhere. It's boring. You've got to "move" your listeners. Find that spark.

♪ A singer or speaker needs to be experienced and practiced enough to that technique is automatic. When the technical aspects of singing or speaking are second nature then that real emotion can shine through.

Dynamics include a mixture of technical and artistic choices that will affect the song or speech - including:

- ☑ Loud and soft, crescendo and decrescendo
- ☑ Rhythmic and melodic interpretive choices
- ☑ Fluidity
- ☑ Phrasing
- ☑ Tempo
- ☑ Tension / release
- ☑ Choices involving vibrato, resonance and tone, and uses of vocal registers
- ☑ The key you choose for the song will affect tone and mood
- ☑ Choices involving format
- ☑ Lyrical interpretation
- ☑ Choices involving emphasis

☑ Mood choices (i.e. spirited, torchy, bright and cheery, dark and sullen, angelic, earthy, spiritual, sad, bluesy) and how these moods might change within the song

An example:
♪ How many different ways have you heard Gershwin's *Summertime* done? How about every way, every mood, every tempo, including 5/4. And each version, as it was processed through the individual artist, projected a different facet of the song; with each interpretation the song could be heard in a different light; with each set of choices the song could impart some different knowledge to the listener.

♪ I've heard *Summertime* done slowly and mournfully; I've heard it done with purity and classical beauty; I've heard it bluesy; jazzy; up tempo and bright; with a Latin beat; with full orchestra and huge string section; with a brassy big band; with lone singer on stool under blue spotlight and hip acoustic bass player; with out and out sobbing; with tears held back; and as an actual lullaby. These are all dynamic choices made by the musicians.

How far can you go?
▶ Gershwin wrote *Summertime* a certain way, and he put in some of his own dynamic choices. The song is also part of the larger plot of **Porgy and Bess**. So lines have to be drawn - as they do in all artistic interpretations of someone else's work - as to how far you can take something without completely misinterpreting, or even destroying, what the composer had in mind.

▶ There's no solid line over which you cannot cross. But you will be in a range of acceptability if you approach a work with:
   ♪ integrity
   ♪ an awareness of what you're doing, technically and artistically
   ♪ a knowledge of the history of the work and the composer
   ♪ respect for the composer
   ♪ a sincere and loving desire to share your personal artistic insights with others
   ♪ some sort of good taste

▶ Dynamics don't have to be intrusive. They can be as subtle as a brief pause taken in a well-chosen spot; a slight slowing down of a particular phrase; a barely perceptible change in vocal resonance; a look.

▶ A song's message doesn't have to be hugely existential, either. (Although it can be.) The message could simply be: beauty. It could be humor. It could be the pure joy of singing.

How does one begin to make these choices?

1. The first decision the singer makes is to define what the song is saying. (Often speeches and lectures are more direct - they will say what they are saying - unless, of course it's poetry or performance art.)

-With music and artistic speech, there is the element of the abstract.

- So: decide what the message of the piece is. What is the subtext? (Examples, using *Summertime*, could be: the song is a lullaby sung to a baby. Or: the song imparts a mournful, sad feeling to adults and children alike. Or: Though the song is mournful, it imparts hope. Or: The song gives a sense of calm and tranquility. Or: It's a richly textured sad song but the interplay of melody, harmony, and lyric are so beautiful that the sadness almost disappears. What does *Summertime* mean to you?)

2. The second decision the singer (or speaker) makes is: How do I get that message or mood across to the audience? The answer to this lies in your dynamic choices.

Examples of dynamic choices

♫ For example: Say you want a blue mood for a song you've chosen. Perhaps you're singing *Angel Eyes* by Earl Brent and Matt Dennis. You might then choose a slow tempo (technical), and project a world weary emotion (artistic). You may choose to quicken the pace slightly on the bridge to give it more urgency (technical decision), and during the bridge you may choose to project more desperation in your voice (artistic). At the end of the song you may choose to repeat the last line a second time, perhaps for emphasis (technical) and you may decide, on the second repetition, to come to a slightly more depressed state about the situation described in the song (artistic).

♫ There's really no line that can be drawn between technique and emotion, since in song singing they each depend on the other. But you do have to have your technique automatic and at your command. i.e. Suppose you have an up tempo song that projects cheerfulness - for instance, *My Favorite Things* from **The Sound of Music.** If you're not technically up to par on your interval jumps, ear training, and vocal agility, you may end up slowing the song down in order not to sing flat - and thus losing some of the cheerful mood that comes with a quick tempo.

♬ In learning about dynamics, <u>technical practice must come first</u>. Your ability to sing with precision, to have your register breaks mastered, to make interval jumps on key, to have your breathing muscles developed - allows you the freedom to artistically interpret a song in the best way you can. It allows you to share with the audience what you hear in your mind.

The ups and downs of energy and emotion

♪ When you sing or speak, your energy must always be "up," even on the most dismal of lost-love ballads. This means being caught up in the emotional content of the song. Even on lullabies, you don't want to put people to sleep!

♪ Emotional interpretation must be tempered with intellectual decisions. You don't want to let everything hang out completely, or sob uncontrollably on stage, or get so overwhelmed by the song that you don't enunciate the lyrics.

♪ No matter how many times you perform the same song or give the same lecture or speech, you must never let it get stale. Each time you do your number, your energy must be as fresh and vital as the first time. Your technical approach may be brilliant, but if that spark is missing, the whole thing will go flat. Keep your fire lit.

♪ There's a certain life experience that you can use to color your performances. It's something that can't be pinpointed, but you know it when it happens. It oozes out of you as naturally as your breath. It usually comes after you've been singing or speaking for a while, and have become really comfortable with the performance experience. Something just opens up - like a clearer channel between your inner, secret self and the inner selves of the listeners. A connection is made with the audience and the place catches on fire.

♪ It's a dynamic that comes from letting go of inhibitions, and trusting that what you have to say is just a fine thing to say. Jazz singer Mark Murphy has this quality, as does Mel Tormé, Ernestine Anderson, and countless others. I've seen singers move from being really good to just blowing a club away - and the main difference was this confidence. So if you're ever up there singing, and your inner voice suddenly tells you to let that light shine through, give it a try. You might surprise yourself.

Is a singer also an actor?

✱Interpreting a song is not the same thing as living the actual situation. A song is a stylized "slice" of some situation. Don't get lost in it. Remember always that you are a performer. If you sing a lullaby so softly that people can't hear you, you've forsaken the technical for the emotive.

✱Energy and emotion can't run aimlessly through a song or speech. It has to have structure, so the listener can be caught up in what you have to say. One way to determine structure is to ask yourself what actors ask of their characters all the time: What is the motivation?

✱Examples of motivation: Say you're singing the song *Sophisticated Lady* by Duke Ellington. Ask yourself: What am I trying to do with this song? Why? How can I accomplish this? Am I "playing" myself, or am I a character acting out a role? How does "my character" react to this situation? Was I in love with this "sophisticated lady" at one time, and am I now feeling compassion for her situation? Or am I still in love with her? Am I her, singing about myself in the third person? How did I get to where I am right now, at the exact moment the song begins. What was I doing two minutes before the song began?

✱In some acting classes, actors are told to be in two places at once: on stage, giving the performance and in the last row, watching as the critic. Even in the most demanding of roles, most actors are aware of technique to some degree.

✱Acting classes are highly recommended. Many singers take private workshops, courses at local theatres, or acting classes at local community colleges, in order to improve their interpretive skills.

✱Pursue interests in the other arts: poetry, ballet, theatre, painting, sculpture, literature. Being immersed in other arts besides singing can give you new "takes" on balance, fluidity, the whole beginning-middle-end thing, on contrasts, and on tension/release. Many artists are inspired by works outside their own scope. A novelist writes a book after seeing a famous painting, a composer writes a choral work after reading a book about history, a lyricist uses images from mythology in song lyrics.

Lord, please don't let me be...static

♪ A song is often best served by treating it as one dynamic unit. That is, the song must have motion, it must move forward, it must go somewhere - but this movement must be the result of well though-out motivation. If a phrase or verse repeats itself, for example, you don't want to sing it the same way the second time.

Something has happened between the first and second repetition of this verse. What? Whatever you decide, let that come through in your interpretation.

♪ What you don't want to do is throw in dynamic movement that is not motivated, that is fragmented, that breaks up the forward motion of the dynamic, or that distracts the listener from the inner meaning of the song. An example of this might be a jazz solo or scat that jumps around the scale with no particular meaning or relation to the main mood of the song. Flying up and down scales can work if it has something to do with the context of the song.

♪ Even as phrases shouldn't usually be static, individual notes can't be static either. If a note is held for any length of time - or it this note is repeated - it can't stay the same. Something must happen with it. In Cole Porter's *Night and Day*, for instance, there are a number of held notes. You may choose to make very slight crescendos on these notes - to keep them smooth and flowing. In repeating a note, too, try to think of a motivation for singing the second note slightly differently. It might be a little louder than the first note. Or it might be shorter in duration than the first note. It could be more or less intense than the first note.

♪ Remember, you want to keep your listeners on their toes. You don't want to simply please them - you want to make them really feel something.

♪ Improvisation classes - those things you do at the local acting school where you get up in front of the class and do skits with no scripts - are incredible confidence- boosters and dynamic de-static-izers. These classes teach a lot about making dynamic choices quickly, effectively, and on the spur of the moment.

Exercises

1. Sing *Twinkle Twinkle Little Star* as an upbeat, jazzy song.
    Sing it as a lullaby.
    Sing it as a sad, bluesy song.
    Sing it again, as an airy bossa nova.
    Go back and sing it yet again - as a serious "message" piece.

What did you do differently to achieve the different versions? List the technical and artistic choices you made (tempo, volume, change in tone, change in lyrical emphasis, key change, etc.).

2. Sing *Row Row Row Your Boat* as if you had just decided to get married.
    Sing it again as if your cat died.
    Sing it as if you were interviewing for an executive office job.

Sing it as if you were alone on the range, on your horse, just you
  the horse and the sky.
Sing it as if you were sending a secret warning, in code, to a listener
  in the audience.
Sing it as if you were announcing the birth of a new baby.

Really do these exercises. They're fabulous eye openers. Take the time to analyze how you changed the song to suit the occasion. A good actor can give a listener goose-bumps singing *Row Row Row Your Boat* as if he or she had just been shot by a jealous lover.

3. Sing *Frère Jacque* as if you were actually singing to a younger
    brother.
   Sing it as if you were actually singing to a monk.
   As if you were a young person (child or teen, perhaps) calling your
    neighbor from the street up to his window, to wake him up for
    school.
   As if you were an adult calling upstairs to your child to wake him
    up for school.
   As if you were an adult in the same room with your child, waking him
    up for school.
   As if you were annoyed at Jacque for sleeping so late.
   As if you were amused at Jacque for sleeping late.
   As if you were Jacque and you were trying to get yourself "psyched"
    up for a job you dreaded.
   As if you were Jacque and you couldn't wait to get to work.

Again, note what you did differently - technically, intellectually, spiritually, artistically, and / or emotionally to produce different results.

4. Exercises for speakers.

   → Find a short monologue from Shakespeare. See how many different
    ways you can do it - based on different motivations you can think up for
    the character. Make notes of what you did vocally, emotionally,
    intellectually, and artistically, to make each version mean something
    different.

   → Take a sales speech you are working on. Read it through as if you
    are the president, owner, and major stockholder of the company.
    Then go back and read it through as if you are in the mailroom but
    sure would like to impress people enough to get out. Read it through

a third time as if you have just been hired to this fabulous position, but you're young and not so sure of yourself. Same thing, but this time you're young and too sure of yourself. Make notes of different vocal registers, artistic and technical choices you made, that make each sales presentation different. Which way would you like to present this speech?

→ Find a few paragraphs from a travel magazine, and use that as a script. You are the tour guide. Read the script as if you have never been to this exotic place before, but you sure need the job. Read it again as if you've been on the job twenty years and you're bored stiff. Read it again as if you're making a commercial for this place and you want people to visit it. And again as if this place brings back memories for you of a lost love. Make note of what mental and vocal techniques produce what results. Keep track of your different "voices" and know how to reproduce them again.

Notes:

**Dynamics:
Loud and Soft**

More About "Dynamic"
- It's the way the song or speech moves.
- It's the way the singer or speaker chooses to use his or her energy.
- It's the interplay of tension and release; of building up and letting down.
- It's the flow of the piece, and the variations of speed, volume, intensity, emotion.
- Dynamics can be subtle or forceful - it's a choice the artist makes.
- Dynamics can be defined as the movement and energy within a song or speech that can enhance the lyrical, emotional, intellectual, and spiritual message of the piece.
- Through dynamics, the artist can impart knowledge that is non-verbal. (i.e. Have you ever been brought to tears by Itzhak Perlman playing the violin? Have you ever had chills run up your back listening to Ella Fitzgerald scat singing? It's not just the technical expertise of these artists that does that, it's the way they use their energy and emotion within the music.)
- Dynamics include many factors (see the segment on "Dynamics: Energy and Emotion"), but in this segment we'll be concentrating on loudness and softness.

Loudness and Softness
♪ Shifts in volume are a powerful dynamic tool.

♪ Usually we shift from soft to loud and loud to soft gradually.

♪ The move from one volume, swelling to a louder volume, is called a crescendo.

♪ The move from a particular volume to a softer volume is called a decrescendo or a diminuendo.

♪ The performer, conductor, or composer makes decisions about:
- how soft the soft phrases will be,
- where the crescendo will occur,
- how quickly the crescendo will occur,
- what volume the crescendo will reach at its peak -
- and the same decisions for the decrescendo.

♪ A crescendo can move from any volume up to any other volume - it does not have to be extreme. It can be subtle, such as moving from very very soft to soft (pianissimo to piano). Or it can begin with a loud sound and move to a very loud sound (forte to fortissimo). A decrescendo, the same - decisions are made as to how loud the sound is when it begins, how quickly it will get softer, and how soft the resulting sound will be.

♪ Shifts in volume often contain some crescendo and decrescendo, rather than just singing softly for one phrase and suddenly singing loudly in the next phrase. Crescendo and decrescendo assure fluidity. Unless you need your song or speech to be jarring for some specific purpose, fluidity is often the best artistic choice.

♪ There are times when the choice would be made to change suddenly from soft to loud or from loud to soft. Examples can be found in much of the dramatic choral literature. In solo song styling, this choice might also be made - perhaps a torch song builds to a high point and then suddenly gets soft on the last line.

Technical Aspects of Producing Loud and Soft Sounds

Singing Softly

♫ "Soft" is hard to sing. It's not just a matter of getting more breath and less sound. It's a matter of keeping the same rich, round, resonant sound you have been developing, and bringing down only the volume. <u>You don't want to lose any tone.</u>

♫ In song styling, you may choose to make your soft notes breathy - but you don't want them breathy simply because that's the only way you can lower your volume.

♫ <u>In learning to sing softly, don't get breathy.</u> You can always add that effect later on. Keep your tone bright.

♫ Soft sounds still need the full support and control of the diaphragm and abdominal muscles in order to remain tonal and bright.

♫ Soft sounds need the same attention given to the vowels and placement as your mid-volume sounds.

♪ Technically, you may notice that your diaphragm is pushing air out of your lungs at a slower rate; yet there is the same intensity and precision that you'd use with your other volumes.

Singing Loudly
- Loud, too, is hard to sing. It's not a matter of yelling or straining. You want to keep your basic round, resonant tone.

- You can increase the volume by increased effort of the diaphragm and breathing apparatus - never by increasing effort or tension in the throat.

- Singing loudly you may notice that you need to take in more air on your inhale; that your diaphragm pushes air out of your lungs at a faster rate (meaning that you may have to breathe more often than you would at a lower volume).

- Remember to keep the jaw dropped and the throat "opened."

- Never force the sound.

- Inhale deeply but not so much that you tense up. (Don't "overstuff".)

- Never go louder than is comfortable or pleasant sounding. Your "loud" may not be as loud as someone else's "loud" - simply because your voices and body / instruments are built differently.

- A big problem for some singers who do live gigs is that once they get on stage they find they can't hear themselves, and must either eat the microphone or shriek into it to be heard. This can be corrected by obtaining better quality monitors - or more monitors; by having a talk with the club's sound engineer, who is often an instrumentalist and may not be sensitive to needs of singers; or by making sure that your instrumentalists don't overpower you with their volume. Sometimes just having the drummer switch to brushes is all that's needed. Other times the instrumentalists are simply not listening for the overall sound and are not aware that there is a problem. The point is, you've got to get your volume without yelling.

Rock
What to do about yelling. This is the big question, because in rock music, part of the desired sound is that rough, shrieking quality. Unless you don't mind a short career with possible nodes as the end result, learn how to get your power and volume from the strength of your abdominals, intercostal muscles, your diaphragm, and anything else that will help you by-pass

using your throat and neck for your volume. Learning a good classical breathing technique can help a rock singer's career-span. Finding a private voice teacher who specializes in producing "power sounds" is also a necessity. (See the chapter "Pop and Belting.")

Power
* ✱ You can sing with power and / or intensity in both soft and loud volumes. Power is not directly related to volume.
* ✱ In singing at any volume, the sound must "come from the diaphragm." <u>Never let it come from the throat.</u>

Dynamic Symbols

A **crescendo** is indicated by this symbol:

Or by the abbreviation: *"**cres.** "* or *"**cresc.** "*

A **decrescendo** is indicated by this symbol:

Or by the abbreviation: *"**decre.** "* or *"**decresc.** "*

Soft is indicated by the word *"**piano**"* or the symbol *"**p**"*

Very soft is *"**pianissimo**"* or *"**pp**"*

Medium soft (a little louder than *"piano"*) is notated: *"**mezzo piano**"* or *"**mp**"*

Loud is indicated by the word *"**forté**"* or the symbol *"**f**"*

Very loud is *"**fortissimo**"* or the symbol *"**ff**"*

Medium loud (a little softer than *"forté"*) is *"**mezzo forté**"* or *"**mf**"*

Exercises

INSTRUCTIONS:
a. On all the exercises, begin in your midrange and transpose each phrase up chromatically as far as is comfortable. Then go back to your midrange and sing the phrases again, transposing them down as low as is comfortable.
b. Suggested syllables are written under the notes - but be creative - do the exercises on a variety of syllables.
c. In the crescendo and decrescendo, the object is to make the volume transitions smooth and flowing.
d. The other objective is to keep your tone, placement, and vowel sounds **uniformly** rich, round, bright, and resonant on all volumes and through all volume shifts.
e. Take the exercises at moderately slow speeds. Then, as you develop these skills, speed up the tempos, still keeping the transitions smooth and the tone bright and even.

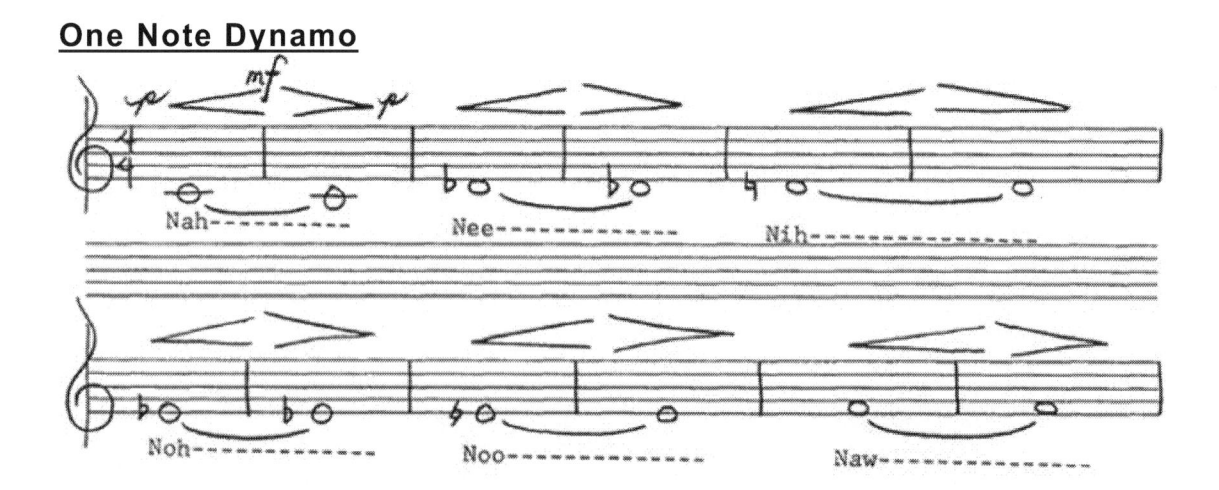

One Note Dynamo

Five Note Dynamo

Basic Crescendo

Basic Decrescendo

Fancy Finish

Hairpin Turn

Stretch Dynamo

Dancing Dynamics

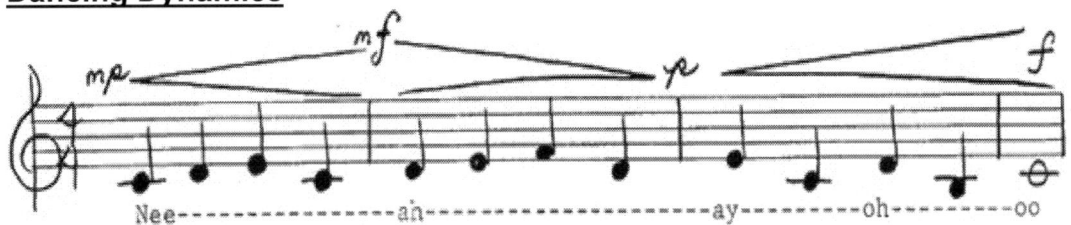

Sudden Shifts

Sudden Shifts Too

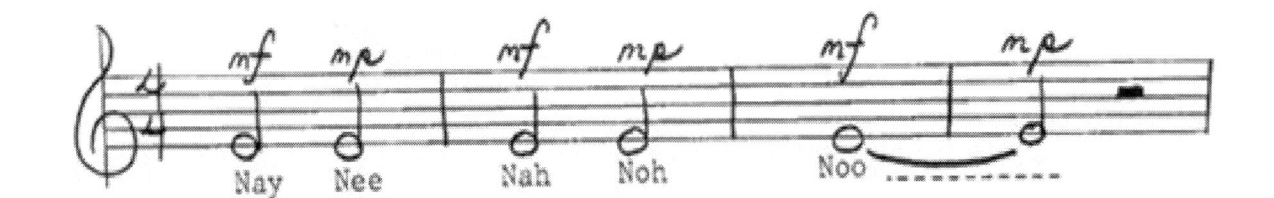

[Musical notation: 4/4 time, notes with syllables "Nay Nee Nah Noh Noo" marked with alternating mf and mp dynamics]

Shifting Speech Volumes

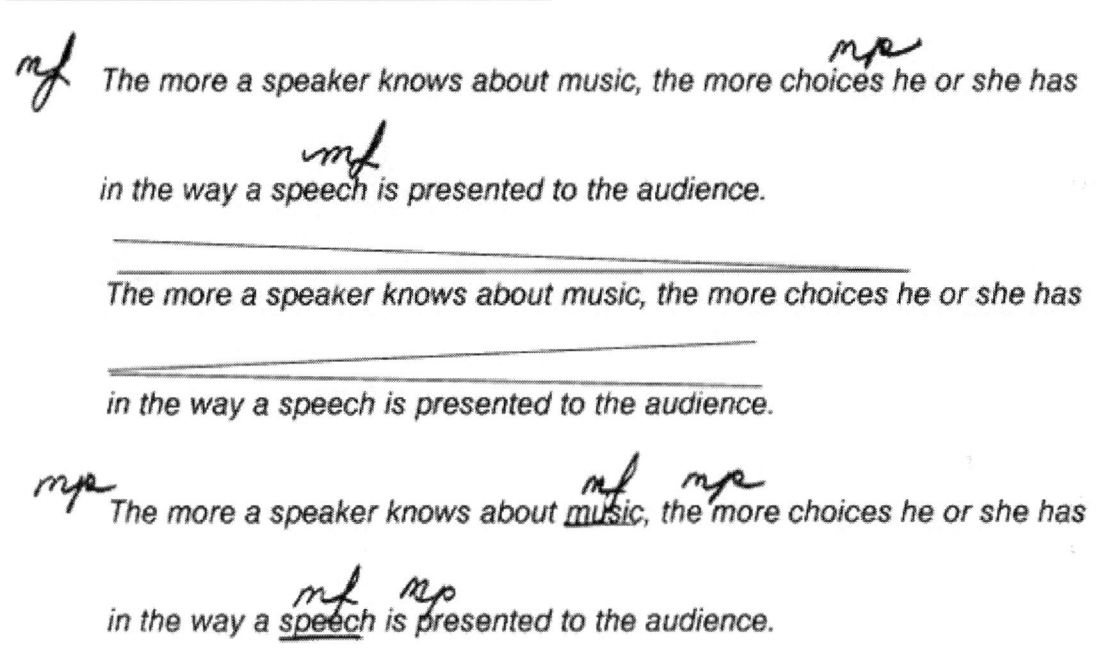

mf The more a speaker knows about music, the more choices *mp* he or she has

mf in the way a speech is presented to the audience.

———————————————
The more a speaker knows about music, the more choices he or she has

———————————————
in the way a speech is presented to the audience.

mp The more a speaker knows about <u>music</u>, the *mf* *mp* more choices he or she has

in the way a *mf* <u>speech</u> is *mp* presented to the audience.

Notes:

Ear Training:

What Key Is Your Refrigerator In?

What Is Ear Training?

This is a big subject, but the fact is we're training our ears all the time. Simply being curious about sound, aware of what you're hearing throughout the day, and willing to carry a pitch pipe around with you, is a good start.

Ear training is learning to hear musical details, and then being able to sing them. Some of these details are:

1. pitches

2. rhythms

3. intervals

4. patterns

5. scale types

    -major, minor, pentatonic, blues, etc.
    -for the advanced singer, modal scales, the various assortment of minor scales, etc.

6. chord types
    -major, minor, augmented, diminished, half-diminished, major seventh, dominant seventh, sixth, ninth, thirteenth, etc.

7. an awareness of tones, overtones, acoustics, other voices, and how other singers and speakers get the sound they do

Where to Begin
1. Pitch
    a) As basic as it sounds, we've all got to sing on key. You can have bad hair days, you can live a life filled with high drama and crises, you can wear a cape and be moody - but you can never sing flat. (Or sharp.) That also means no slurring up to a note when you make an interval jump in a song or exercise (unless you choose to do that for an effect).

    b) If pitch is not a problem for you, go ahead to the next section. If it is a problem, even if only occasionally, you'll need some way of checking your pitch when you practice alone. A piano (it's got to be in tune), electronic keyboard, or pitch pipe will work.

    c) Some ideas for working by yourself:

        ♪ Whenever you sing, hear your pitch <u>mentally</u> before actually singing it. Don't just go for a note hoping it will be right. <u>Think it, then sing it.</u>

        ♪ Keep a tape recorder next to your keyboard and tape yourself vocalizing and singing. Play back each scale or exercise you sing. Don't let yourself get away with even the slightest pitch inaccuracy. Go over each off-key segment again and again, until you can do it perfectly.

        ♪ When listening to other singers who sing in your range (and who sing on key), match your pitch with theirs. (Easier to do on slow songs, ballads, or even on the ends of phrases if a note is held.) Listen to your voice singing along with the other singer. Do you hear any discrepancies? If so, make adjustments in your pitch. Tape yourself singing with the other singer. Are you together, or are you hearing flat notes? If you hear flat notes, go back and find out exactly where the flat notes are occurring and practice those specific segments.

        ♪ For more basic pitch practice, stand by your keyboard and strike a note at random. Then sing that note. Strike another note at random (but within your range), and duplicate that pitch. And so on. Again, a tape recorder will help you if you can't hear your accuracy on the spot.

        ♪ If you play a stringed instrument or tune pianos, chances are you've got a great ear. I love to listen to the piano tuner as he adjusts the strings - there's something satisfying about the sound coming together just right. If you sing with a choir, get there early and listen to the harpist tune up, or go backstage and listen to the violins. Listening to instruments tune is an excellent "ear trainer."

♪ This is not work - this is fun. It's games. For example, when you hear a pitch during your day, sing it. There are pitches everywhere - train whistles, doors creaking, refrigerator hums, birds singing, crickets, car radios next to you at red lights.

d) Pitch trouble-shooting

♫ If you are going flat, especially if you're usually on pitch, you are probably not breathing correctly. Check out the chapter on breathing.

♫ If you expand your lower ribs to breathe, as per the segment on "The Inhale," that can add to your support and help you stay on key. But it's got to be done right. The proper way to support the diaphragm with the ribs is to gently expand the lower ribs - not raise them. If you raise your rib cage unnaturally and force yourself to keep it raised while you sing, this can cause fatigue, stress, and flat singing.

♫ If you are going flat and you are breathing correctly, you might simply be tired.

♫ You're breathing correctly and you're not tired. Have you done your daily warm up exercises?

♫ Perhaps the song is in the wrong key for your voice.

♫ If you're singing in an adverse situation and you can't hear yourself - for instance, with a stage band that has no monitor speaker - you could go off key and not know it.

♫ Here's an interesting concept: Pitch can be remembered, not just heard. Remember what it **feels like** to sing certain pitches, and duplicate that sound during times when you cannot hear yourself.

♫ Stage fright and tension can throw you off pitch.

♫ Singing with a microphone through an unfamiliar sound system, or a sound system with too much reverb - can throw you off pitch. Ditto for singing in an unfamiliar room with unknown acoustics.

If possible, practice your songs in the room where you'll be performing.

♪ Some pitch problems are caused by the need for more practice in hearing and singing intervals. If the song calls for an interval jump of a sixth, and you sing up an augmented fifth, you'll be flat. Know what a sixth sounds like. Know what an augmented fifth sounds like.

♪ If you are a solo singer who likes to slur or slide up to a note, be very careful to actually reach that note before going on to the next note. Sarah Vaughan slides up to notes, but she always ends up on the correct pitch. Here's the rule: If you're going to slide, slide up all the way.

♪ If you've listened to one too many Sarah Vaughan albums, here's what you do: Practice your song with no glides or slurs at all. Tape it and make sure you make all your interval jumps with <u>precision.</u> When you've memorized the correct pitches, then go back if you must, and put your slurs back in. Tape yourself and make sure you're still hitting the correct pitches.

♪ Choral or small ensemble singers can <u>never slide</u> up to a note.

Intervals, Patterns, Scales, and Chords

a) An interval is the distance between two notes.

b) A singer must know intervals, must be able to repeat patterns, and must have some feel for scales and chords.

c) Practice with a tape recorder. Try playing an interval on the piano, then singing it. Listen to yourself on tape to make sure you were right on.

• Practice singing intervals of seconds, thirds, fourths, fifths, the sixth, the seventh, the dominant seventh and the octave. Practice major and minor seconds and thirds, and augmented and diminished fifths.

• Practice intervals going up from the root note, and also from the root going down.

• If you're not familiar with these intervals and you don't have a voice teacher, check out the chapter on reading music for ideas for home study books on music theory.

d) Memorize intervals as if they were melodies. Or find songs you know and analyze the intervals.

▶ The first two notes of *Frère Jacque* are a major second. If you know that song, you'll always know how to sing a major second (also called a whole step).

▶ The first two notes of *The Long and Winding Road* by Lennon / McCartney area minor second (also called a half step) ("The long and winding road...").

▶ The first interval jump in the chorus of Gershwin's *They Can't Take That Away From Me* ("the way you wear your hat") is a major third.

▶ The first two notes of *Someday My Prince Will Come* by Frank Churchill and Larry Morey are a fourth.

▶ The first two notes of *Twinkle Twinkle Little Star* are a fifth.

▶ The first two notes of *My Bonnie Lies Over the Ocean* are a sixth.

▶ Sing through the first measure of *The Glory of Love* by Billy Hill (not counting the pick-up). The very next interval jump - the jump going from the last note of the first bar to the first note of the second bar - is your dominant seventh. ("You've got to give a lit-tle, take a little...")

▶ The first two notes of *Over the Rainbow* are an octave, as are the first two notes of *Willow Weep For Me* by Ann Ronell. If you ever need to sing an octave, think of one of these songs.

▶ You can play with scales the same way - for instance, "Joy to the World, the Lord is come", from the Christmas carol, is a descending major scale. If you know that song, you'll always know that scale.

e) Go ahead and make up your own exercises. Play a scale and sing it. When you're vocalizing, instead of going up and down the usual major scale, try vocalizing on, say, the relative minor scales. Vocalize on a blues scale. Sing up and down the different modal scales. If you're singing arpeggios to warm up your voice for the day, why not alternate the usual major arpeggio with a minor or a half-diminished arpeggio.

f) Listen for these various scales and chords and identify them. If you've got your car radio on, ask yourself: Is this a minor or major scale? If a minor scale, which minor scale is it? Am I hearing a major or minor chord? Is this a major seventh or a dominant seventh? Was that interval jump a third or a fourth? Any questions you can't answer, try out for yourself when you get back to your keyboard. (Or pull your car over and take the pitch pipe out of the glove compartment.)

Rhythm

✱The best education in rhythmical articulation is fun, easy, and free - it's just listening.

- Listen to both vocal and instrumental music. Listen to classical music, jazz, Brazilian polyrhythmic percussion. Even if you're not a jazz fan, listen to the solos and see if you can keep a handle on the beat while the soloist plays around the rhythm. Tap your hand on beats one and three. Tap your hand on beats two and four. Tap your hand between the beats. Listen to Jean Luc Ponty's album *No Absolute Time* and get a feel for syncopation. Listen to Dave Brubeck's *Take Five* and get a handle for 5/4 music. Listen to waltzes and feel the 3/4.

✱If you're a beginner, you can learn rhythm theory and practice from most children's piano instruction books. If you're more advanced, you can work your way through **Rhythmical Articulation** by Pasquale Bona or **Elementary Training for Musicians** by Paul Hindemith. Also, books on sight singing usually open with basic rhythmic notation.

✱Practice with a metronome.

♪ Try singing scales with the metronome, going on and off the beat.

♪ Clap your hands or sing a scale using the metronome as beats two and four only. Then change and use the click as beats one and three.

♪ Sing a scale in 3/4 using the metronome on all beats, but accenting beat one in your singing. Then, without touching the metronome or skipping a beat, change to 4/4, putting the accents on beats one and three.

♪ With the metronome as 4/4, practice your eighth notes, dotted eighths, sixteenths. Practice half notes. Again, any basic child's piano instruction book will have these rhythmic phrases written out and defined for you if you need them.

Checklist for Singers:
1. Sing on pitch.

2. Sing with the correct rhythm, and with correct rhythmic accents.

3. Have a basic knowledge of musical notation.
   -You must know what keys your songs are in.
   -You must know what time signatures mean.
   -Better yet, learn to read music if you don't already know how. You don't want to fall into the stereotype of the "singer" as something other than a musician. You want to be a musician.

4. Have a basic knowledge of music theory and harmony.
   -Can you hear the difference between, say, major and minor?
   -Can you hear the difference, say, between a second and a third?
   -Between a dominant seventh and a major seventh?

5. Can you hear musical patterns?
   - If you hear a musical phrase, can you repeat it?

Checklist for Speakers:

1. Be able to hear pitches - and keep your speaking voice in a range that's comfortable and effective for you. If you're an actor, be able to use various pitches for effects or characterizations. Voice actors who do animation are very aware of pitch, placement, and resonance.

2. Be aware of rhythmic patterns, and the effects they have - and incorporate varieties of rhythms in your speech, lecture, or presentation.

3. Can you hear what you really sound like? Are you aware of your placement, your resonance, your tone - and do you sound the way you <u>want</u> to sound?

Ear Training Appendix:

Practice the following scales and interval jumps until you can sing them on key, a capella (without accompaniment). Sing on "nah" or any syllable that works for you. Check yourself by singing into a tape recorder and checking your recorded pitch against a piano or pitch pipe. Keep a mental note of what each interval sounds like <u>and feels</u> like.

The Basic Intervals in the C Scale

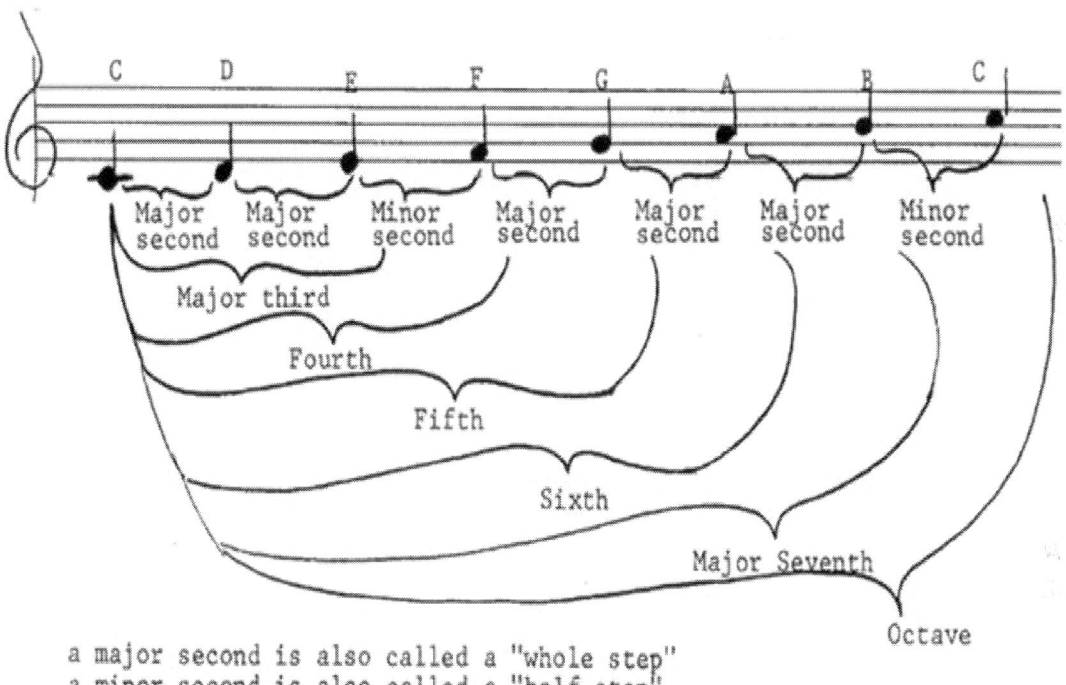

a major second is also called a "whole step"
a minor second is also called a "half step"

The Basic Intervals in the C Aeolian Scale

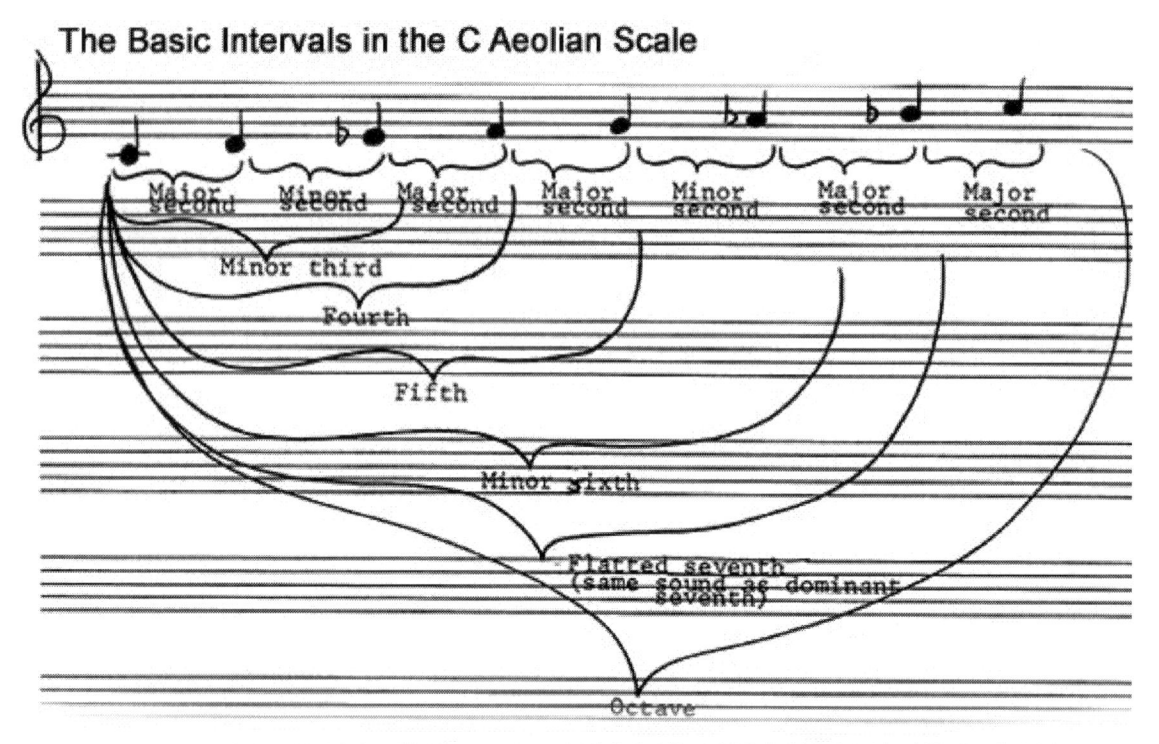

(The Aeolian is a common minor scale, also called "Relative Minor," or "Natural Minor.")

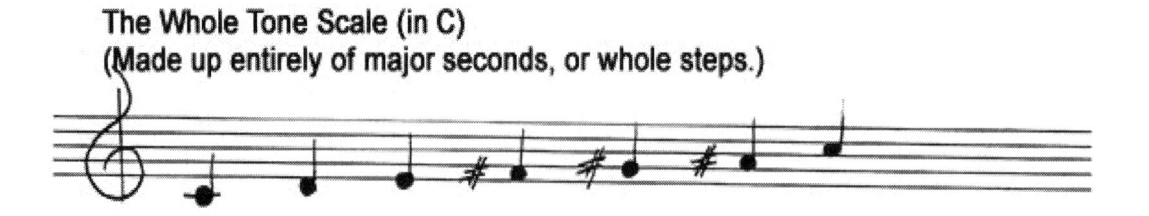

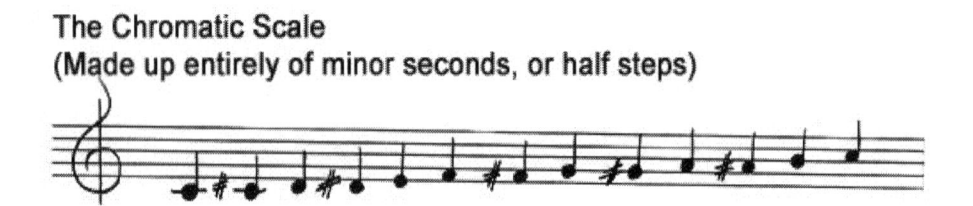

The Whole Tone Scale (in C)
(Made up entirely of major seconds, or whole steps.)

The Chromatic Scale
(Made up entirely of minor seconds, or half steps)

The Pentatonic Scale (in C)

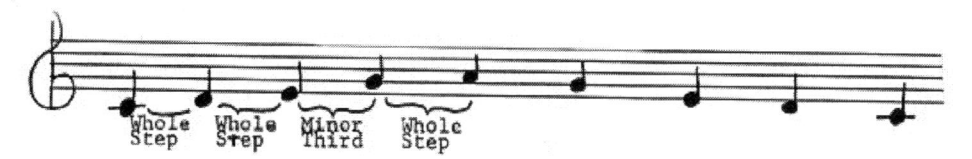

Whole Step, Whole Step, Minor Third, Whole Step

Basic Interval Jumps (using C as the root)

Major second
Minor second
Major third
Minor third

Fourth (also called Perfect Fourth)
Augmented fourth (also called Tritone)
Fifth (also called Perfect Fifth)

Augmented fifth
Diminished fifth (also called Flatted Fifth)
Sixth (also called Major Sixth)

Minor sixth
Major seventh
Dominant seventh (also called Flatted Seventh)

Octave
Ninth

Note: Some of the different intervals have the same sound, i.e. the augmented fourth and the flatted fifth. You should know them by both names. Whether it's called an augmented fourth or a flatted fifth will depend on the key the song is written in, and the maneuvers of the composer.

Notes:

What Do You Study When You Study Voice?

Sometimes it helps to get an aerial view of the entire gold mining town. That way you can pick out the parts of it that you'd like to explore - and avoid spending precious time in places you already know.

Following are the aspects of voice study. Pick, choose, boogie.

1. Breathing
2. Articulation and vowel sounds
3. Agility, fluidity, and precision
    - ♪ small intervals
    - ♪ large interval jumps
    - ♪ various scale patterns
    - ♪ handling intervals and scales at different tempos and volumes, and in different registers
4. Placement, resonance, tone
5. Pitch
6. Rhythmical articulation
7. Dynamics
    - ♪ tempo
    - ♪ volume
    - ♪ crescendo, decrescendo
    - ♪ use of staccato, legato, and other effects
    - ♪ dynamic variety
8. Control
    - ♪ smoothness
    - ♪ vibrato
    - ♪ mastery of the registers and "break notes"
    - ♪ special effects
9. Posture
10. Increasing the range
11. Song interpretation, technical
    - ♪ where to breathe
    - ♪ choosing a key
    - ♪ how to phrase the song

♪ tempo, etc.
12. Song interpretation, emotional
13. Ear training
14. Music theory; reading music
15. Sight singing
16. Your personal style; choosing a repertoire
17. Ensemble singing
    ♪ blending
    ♪ dynamics
    ♪ harmony
    ♪ precision, agility, pitch
    ♪ diction
        -vowels
        -consonants
        -ends of words
        -breathing
    ♪ group projection of the emotion behind the music
18. Performance techniques: microphone, eye contact, stage movements, etc.
19. Auditioning
20. Handling stage fright
21. Care of the voice and physical well-being
22. Relaxation
23. Freedom from having to think about any of the above
    ♪ getting to the point where everything falls together naturally
    ♪ being able to let go of technique and concentrate on feeling and projecting the spirit behind the song

Notes:

Ensemble Singing

Why sing with a group?

-Singing in an ensemble - whatever the genre - can be exhilarating. To sing with others is to be engrossed experientially in harmony. To sing in harmony, to work closely with others as part of a team with a mission, is to live in a magical (but real) world of beauty, art, balance, and joy. It gives us a feeling of what it could be like in a world filled with order, give-and-take, and long range thinking; of what it feels like to be an integral part of something that really makes a difference. Ensemble singing reminds each of us that we are unique and <u>needed</u> for exactly the voices we have. Knowing your part is knowing what your role is and knowing that no one else can take your place. Being in the middle of harmony is being in sync with fellow humans. If this sounds idealistic, just give it a try! You'll see...

-Ensemble singing can also give you a feeling that you can create something beautiful without having to "carry the burden" alone. With many people close together working toward the same goal, each with his or her own unique vocal contribution, the "burden is easy"." Why do people sing, unpaid, in church, civic, and school choruses? Why do people love to harmonize? Why do people even <u>pay</u> to sing - as many in civic choruses do, through annual dues, the purchase of music, and ticket sale obligation? Why do we revere the great choral literature? Perhaps it gives us a glimpse of something we can't get anywhere else...

-And by the way - unison singing can be as rich and full of harmony as singing in parts. Whenever there are voices together, you've got blend. You've got the overtones of people's life experiences and vocal instruments coming together to create a new, intricately textured sound.

It's as much listening as singing

OK. You're sold. You want to do this. But what to do? Where to start? The first thing to do is: sit there. Sit there and listen. And analyze. And hear how other groups make the sounds they make.

♪ Ensemble singing is 90% listening.
- ♯ A bold statement that can't be backed up. But the point is, you can improve your contribution to your vocal ensemble by listening to other groups and learning from them.
- ♯ And don't get stuck listening to groups that are just in your own particular genre. I sing jazz, but I also listen to classical, and folk groups from other countries. A classical singer I know listens also to barbershop. Whatever your musical tastes, you can benefit from listening to all genres, for they all have something to teach us. Listening globally is guaranteed to bring more depth and experience to the particular group with which you sing.

♪ What to listen to?
- ♯ Support your local musicians. Haul yourself away from the TV and go out and hear live music at night. Get to know the various ensembles that perform in your town. Catch the acts that travel through your town. If your city has a Handel Haydn Society, go hear them. Analyze the different groups, watch their development over the years. (And when you're out there singing, hopefully others will brave the cold to go hear you!)

- ♯ If you live near colleges or universities, you probably have access to faculty and student recitals. Often these recitals are free or reasonably priced, and you'll be able to broaden your scope by listening to all genres of music: Renaissance, Madrigal, Baroque, Classical, Romantic, Twentieth Century, as well as original compositions, art songs, music from the Church, well known pieces and obscure works.

- ♯ Get to the library. Browsing works.

- ♯ Get a great education for $15.00. Buy one of dozens of available CDs by The Tallis Scholars. They perform motets, masses, anthems, Anglican service music and other pieces, and from them you can learn just about anything you need to know about ensemble singing. Each of their individual voices is trained and gorgeous on its own, yet within the group there is a purity and focus of sound that is breathtaking.

- ♯ A hot contemporary group called Zap Mama is another listening route to take. They cannot be categorized, except to say they should require seatbelts. The material is new, it's tight, the voices blend like thick, heavy silk, and their rhythms are so magical they are capable of picking you up and carrying you away.

♯ Groups like The Manhattan Transfer, Rare Silk, Take Six, The New York Voices, Singers Unlimited, and others are thrilling examples of rhythmic precision, hot dynamics, and the blending of voices on intricate and complex harmonies and counterpoint. To get to the roots of this jazzy "vocalese" sound, check out Lambert, Hendricks and Ross, the "vocalese" pioneers. Their voices weave in and out of each other in jaw droppingly complex ways, yet the sound is fluid and effortless, and no one has sacrificed his or her own unique timbre.

♯ Listen also to recordings of:
- Ladysmith Black Mambazo
- The Robert Shaw Chorale
- The Gregg Smith Singers
- The Westminster Choir
- Atlanta Symphony Chorus
- The Dale Warland Singers
- The Choir of King's College
- The St. Olaf Choir
- The Cambridge Singers
- Anonymous 4
- Chanticleer
- The Swingle Singers
- Gothic Voices
- The Muungano National Choir, Kenya
- Tubuai Choir, Polynesia
- The Rustavi Choir, Georgia
- Varttina, from Finland

♯ Subscribe to any choral journals or Internet lists/newsgroups that you can find. These invaluable resources will give you more ideas for listening, and for improving your own ensemble sound.

♯ Opera choruses, Broadway music choruses and other big performance ensembles have their own lessons to teach us - among others, the lessons of group projection of emotion, of dynamics, of movement, of supporting the main characters emotionally and technically.

♯ Studying barbershop quartets can reveal useful information, especially about precision and blend, and about the strength of harmonies working off each other in a bold way.

♯ Madrigal groups offer impeccable lessons in precision, artistic dynamics, and blend. A good madrigal group is so tight, so rehearsed, that the resulting sound is seamless. Like jazz musicians, madrigal singers are intensely "in tune" with one another, to the point where they each know when the others breathe.

An ensemble singer's personal responsibilities:

How can you get your group to sound as good as the groups on the recommended CDs? Many ways. Let's start at the beginning, with the most basic of requirements: personal accountability. What does this mean?

- ✓ It means taking the time <u>before</u> rehearsals to go over the music by yourself, so you come to rehearsals prepared.

- ✓ It means working on your voice individually or with a voice teacher, so you can bring to the ensemble your very best sound.

- ✓ It means vocalizing daily, by yourself.

- ✓ It means being open to constructive help from the artistic director or conductor. (Translation: Leave the diva-ness back home.)

- ✓ It means being there at rehearsals. In mind as well as in body. (Translation: Write notes in your score. If you're asking a question that everyone else knew the answer to two weeks ago...)

- ✓ Bring a loving attitude to rehearsals. If someone near you is singing in an annoying way, try approaching the problem from a forgiving and helpful place. Snapping at them will simply make them defensive.

- ✓ If you're in a small ensemble and someone just isn't singing right, the first course of action is to follow protocol: Take it up with the group's leader or producer, and let him or her handle it. Tactfully. If you're the leader, then you must say something - but make sure it's constructive, loving, and devoid of hidden agenda or malevolent subtext. "Let's go over that section again, it was sounding a little flat" is probably a better choice than "You worthless idiot, where did you learn to drive?"

- ✓ In a large choir, another solution to having someone sing flat in your ear is to help them by sitting where they can better hear <u>you.</u> Perhaps your singing correctly in <u>their</u> ear will help them with their pitch (or other vocal problems).

✓ Also in an ensemble, avoid wearing perfume or scented hairspray, and don't smoke just before rehearsal. You don't want to start a wheezing frenzy or sneezeathon.

General issues for ensemble singing

Whether you've got four singers or two hundred singers, there are certain issues that must be addressed in order to get an optimal sound. In a choral setting, the artistic director will make these choices and pass the instructions on to you. In a small ensemble, you must personally make sure these points have been covered:

1) Blend. How do you want the blend to sound? This is an artistic choice.

- ♪ In groups like The Gregg Smith Singers, The Robert Shaw Chorale, or Take Six, there is a seamless blend - the listener hears one integrated sound. No one voice can be distinguished. These groups have their own tone, their own character. The group is, in effect, one instrument.

- ♪ Conversely, a group like Lambert, Hendricks and Ross allows for each singer to have a special timbre - the listener can identify who is singing what part (still within a certain blend, however). Lambert, Hendricks and Ross provides a seamless sound, but a different choice has been made about the blend.

- ♪ There is a controversy about choral singing and blend. Most people agree that a chorus must have a smooth blend, and no one voice should stand out. However, some trained singers who sing in choirs complain that in order to blend in this way they must stifle their voices, hold back, and refrain from using their natural vibrato. They say that these practices hurt their voices and are generally frustrating. There are two trains of thought here:

    -One is that the singers in a chorus must indeed blend. Holding back a little, toning down large vibratos, and listening to the other singers and other sections is a skill in itself. It does not harm the voice.

    -Another alternative is to allow each singer to use their full, trained voice. The key to a blended sound here, according to many, would be to carefully arrange the seating so that voices are next to one another that complement each other, or blend with each other naturally.

-A neutral tidbit here: It's amazing how you can take a choir of just about any size, and by moving people around, change the entire sound! You move one person here, another there, a threesome over there, this person up to the front next to that person, this loud one goes to the back row, and voila - here's the sound, the blend, you've been looking for. Quite magical.

-Blending within an ensemble is quite an art. It will depend on many factors, including those mentioned above. Also to take into consideration: Is this a live performance or a recording? If a recording, the sound engineer will need to have input into where people are placed. If a live performance, how many microphones, if any, will be used - and where will they be placed on the stage? How will the microphone placement affect the balance of voices? If you've got the budget, a sound engineer can help. If not, you will need to read up on this subject, and experiment within your group to get just the sound you want for the situation you're in.

2) Tone and depth. Yet more controversy surrounds decisions about a particular group "sound." Does your ensemble want to be known for a particular sound, a unique tone? Or do you change your sound as you change your repertoire, to best reflect the work you've chosen to do?

♪ If you're in a large choir or chorus, you can leave these decisions up to the artistic director.

♪ A small ensemble often does have a signature sound; a particular tone or depth that is recognizably unique to that group.

♪ Whatever the blending decision is, the result is still somehow "one sound." Each ensemble must make decisions as to what "character" that sound wants to be. What kind of warmth, intimacy, or sophistication will the group's sound project (although this will also vary with the different choices of music)? A Broadway chorus will have a different approach to tone and depth than a night club revue. A sacred music ensemble will make different tonal decisions than a pop group. What is the overall message your ensemble wants to deliver? Are you a "Yes, in-your-face, smiling energetic alive" type group? Are you a sweet, celestial, sacred and thoughtful group? Does your group just wanna have fun?

3) Acoustics. What kind of acoustics will you be dealing with? If you're a four voice group using microphones in a night club, you'll have different vocal issues than a thirty voice group singing in a big church. You'll need to adjust your tone and approach to make optimal use of available acoustics. (i.e. In a big church or hall you might choose a precise and reasonably vibrato-less sound in order to avoid possible muddiness. In a small room with a low ceiling and lots of draperies and carpet, you might want to add more depth of tone and richness to the voice in order not to sound too dry. Or hey - you may <u>choose</u> to have a dry, very "present" sound.)

4) Pronunciations. No matter what the size of the group, decisions must be made as to:

> ♪ how words and vowels will be pronounced. Regional accents generally don't work in most ensemble literature. Diphthongs must be carefully attended to. Whether the music is in English, Latin, German, or any other language, different people have different ways of pronouncing words - and this must be cleared up.
>
> ♪ where final consonants will go within each measure.

5) Large and small groups develop a "**group consciousness**." That is, often decisions are made that no one ever discussed - yet the entire group knows what they are. For instance, recently an eight-voice ensemble sang a piece together for the first time. Each person was reading from the sheet music. It was a samba, with some syncopated rhythms. There were four or five instances in this read-through, in which the group mis-read the rhythms - but they ALL did it wrong in the SAME WAY! The group was together, even in their mistakes. (Later, it was decided to leave the "mistakes" in, as the group preferred the rhythm that way.)

6) Ensemble singing must always **begin with vocal warm-ups** and tune-ups. The ensemble is an instrument. You wouldn't think of picking up, say, a violin and playing it without tuning up. The same applies to a group of singers. Even two people working together need to tune to each other at the beginning of rehearsals, and before performances.

Small ensembles

✻ The most important thing singers in a small ensemble can do is to **listen** to one another. As you listen, your awareness changes your voice to best suit the total sound. It's magical. All you have to do is focus your awareness outside of yourself, and onto the sound of the others, and your body/instrument usually makes any necessary adjustments without you having to think about it.

✱ All the issues mentioned above: diphthongs, vowels, decisions about pronunciations, decisions about tone and vibrato - are intensified when singing in a small group. You're not buried in a 150 voice choir, you're much more "on the line."

✱ **Precision**. That's all, just precision. A small ensemble can't afford the tiniest bit of sloppiness in blend, in dynamics, in phrase attacks and cut-offs, in rhythmical details. Practice each piece until you know each other so well that every nuance of every song is tight and defined. Precision in pitch can never be taken for granted.

Large ensembles

♪ All of the preceding points apply to choruses as well: precision, pronunciations, focusing the awareness outside of yourself and onto the sounds of others.

♪ Read books. It adds depth to the choral experience to read up on the composer whose piece you're doing, and to know the history of the piece. When was it written? Under what circumstances? How was it received by its first audiences? It's also interesting to read up on the critical and technical aspects of the piece you're singing, and on choral literature and trends in general. Many excellent books have been written, devoted entirely to choral singing. Why not try to find **The Choral Experience: Literature, Materials, and Methods** by Ray Robinson and Allen Winold, **A Survey of Choral Music** by Homer Ulrich, **The Choral Singer's Companion** by Ronald Corp, **Concertos and Choral Works** by Donald Tovey, or other excellent books?

♪ Join a chorus you love and whose music director you trust. Joy is the name of the game.

♪ Know the music well enough <u>before</u> rehearsal so that you can watch the conductor <u>during</u> the rehearsal. You can't contribute to the overall sound if your head is totally buried in the music. Watching both music and conductor at the same time is one of the more sophisticated art forms a good chorister develops, since it requires two sets of eyes per person. But it can be done. (Hold the music up, sit up straight, and use your peripheral vision - that's the vision you used when your kids were young and you were able to watch them, balance your checkbook, and stir the soup all at the same time.)

♪ No matter how fierce your choral director, most will never go so far as to single out one singer by name for reprimand. Since you will seldom hear, then, "George, you idiot, you're singing flat again," be alert for more subtle feedback. For example, if the director keeps looking at your section and suggesting that pitch is a problem, don't assume it's not you. Listen to yourself. Is it you?

♪ Bring a pencil to rehearsals.

Exercises for ensembles

Your unique sound will be acquired through practice. The following warm-ups and tune-ups can be used before the song-singing segment of your rehearsals. Choose the ones that suit your group, or make up your own exercises.

♪ **Practice phrases using different dynamics.** Practice crescendos and decrescendos so that the group gets louder together at the same rate, turns around to the decrescendo at the same time, and then gets softer, with everyone softening at the same rate.

♪ **Practice vowel sounds and more vowel sounds.** Make sure you all turn your diphthongs around at the same time (see the chapter on vowels). Sing phrases together listening for these particulars. These can be phrases from songs you are working on, or you can use traditional vocal warm-up vowels such as "nah," "nee," "nay," "noh," "noo," and "ni," going up and down scales.

♪ **Practice consonant placement within phrases**, and make sure you all do it at the same time. Especially important would be the end consonants of words and phrases. The real killer is the "s" sound - if you've got singers all ending the lyric "highways," for example, at different times within the music, you've created a rotating hissing sound that is what the audience will hear. If the lyric is "Traveling the highways," the decision must be made as to exactly where that final "s" will be placed. And everyone has to do the "s" at the same time. (If this presents an enormous problem, you can always tell all the singers except one or two to leave the "s" off completely. The one or two "s"s that remain can produce plenty of sound.) Same thing with "t" - if a lyric ends with "t", for instance "cat," a decision must be made as to exactly where the "t" will come. Otherwise it sounds to the audience like "cat - t - t - t - t."

♪ **Practice attacks and cut-offs.** You can do this using a phrase from a piece you already know - take it and go over it a few times, concentrating as a group on precision entrances and phrase endings. Listen for any sloppiness and go over the exercise until it's all cleaned up.

♪ **A good tune-up exercise** is to have the group sing one note, on any chosen vowel sound, in unison. As this unison note is being sung, have each person consciously listen to the total sound. Aim for a unison that meets your group's requirements for blend and tone.

♪ **Another tune-up:** Same thing as the unison exercise, but in octaves. i.e. Have the low voices sing "noo" on the F below middle C, the medium voices sing on the F just above middle C, and the high voices on high F. Again, listen and tune for the precision and blend you want. When you get it, go up half a step. Listen and blend again. Go up another half step, etc.

♪ **Scales.** Divide the group in half and have Half #1 sing a scale from the root up to the eighth and then down again, while Half #2 sings the same scale starting from the eighth going down to the root and then up again. You can use any vowel sound, or a series of vowel sounds. Repeat the exercise, going up chromatically. Then go back to the midrange and repeat the exercise going down chromatically. Listen for balance. It looks like this:

♪ **Intervals.** Tune-up the group on interesting intervals. For instance, divide the group in half and have Half#1 sing "nah" on a G, while Half #2 sings it up a third on a B. Then have Half #1 stay on the G while Half #2 goes down to a B-flat. Go for pitch precision. Then have Half #1 go up to an A-flat while Half #2 stays on the B-flat, etc. Make up your own interval challenges. This one looks like this:

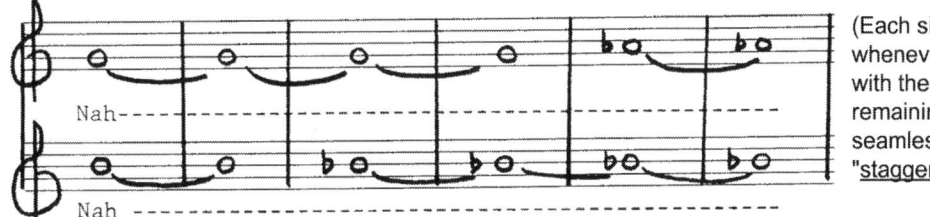

(Each singer breathes whenever necessary, with the total sound remaining smooth and seamless. It's called "staggered breathing.")

♪ **Agility.** Take an especially quick and difficult passage from a piece you are working on, do it on "nah", and use it as an exercise in precision.

♫ **Son of Agility.** Or choose a favorite and elaborate melisma (a "spinning" passage) - from a Bach or Mozart choral work and have the ensemble do it - either in unison or with harmony. Make sure each singer is hitting each note perfectly, listening for pitch, rhythmic precision, and fluidity.

♫ **Daughter of Agility.** Take the same melisma and add dynamics to it. Make sure, in the excitement of dynamics, that the fluidity, pitch, etc. are not lost.

♫ **Cousin of Agility.** On top of precision, fluidity, and dynamics, add another depth to your melisma: emotion. For instance, suggest to the group that the passage be done with melancholy. Then go back and do it again, this time projecting joy. Then again, with, say, intimacy. With royalty. Make up your own.

♫ **Emotional tune-up.** Have the group sing something familiar - this could be a piece you know, an exercise or scale, or even a nursery rhyme. Go through it a few times, each time suggesting the projection by the group of a different emotion. i.e. If everyone's singing "Twinkle Twinkle Little Star," have them first sing it to try to get a teething two-year old to go to sleep. Then have them sing it as if each person is an adult wishing on a star during a sleepless night of insomnia. Then do it as if you're wishing on a morning star after a good night's sleep. Do it as if there is a great sadness - say someone has passed away. Sing the song again as if you've just been given a million dollars.

♫ **Tone, color, and emotion.** Have the group hold a note in unison on "nah" (or add a simple harmony, if desired - a fifth up works well with this). Let people breathe whenever they want (staggered breathing), so the sound is continuous. Give the motivation to make the sound:
> round
> then change to nasal
> then angry then celestial
> then lush and romantic, a la "Sound of Music"
> then streety, a la "Peter Gunn"
> then large, as in Aaron Copeland and the big sky
> now think Tahiti and soft tropical breezes
> then change the mood to bustling Broadway
> now be timid, now sacred now bold
> operatic, etc.

Afterwards, ask for some brief feedback from the group members.

♫ **Listening exercise.** Have the ensemble stand in rows (or in a row) and sing a brief passage from a piece you're working on. Then have everyone stand in a circle or horseshoe, and have them sing the same thing again, being conscious of the change in blend and acoustics. Now have everyone face the wall and sing it. Now bring people back to the circle, but standing next to different people. Discuss the differences you all hear as each individual's physical relation to the group changes.

♪ **Vowel check.** Do 5-note scale passages on each vowel, making sure you all pronounce the vowels the same way. For a heightened vowel check experience, do it in harmony (i.e., half the group can do the scale up a third). For instance:

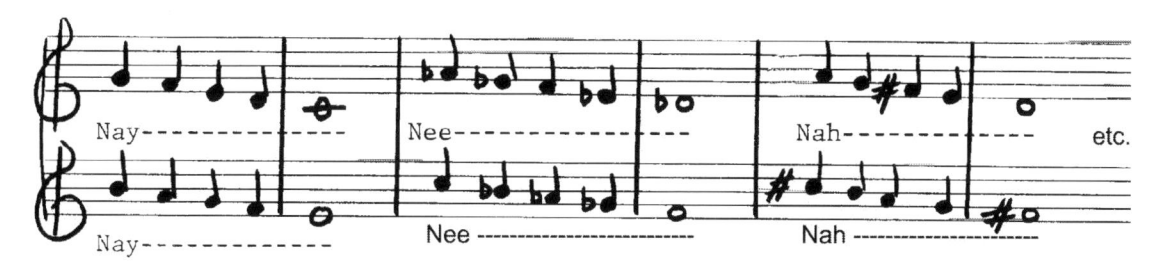

[musical notation: Nay—, Nee—, Nah— etc.]

Ensemble singing appendix: What to do with your pencil

Here are some common marking symbols to write in your score where appropriate:

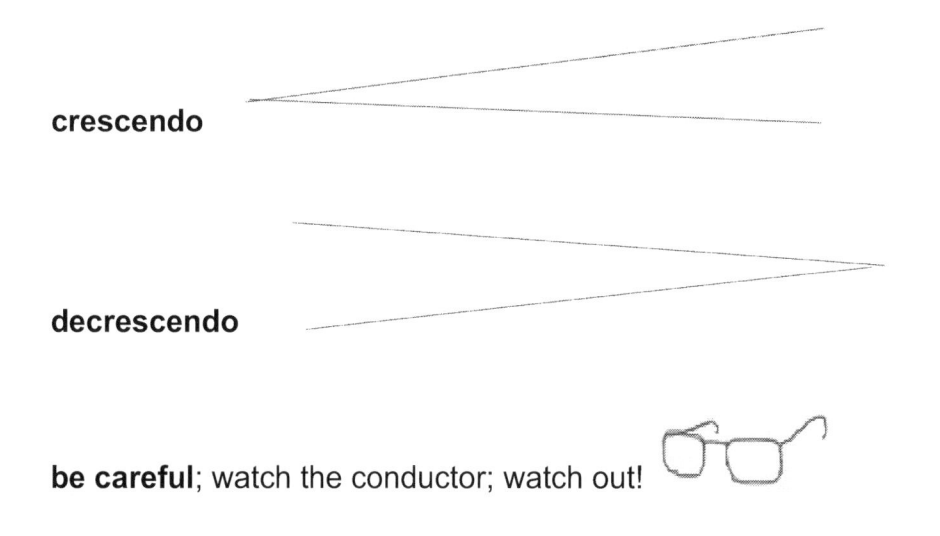

crescendo *[< symbol]*

decrescendo *[> symbol]*

be careful; watch the conductor; watch out! *[glasses symbol]*

soft   *p*

medium soft mp

very soft pp

louder f

medium loud mf

very loud ff

accent (*marcato*)

stress (but don't accent)

accent each note, but don't separate them (*ben marcato*)

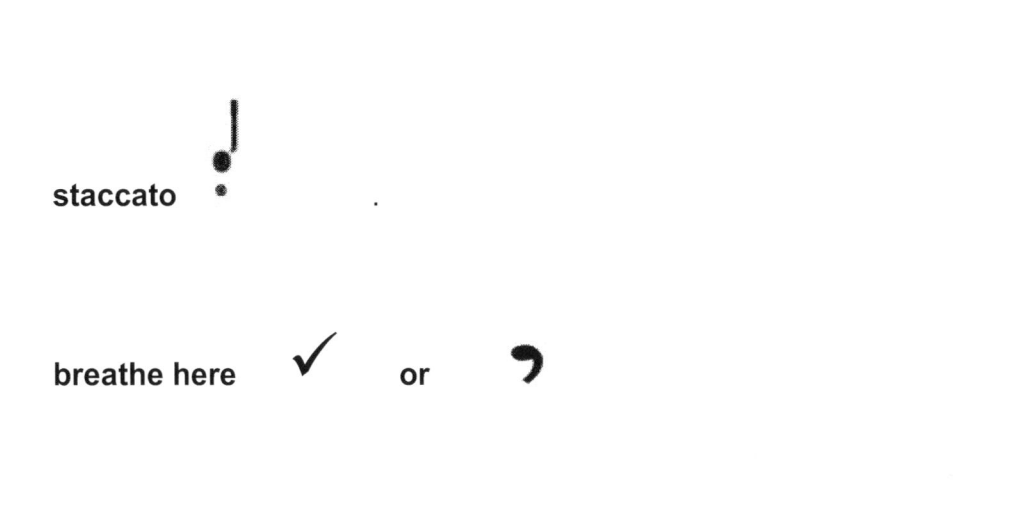

staccato

breathe here   ✓   or   ❜

don't breathe here (make it one phrase)

Your own marking symbols:

Notes:

Ensemble Singing:

Anatomy of a Jazz Ensemble

Whether you sing madrigals, barbershop, background studio "oo"s, rock, pop, or with a chorus, a lot can be learned by studying the personal and musical dynamics of a jazz ensemble.

You've heard this sound if you were ever fortunate enough to get to a Miles gig. Find Youtube footage of ensembles led by Coltrane, Monk, and the other giants - Tom Scott, Stan Getz, Herbie Hancock, Gerry Mulligan, The MJQ, Steve Turre, The New York Jazz Quartet, and hundreds of other trios, quartets, and quintets.

What's Happening to Get This Tight a Sound?

1) First of all, each musician is listening to the other musicians - sometimes listening more to the other musicians and the total sound than to themselves.

2) Each individual musician brings a high level of energy and excitement to the group. The atmosphere is charged. The feeling is that anything can happen, and as the musicians work off each other and the evening goes on, more and more innovative and creative musical things do happen. (Conversely, musicians who must drag themselves to the gig, who slouch in the chair, who have had too many years of too few sit-ups, will lack any kind of magic or intensity.)

3) The musicians respond to one another. Often the person who picks up a solo will pick up where the soloist before left off, both rhythmically and melodically - so they work together and support each other. When one is soloing, too, the others are always responding to that solo, listening intently, laughing quietly at little musical puns or "in" musical jokes, nodding in appreciation if the soloist does something new or particularly appealing. Jazz musicians play for one another almost as much as they play for the audience - thus the after hours jam sessions, the all night "hangs." The interaction is intense.

4) They agree on rhythms. Often the difference between a capable jazz quartet and a burning (actually, it's burnin') jazz quartet is how the musicians relate to each other rhythmically. If it's burnin', the bass and the drums are so linked together they often think of the same musical idea at the same time, even in improvisation.

> -Rhythms are subjective. Some players play on top of the beat, some smack dab in the middle, and some play on the tail end of the beat. A beat can be interpreted in many ways. A really tight ensemble has agreed, verbally or nonverbally, on where to play it.

5) They agree on nuances of interpretation. Even a big band can get this kind of tightness, this incredible telepathic agreement on detail. Witness the high energy, hot licks of the GRP All Star Big Band, Rob McConnell and the Boss Brass, The Tonight Show Band with Doc Severinsen, Bob Mintzer's Big Band and so many more. Or the cool, captivating nuances of the Bob Florence Big Band and other excellent groups. Large or small ensemble, all the musicians work the same slide, the most subtle (or not so subtle) grind, the same attack and delay, the exact groove of the mood. I'm not saying these grooves are not written into the charts - but the nuances can't be written in, and that's what I'm talking about.

6) The egos have been dispensed with long ago, and the dynamic shifts in the group always put the music first. When jazz musicians play the "head" or main motif of the piece, they listen to each other, they blend, they create their one unique voice. Even though they are blending instruments with different sounds, such as piano, bass, drums, and sax, by being aware of each other they are able to project a voice, a timbre that is different, and more than, any individual instrument in the group. Yet no one is sacrificing or holding back the fullness of their own talent.

> -And then when they solo, the instruments that are "comping" (playing in the background in support of the soloist)

become that one voice; the instrument that is soloing moves out front to become the focal point. It's a dynamic shift that's always balanced. (You can see this kind of dynamic, too, in opera choruses or Broadway musical choruses when they sing a piece, and then sing behind the main character. There's always a blend, it just changes, and everyone knows where they fit in.)

7) Decision making in a hot small ensemble is often spur of the moment - yet no one misses a beat.

-Often the musicians will decide <u>on the stand</u> what order the solos will go in, and how many verses each soloist will take. Or they may decide, during the last measure of someone's solo, that the next thing they will do is "trade fours" between the drummer and the sax player. ("Trade fours" means that they solo over the song's chord changes, alternating players every four bars. You can also "trade eights" or anything you want.) These decisions are fluid; they are made as it's happening. They are communicated with a glance, a nod, a slight gesture (or sometimes yelling across the stage, but hey). Each musician is aware of these dynamics at all times.

-And after all the solos, even the most extended atonal, arrhythmic rendition, the group will know exactly - to the fraction of a beat - when to come back in with the closing motif. They know when each player is done soloing; they feel each others' phrasing.

And the magic of the whole thing is that not only do the musicians establish this kind of intimate rapport, but if you're sitting there in the audience, you become a part of it.

Notes:

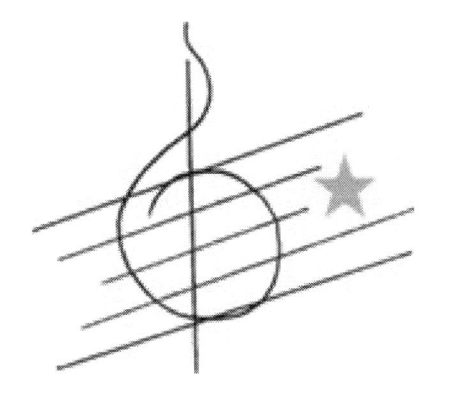

Expanding Your Range

Singing: Its Highs and Lows

A large range is not a mystical occurrence. How high you can fly - and how low you can go - are results more of simple, daily practice than of innate talent. A range of 1 1/2 to 2 octaves is a good range. Many singers have ranges of 3 octaves. If you'd like to extend your range, in both directions, read on.

Key #1: Patience
Here's the thing about the voice: It can't be forced. There's just no way around the fact that developing your voice is a lifelong pursuit. Don't forget that even the most accomplished opera singers still see their coaches regularly.

Expanding your range happens slowly. Be happy with a half step higher or lower each week. And, too, you will hit plateaus where your voice just won't go any farther. When that happens, vocalize over your newly acquired range, but don't push it until - and if - it feels easy again.

Key #2: Ease
When you begin to hit new high or low notes, it should come easily. Straining to hit a note, getting sore throats from vocalizing, or simply sounding awful are warning signs that you're pushing your voice to expand too far too fast.

How to extend your range? Just keep vocalizing.

Here's the good news: ***A singer's range expands naturally as he or she studies and vocalizes daily. It's a by-product of regular singing.*** Go through the chapter on how to vocalize, work with your voice teacher on whatever your other vocal challenges are (agility, fluidity of tone, or whatever), and you will experience the magic of an ever widening range.

I would suggest keeping track of your range, so you can see the progress. Once a week, jot down the date and the average range for that week. You might even note your extreme highs and lows. The very high or very low notes that only grace your routine on occasion, will soon become easy-to-reach notes that are a part of your every day song singing.

An expanded range is also a by-product of good breathing technique. So as you include your breathing exercises in your daily routine, and use a supported breath in your song singing, you will naturally see your range increase.

Range expansion by developing the registers:

If you want to go about expanding your range in a more methodical way, here's another approach. Review the chapter on registers if you need to, before proceeding.

1. Expand the range of your chest register, both higher and lower.

2. Expand the range of your head register, higher and lower.

3. Polish the "break notes" that occur between the registers, and match the tones as best as possible. By expanding your chest register upward and your head register down, you'll have a larger number of overlap notes - these are notes you can do in either head or chest, depending on the demands of the song.

4. For women, you'll want to develop and work on the "high head" or "super head" register, if you want to hit that high C.

5. For men, you'll want to make decisions about your head register, or your falsetto. You can go up higher than you ever thought possible, if you're willing to use your falsetto. You can work on the tone of your falsetto so that it blends in with the chest tones. In listening to a good singer who generally sings in chest, it's often impossible to tell when he has switched to falsetto in order to hit a few high notes. Also, working on your head tones has the side benefit of improving the overall tone of your whole voice.

> -Many voice teachers hear more than just chest and falsetto in the male voice. They hear chest, head, mixed falsetto, and pure falsetto. Depending on how involved you want to get, these are all doors of opportunity for you in developing your range.

Examples

Chandra begins with a range that goes up an octave from the B just below middle C. She naturally sings in chest from her B up to an E-flat, then breaks into head on the E.

- ✓ She works her chest register, slowly expanding the range over which she vocalizes, eventually getting it down to the F below middle C, and up to the F above middle C. She's now got an entire octave she can work with, in her chest voice alone -At the same time, she gently works her head voice, extending the range over which she vocalizes in this register from the E above middle C, down a whole step to D. On the upward expansion, she vocalizes a little higher each week until she can comfortably hit two D's above middle C. She's gone up by a minor third in this register.

- ✓ With the help of her voice teacher, she learns how it feels to sing in "high head," or "super head." This entire register is new to her, and as she becomes comfortable with it, she finds that a whole new door of possibilities has opened up for her - for without trying, using no stress or strain whatsoever, she is able to sing from her previous high note of D, all the way up to a high A-flat.

- ✓ Now she also has the luxury of an overlap in her registers. She can sing over the D, E, and F in the middle C scale using her choice of either head or chest - whichever she prefers. She will also work on those three "break notes" to make sure their tones blend in with both her chest and head registers. In her "high head" voice, too, will come the luxury of an overlap with the head voice.

- ✓ She's now got a range of over two octaves.

Steven has never worried excessively about registers, break notes, or changing from chest to falsetto. His voice does change registers easily and fluidly, and it's something he's never had to worry about. He sings with a supported breath and a relaxed jaw, and trusts his instrument.

- One of his favorite exercises is a quick, light scale, on various syllables, going up a ninth and down again. (An example of this exercise follows.) He begins in his midrange, and transposes this exercise up by half-steps, stopping before he becomes uncomfortable. Then he goes back to his midrange, and does the exercise again, this time transposing down by half-steps each time he does the scale. Again, he stops before he hits any uncomfortable notes. Later in his vocalizing session, when his voice is thoroughly warmed up, he goes back to this exercise and does it again, but this time he makes it a point to transpose up and then down to a scale that lands him a half step higher and then lower than was previously comfortable. Each week he adds a half step in both directions, thus expanding his range gradually and comfortably.

- Once he gets to the point where his new notes are part of his "comfortable" range, he does slower scales, and holds each note a little longer, instead of quickly moving through the scales as he had done before. This helps him develop the <u>tone</u> he wants for his new notes, so they will blend in with the rest of his range (an example follows).

<u>Key #3: Lightness</u>
When practicing scales and working on range expansion, you generally want to keep your tone light and your volume soft. First of all, light dynamics and brighter tones are easier to blend. Secondly, the voice is more agile when it's light. And third, this will help prevent damage to the voice. Stomping around like a rhinoceros in new parts of your range can cause problems. (Don't forget that soft volumes are still tonal, focused, pure sounds. Don't be breathy.)

Remember, too, when we talk about registers, that your voice will be different every day. So you've got to be easy-going and fluid about the whole register-changing process. The overall feeling in changing registers is not one of forcing a change at a particular note, although you can consciously change at a particular note, but rather of <u>letting</u> it change. It's a mental image thing, with tangible results. Everything in voice must feel smooth and easy, never forced or strained. If you're a woman working on your "high head" voice, you'll find that it simply won't go into that register by force. The only way to get to that register is through relaxation; letting it flow there.

<u>Key #4: Overshoot</u>
Most singers actually have two sets of ranges: one that they vocalize over, and another, smaller, range that they actually sing over. It's a good idea to vocalize over more than you will ever sing over. For one thing, your very high and low notes will usually always need some work. For another thing, overshooting during practice will give you confidence for performances. If you regularly vocalize up to a high C, for example, singing that high A for your performance will be a piece of cake.

<u>Key #5: Physical relaxation</u>
You can't sing well if you're tense, and you certainly can't reach your highest and lowest notes if you're tense. I've seen singers actually stand on their toes with their eyes looking upward and their shoulders up around their ears, in an attempt to hit a high note. Imagine how this sounds. It's like when you go to the doctor for a shot. If

you're tense, it's going to hurt. Conversely, trying to hit very low notes by bending your head forward and creating double chins will do nothing but scrunch up your tone. For each half step you take that's higher or lower, you must consciously relax your body one degree more.

Exercises
Quick, light, stress-free scales are your best exercises. Here's an example of the nine-note scale Steven used:

Another good set of exercises are slower 3-note major triad arpeggios. On the slower exercises you'll want to listen for depth and richness of tone, and a certain ease and beauty in your very high and low notes. Here's an example.

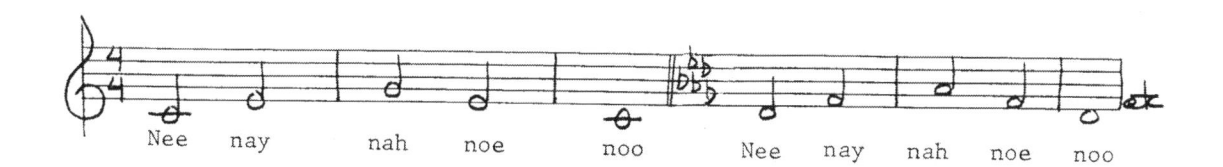

Key #6: Help for high notes
♪ Because singing your very high notes can be such an emotional, stressful event, I would have to conclude that tension and lack of confidence are the two biggest enemies to a gorgeous high register. Assuming, of course, that you're breathing properly, your best "technique" in singing high notes is mental. It's a feeling of physical ease, of mental ease, of "letting go." A

mental image that helps me is one of "floating." As I go for the high notes, I imagine myself small and light. I also imagine myself gently landing onto the high note from some cloud up above it.

♪ Some singers use the mental image of "coming down to the high note from a note above it," even if they never sing the note above it. What you never want to do is imagine yourself climbing up a slippery ladder. Bracing yourself and saying, "Oh rats, here it comes," as you approach your high B-flat is dangerous business. If you're singing the lyric "On that clear day, how it will astound you..." and in your head you're thinking "I promise, God, if you help me through this upcoming high note I will never (whatever you do) again, and in addition if I can just get through this without utterly annihilating humiliation, I will live a quiet and secluded life in a monastery," you're in trouble.

♪ Also in singing high notes, you don't want to hang on to your consonants. Remember that music travels on vowels. Get the consonants out of the way crisply, clearly, and quickly.

♪ Get that jaw dropped. You cannot sing high notes through gritted teeth.

♪ Modify your vowels if you need to. Many singers take slight liberties in their upper ranges, trying to go for an "ah" sound as much as possible, no matter what the actual vowel is. For instance, if you're singing the vowel "ee," you might want to modify it slightly in your high range. Do this by thinking "ee" but singing a slightly more "oh" sound. The audience will hear it as "ee." The chapter on vowel sounds goes into more detail about modifications.

♪ You need lots of breath support, but not more volume.

♪ The throat should feel "open." You never want to feel constricted, pinched, or tense in your throat or neck area. There should be a feeling of ease, as if all the power comes from the lower abdomen and the rest of your body just lets the sound float out.

Key #7: In search of non-booming low notes
♦ When you sing low notes, remember to keep the tone bright, focused, and forward; never breathy or boomy.

♦ As with high notes, the mental attitude in singing low notes is one of ease and relaxation. If you push for low notes, furrow your brow, or get nervous as you go down, it will make you sound like you're singing from a swamp.

♦ Also as with high notes, approach low notes "from above." This is a mental image that helps keep the tone bright and matched with the tones of your midrange.

♦ You use more breath in singing low notes. That doesn't mean you must take in more air; rather it means you must be stingy with the amount of air you let out on the exhale. Also, don't fall into the trap of making your low notes louder than the rest of your range. If anything, practice them at a soft volume.

♦ Your jaw on the low notes need not be dropped as far as you drop it for the high notes. In fact, dropping the jaw too much will produce an unwanted boomy quality. If the lamps rattle on your low notes, your jaw is dropped too much.

♦ If your low notes tend to get boomy, practice scales on the forward vowel sounds, such as "ee" and "ay," or practice your scales on a hum. The hum will bring the sound forward. (The "Placement Waker-Upper" exercise from Warm-up II is one of many humming exercises that can help.)

Notes:

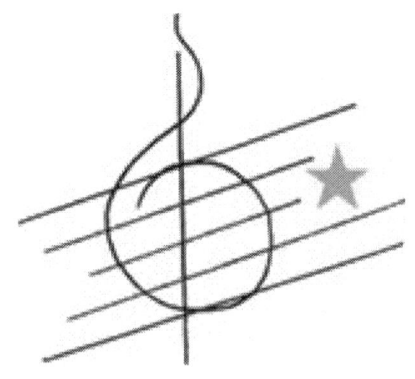

Eye Contact:

When to Go Eyeball to Eyeball

Eye contact - a subtle but mighty issue. The use and misuse of the eyeball can have a big impact on your performance. Unless you're an excellent actor, which you might indeed be, making eye contact with someone is allowing them to see exactly what you're thinking and feeling. Plus, you get eye contact back from them - so there's a whole lot of energy being exchanged. Here are some suggestions:

♮ **While auditioning,** don't make eye contact with anyone. Instead, keep your sight just above their heads. There's no reason they need to see the terror in your eyes. (Of course if the producer speaks to you after you're done singing, definitely commit to eye contact.)

♮ **While performing,** eye contact is optional - but you must at least look up and out. If it's a small, intimate club, eye contact might be nice. If it's Lincoln Center, you can't see anyone out there anyway. In a medium sized room you might want to look out just above people's heads. Making eye contact can be distracting. Or worse, if you make eye contact with someone who is frazzled, sneering, or flossing their teeth, it could dampen the mood.

♮ **While speaking at a business presentation** you must make eye contact in order to be sincere. Lack of eyeballing makes you look like you're hiding something.

♮ **Speaking at a large convention, or lecturing,** you need to make eye contact to use as feedback. Are people looking totally confused? You want to know this right away, so you can explain the material in better detail. If everyone's asleep, this is information you need to have to make your lecture more interesting.

♮ **In any situation,** you never want to look down, close your eyes for too long, or look too far above or away from your audience or listeners. Some singers, in an attempt to be torchy or deep, close their eyes for long periods of time. This can distance the singer from the listener, and eventually the audience will get bored. Even if you're not looking people directly in the eye, they must be able to see your eyes.

♮ **On video or television,** you and your producer must make decisions about when to look directly into the eye of the camera.

Notes:

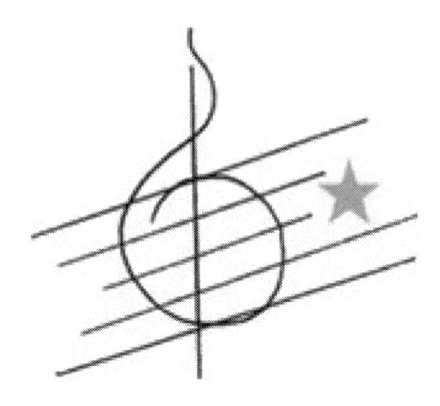

Finding a Voice Teacher

How to find the perfect voice teacher
It's more important than finding the right therapist, attorney, or gym. Finding the perfect voice instructor can make or break your voice, and consequently your career, your hobby, or simply your enjoyment of music.

You can start out with almost any kind of voice. A good voice teacher - one that's perfectly attuned to your individual vocal needs - can take that voice and develop it into its fullest potential. Whether you are looking for a new teacher after many years of previous study, or whether you're just starting out, this is one of the most critical choices you will make.

What is "a good voice teacher"?

1. Someone who understands and respects your individual vocal needs:

    a) the technical needs of your voice;

    b) your artistic needs as a unique and important person.

    c) And if you don't know what your goals are, a good voice teacher will help you find out, rather than automatically imposing their goals on you.

2. Someone who has the training, experience, and/or expertise to get you where you want to go.

3. Someone who asks <u>you</u> questions!
A good voice instructor will want to know where you want to go with your music. He or she will want to know what music you listen to, who your favorite singers are, and what your professional goals are. You might already be a professional singer - the teacher will want to know that. He or she will want to know what your previous training has been, and what vocal techniques you already practice. He or she will ask you what <u>you</u> feel your strong and weak points are, and what you'd like to hear your voice sound like. If you are a voice teacher, are you asking your students these

questions?

4. Someone who is experienced in the kind of music you want to study.
Many voice teachers have certain areas of specialty. Some teach with classical techniques, some specialize in belting, some are rooted in a certain pop sound. Some teachers have the students do exercises and scales for a long time; others start right away with song singing. Some teachers teach bel canto basics and can apply those basics to any genre of music. You need to know ahead of time how your prospective teacher likes to work. Then you can decide if that fits in with your needs.

How do you find such a person?

* Word of mouth, if the recommendation comes from someone you trust.

* Go out to hear people's gigs. If you hear singers you love, ask if they teach privately. If not, ask who they study with.

* Call your nearest music school, and ask for a list of graduates who teach privately.

* Invest in lessons from at least two or three different teachers, before deciding on one.

* Enroll in short term classes, and make connections that way. Many towns have acting schools, adult education classes, weekend workshops given by local singers or actors, informal university courses, or summer workshops. These classes are not only fun, but they're great for meeting people who teach.

* Join the civic or church chorus - you'll meet people there who teach, or who know of good teachers.

* If you know and trust the people on your Internet singing list or newsgroup, post an inquiry there.

* Check out the ads in your local alternative paper, your music & arts weekly, or the university paper.

What to ask a prospective teacher?

1) Tell them what your musical needs and goals are, and ask them if they are comfortable with that.

2) Ask them where they studied, who they studied with, or what kind of performance experience they've had.

3) Ask them what kind of music they prefer. If it's vastly different from your preferences, find out if they are familiar with the music you like, and if they can get you where you want to go.

4) Ask how much they charge. Remember, someone who charges an absolute fortune is not necessarily a better teacher, even if everyone in town is going to him. Unless you're preparing for an audition at the Met, you need not pay a voice teacher more than you pay your attorney.

5) Find out if this person is a technical voice instructor, or a vocal coach. There is a difference. If they teach the basics such as breathing and vowel sounds (how to sing), this is an instructor. If they are more into repertoire and stage presentation, they may be a coach. Generally, voice instructors can also coach, but not the other way around.

Your part in this duet

You can have the best voice teacher in town and still not learn anything. Why? Because it takes two to get this thing on the road. Your teacher can only take you so far - most of the actual work is up to you.

1. You must show up every week. I know this sounds fairly basic, but you'd be surprised how many people want to learn to sing, but don't have the organization in their lives to get to their lesson every week. The teacher cannot weed you out of your chaos and drag you to your lesson.

2. Every day, you must practice the material your teacher gave you for that week. Your teacher can only show you stuff. You yourself have to actually do the work.

-With singing, I promise you <u>there will be no progress without daily practice.</u> That's how the voice works - it develops slowly, with care and patience. On the flip side, no matter how hopeless a vocal task seems to be, it will get easier and smoother with each day that you practice it.

3. Remember that developing the voice takes times. That's the nature of the instrument. You force it, you hurt it. So be patient with the lessons.

4. If you have found a voice teacher you trust, then be willing to try what they want you to try. If you want to be a jazz singer, and your teacher wants you to learn Italian arias, my suggestion is: Learn the arias. You've got to trust that she knows what she's doing. Also, when you get what might be construed as "weird" vocal exercises to do, do them. Singers make strange noises in the process of training and maintaining their voices. Uses of non-musical noises, creative mental imagery, and unusual breathing exercises are part of the process.

5. About trusting your teacher. Many people have preconceived notions about singing in chest versus head register. If you do trust your voice teacher, you need to at least give her or his suggestions about this a try. You may develop your head register and then decide you only want to sing in chest after all. This is fine. Nothing has been lost, and you've got the use your head register any time you want it. Conversely, if you're a die-hard soprano and singing in chest is something only altos do...

6. Leave your ego outside. When you go in for a lesson, you can't become a sulking diva if your teacher says you're singing flat. Better to know you're singing flat so you can fix it, then to empty out the local pub every time you sit in with the band, and not know why.

7. You can't expect your voice teacher to work miracles for you if you smoke. If you want to sing, smoking is not an option so don't even bother angsting out over quitting. Just quit and be done with it.

8. You simply can't vocalize in the car. How can you vocalize if your instrument is bent in the middle? Would a flute sound its best if you bent it in the middle and then played it? You've got to be standing up to vocalize.

When to bail out:

♩ If your voice gets hoarse or your throat sore, check with your teacher. You may be doing something wrong, or you may have misunderstood what your teacher wanted you to do. But if you're constantly sore or hoarse because of vocal techniques you are supposed to be doing, it's time to leave Dodge.

♩ You feel like a miserable, talentless worm. Time to look for another teacher.

♩ You used to sound OK, but with this new breathing technique this teacher taught you, you're now starting to sing flat and get tired easily. It doesn't matter that every other person in town is going to this teacher - if you are sliding backwards from his or her techniques, it's time to check out. (By the way, this does not mean he or she is not a good teacher - it simply means that technique doesn't work for you.)

♩ You feel you are being treated like a cow in a herd of cattle. Your teacher never remembers your name, doesn't ask how your practicing went that week, takes phone calls during your hour, or wears a cape. Time to find someone who cares.

♩ We talked about the prejudices some singers have about head versus chest registers. I usually like people to develop both of these registers, if that's in keeping with their own goals. But some teachers teach only head voice - and some teachers who specialize in certain forms of pop music teach only chest voice. If this suits you, fine. But if the teacher is forcing your voice up too high in the chest register and you're getting sore throats, or conversely is not allowing you to develop your chest register even though you want to, it's time to change airlines.

♩ Listen to your instincts. Your inner voice already sings. It already knows the score. It's the best voice of all in guiding you to your best singing teacher.

Notes:

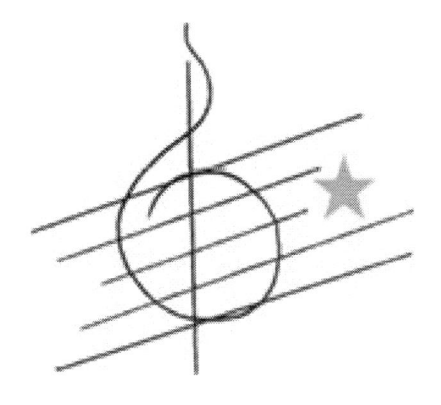

Glass Breaking

How to Break Glass

Of course you could just throw it into the fireplace. But why make it easy on ourselves? Here's how to do in your fine crystal the artist's way - by singing it to shreds.

First, you'll need to obtain a very fine, delicate wine glass. It's got to be basically fragile, let's face it. Heavy lead crystal with lots of supportive ridges would take a rhinoceros to shatter it with sound, so stick to simple, light-weight glasses with no decorations.

Assuming that you will actually be able to break this glass, you should also wear a pair of safety glasses. I personally don a pair of rubber gloves as well.

The next thing you'll want to do is assemble together all your singer friends. In case your voice just doesn't have that oomph it takes the break the glass, you'll want someone to be able to break it. Why waste all this preparation, not to mention the anticipation and the emotional investment of this project?

Next, clear out all your cats, dogs, and children. You don't want any little creatures hobbling around with shards in their tippers because of your career.

Most importantly, tell your neighbors not to call the police, that everything is relatively OK no matter what shrieks, piercing blasts, or yodels they may hear coming from your apartment.

Now you're ready to do this thing:

- Go into the bathroom. It's got to be a bathroom with no carpeting or draperies. You want lots of sound bouncing around in there. Find a spot where the acoustics seem to be the most alive. In my downstairs bathroom, this spot is actually in the shower stall.

- Put the wine glass on a stool, chair, or plant holder of some kind. You'll have to experiment with placement of the glass, but you don't want to place it on something that will soak up too much sound, such as a heavy wooden table. I have a little shampoo holder attached to the shower wall on which I put the glass. As for height, try putting the glass at the level of your mouth. You can't break it singing down into it, and it won't break if it's up higher than your head.

- Now tap the glass with a spoon and find out what key it's in. If you've gotten this far in this chapter, finding out what key a wine glass is in is not going to strike you as eccentric at all. You probably go around guessing what key train whistles are in - I know you.

- Well, here goes. In your most tonal, vibrant, supported, formant-laden voice (see the chapter on singer's formant), sing the note that the glass is in. Sing it in the highest octave you can. I've found that a syllable somewhere between "oo" and "oh" seems to have the most power. But you might also try "nah" or "nee." Stand in front of the glass, and then try standing at different places in relation to the glass. Try different levels of vibrato - although a very large vibrato may not have enough focus. Keep the sound going for as long as you can.

What you want to do is resonate with the glass. You want to duplicate its frequencies. Sound, as you know, is made up of actual waves. If the glass rings at, say, a high A-flat, then you want to sing a note on that high A-flat in an attempt to get the exact sound waves going that will cause the glass to resonate.

If you've broken the glass at this point, you're probably not reading this chapter anymore. You're now in the process of picking up small slivers of glass (thus the rubber gloves), wondering if there is an easier way to make a living.

If you haven't yet broken the glass, it's time to let your friends give it a try. Don't worry if you can't do it. Not everyone's voice can break glass, and quite frankly, I'm not sure if the ability to break glass necessarily makes for the most pleasant singing voice. My own voice simply will not do it, although I have seen singers routinely make the glass rattle. Rattling is good.

But either way, hey. There you are, a bunch of singers, standing in your shower stall together, wearing rubber gloves and welders' helmets, shrieking at a wine glass.

What more could you possibly need from your daily vocalizing session?

Notes:

Glossary:

What Do You Actually Mean When You Say I'm Singing Flat?

Categories of Ourselves

Alto: A singer whose range extends up approximately one and a half octaves from the G below middle C. Men or women can be altos. In contemporary singing, altos are usually women who take the lower of the female parts. In ensembles, you may also find **first** and **second** altos, with the first altos taking the higher of the alto parts, and the seconds the lower. An alto may also be called a **contralto**.

Baritone: Sits on a fence between tenors and basses, with a range extending up approximately an octave and a sixth from two G's below middle C.

Bass: A very nice guy, like a rock. Sings up approximately an octave and a sixth from two E's below middle C. In opera, a **basso profondo**'s range is exceptionally low and powerful, and he often sings serious parts, whereas a **basso cantante** has a lighter quality - for a bass.

Contralto: The same as alto. However, in talking to altos, many who sing contralto describe their voices as being lower than the typical alto range. In classical music, there is also the **dramatic contralto**, whose range is slightly lower than the dramatic soprano, but who has that same kind of power and richness of tone.

Countertenor: A very high male voice, with a range similar to that of an alto, or even a mezzo soprano.

Diva: The center of it all. Can be an alto, soprano, tenor, baritone, or bass. More of a mind-set. I say, go for it. If, however, someone calls you a diva during a rehearsal, this should probably not be taken as a compliment. Many singers are closet divas, with diva-ness deep in their hearts but the common sense not to let it show in public. My personal feeling is that closet diva-hood can be a healthy, life-affirming thing.

Fach: Categories of ourselves. "Fach" is German for "compartment." It often means soprano, alto, etc., but it can also carry the connotation of what *quality* of sound we produce. For instance, a **basso profondo** is a separate fach from **basso cantante**; **bass** is a separate fach from **tenor**. There are no set number of categories. Some people think in terms of four: **soprano, alto, tenor, bass**. Some think in terms of twenty or twenty-one: from **lyric coloratura** and **spinto soprano**, to **basso buffo** and **kavalier-bariton**. The term comes from an operatic tradition, but is now being applied to other genres as well.

Mezzo soprano: A singer whose range extends up approximately an octave and a sixth from the A below middle C.

Soprano: A singer (male or female) whose range extends up approximately two octaves from middle C. In ensemble singing, you may find the terms **first** and **second** soprano, with the first sopranos taking the higher of the two parts, and the seconds the lower. (The second soprano is still usually higher than the first alto.) If you're really into categorizing, you can divide female sopranos into **coloratura** (who can make your spine tingle by hitting those incredibly high notes, and who also have great agility), **dramatic** (bring the box of tissue to the opera, for her acting talents and power will make you weep), and **lyric** (who typically has that light, crystalline, angelic quality).

Tenor: A singer (male or female) whose range extends up approximately one and a half octaves from two B's below middle C. If you go to the opera, your tenors will be male - and you'll need to know that a **Heldentenor** (a.k.a. **heroic tenor**) is a dramatic, agile tenor with a lot of brilliance and power to his voice, whereas a **lyric tenor** has a lighter quality.

Fach Hierarchy: OK, from highest in range to lowest:
    Coloratura
    Soprano
    Mezzo
    Alto
    Tenor
    Baritone
    Bass

Fach Hierarchy in Jazz:
    Singer

Hieroglyphics for Pitches

If you're having a conversation backstage after the opera, or at the dinner table, there's an easier way to describe what note you're talking about besides saying, "Two G's below middle C." Here it is:

c^I = middle C
c^{II} = the C above middle C
c^{III} = the C above C^{II} (a.k.a. "high C")
c = the C below middle C
C = two C's below middle C

The rest follows. For instance, if you say "**d** to **b**" you'd be talking about the d below middle C up to the b just below middle C. If someone says to you, "**d^I** to **b^I**" they would mean the d just above middle C up to the b above middle C.

Italian Terms You Will Come Across (even in pop or contemporary music):

A tempo: The direction to return to the original tempo.

Con brio: Sing it with fire.

Doloroso: Sung sadly, as if grieving.

Messa di voce: This is a dynamic in which you begin singing a note softly, swell to a louder volume, and then diminish back to soft. For example, you sing and hold one note piano (soft), you crescendo to forte (loud), and you decrescendo back to piano.

Mezza voce: Sung with half your regular voice. Save the full voice for the gig.

Segue: Continuing with no pause.

Sotto voce: Softly. In a low voice.

Tessitura: The predominant pitch-range of the piece. If most of the song stays in the high part of your singing range, you can tell people the tessitura is high. Any vocal part can have a high or a low tessitura. A soprano, for example, may sing a song with a low tessitura.

Tutti (**tutta**, **tutte**): Everyone. If your choral score is marked "tutti," that means the whole chorus sings - as opposed to just the soloist singing, for example, or just the tenors.

Moods and Styles**

A cappella: Sung without instrumental accompaniment.

Bel canto: The Italian term meaning literally "beautiful singing." There are many books out devoted to the bel canto style of singing, and almost as many definitions. But basically it means you're not shrieking, shouting, banging your guitar on the stage floor, nor are you belting, straining for notes, or grinding your vocal cords. In bel canto, you're singing mellifluously, with great beauty of tone and with apparent ease. Your breathing is powerful but smooth. Your vowel sounds are attended to. Your timbre is rich and round, expressive but not heavy. Your song interpretations are intelligent and compassionate, but you'd never be sobbing on the floor, or letting your guts spill out on the stage. You sing with fluid dynamics - you don't whack your audience on the head with emotional two-by-fours. Your listeners leave refreshed, not drained. You go home ready for a cool glass of fine white wine rather than an immediate need for a tequila shot. Many contemporary voice teachers teach this style - it's a perfect technique to learn as your main, basic vocal style. You can always branch out from it, and you can always use parts of it in other genres. For instance: rich tone and a smooth style - how bad could that be for almost any genre?

Legato: Smooth. A legato phrase is sung without any perceptible break between the notes. It's not as exaggerated as a glide, or a slide like a siren, where one note bleeds into the next. In legato you do hear each individual note, but each note flows into the next. There are no accented notes in a legato phrase.

Marcato: Stressed. I mean, the *note* is stressed.

Melisma: Not, as some have thought, an unsightly skin situation. A melisma is an extended vocal phrase on one syllable, often at a quick tempo and/or a repetitive melodic and rhythmic pattern.

Portamento: When you sing in this way, your voice glides from one note to the next, sliding evenly through all the microtones as it goes.

Solfege: The study of intervals. Vocal exercises in which a syllable is assigned to each note of the scale. The solfege syllables for a major scale are: do, re, mi, fa, sol, la, si (or ti), do. You can have what's called a **moveable *do*** solfege system, or a **fixed *do*** system. With moveable *do*, *do* is the root note of whatever key you are in. With fixed ***do, do*** is always C.

Staccato: When you sing a phrase in a staccato style, each note will be short and detached from the next note. The notes are not held, they do not flow as they do in legato singing.

Unison: All the voices sing on the same pitch, as opposed to singing in harmony.

Vivace: Lively, quick.

Vocalese: See the chapters on ensemble singing and on scat.

**See also the chapter on song singing.

Noises. Non-Musical
Mouth noises: If you're on mike in a studio situation and you've got a dry mouth, the mike will pick up mildly embarrassing noises. Taking small sips of water during your studio session will eliminate mouth noises.
Pop: Overdoing the consonants. A commonly popped consonant is the "p" sound. Don't pop your "p"s.
Sibilant: Hissing or frying "s"s. Not contagious, and entirely curable.

Pieces of Paper
Chart: This is music encoded specifically for an instrumentalist. You can hand the piano player some sheet music you bought at the store, and the pianist may say, "Yes, but where's your *chart*?" Instrumentalists can use sheet music in a pinch, but if you're a contemporary singer (pop, jazz, fusion, soul, etc.) you've got to provide your players with charts. Depending on the complexity of the piece, you might need separate charts for your drummer, your horn player, and your pianist. If there's a special bass line in a piece, for example, your bass player will need a special chart written up. Charts do not contain lyrics, unless the instrumentalist needs them for a particular cue or cut-off.

Charts are personalized for you. You can't really buy them anywhere, like you can buy sheet music. You have to have them done for you by a local musician, or learn how to do them yourself. Thus your charts will be in your personal keys, with your own chosen forms and endings. Let's just say that singers would rather exchange toothbrushes than charts. (Classical singers don't usually use charts.)

Fake book: A thick, spiral-bound book filled with hundreds of lead sheets. You can get fake books for any instrument in any key. There are singers' fake books, guitar fake books, wedding fake books, harp fake books.

Lead sheet: A lead sheet is more singer-friendly than a chart. It has the melody line of a song written out, and it includes the lyrics. Above each measure are written the chords that are in that measure. So sometimes a lead sheet can be used in place of a chart. It does not have an extensive two-handed piano part written out, as sheet music has.

Score: Usually refers to a more elaborate chart - perhaps one that has been written for a big band or orchestra.

Sheet music: This is the music you buy at the music store. It has the two-handed piano part written out, note for note, plus it's got the melody, the lyrics, and some basic glossy photo of someone on the front. Classical sheet music does not usually contain the chords above the measures, but other genres of music do.

Song Anatomy:

A cappella: Singing without instrumental accompaniment.

Bar: Measure.

Bridge: The part of the song that connects the main verses, but has a markedly different melody and chord progression than the verses.

Changes: When you hear musicians talk about changes, they are talking about the chords and the chord progressions in a song.

Coda: The concluding passage. It differs from a tag in that the coda is a part of the way the composer wrote the song. A tag may be part of the composition, but it also can be improvised or written in at the whim of the singer.

Downbeat: Within each bar of music, there are certain beats which are stressed, and certain beats that are unstressed. The stressed beat (or beats) of the measure is the downbeat. Since the conductor's baton traditionally goes in a downward motion on the first beat of each measure, the first beat is often the downbeat. For example, in a 4/4 piece, where the beats are counted 1, 2, 3, 4, the typical downbeat is beat #1. Beat #3 might also be stressed, but perhaps not as strongly as beat #1. Yes, it's also a magazine.

Measure: Bar.

Pickup: A note or phrase that comes in just before the actual rhythmic body of the song or verse. In "God Bless the Child" by Herzog and Holiday, the first verse starts with: "Them that's got shall get...". The body of the verse, rhythmically and melodically, starts on the lyric "got." The first two words, "Them that's," come in on a pickup (in this context, also called an upbeat). You can have pickups of any length. In the song "How High the Moon" by Hamilton and Lewis, the pickup is nearly a whole measure: "Somewhere there's music" is the first phrase, but the body of the song starts on the word "music." The words before it, "Somewhere there's," constitute the pickup.

Pickup: A truck used in Texas to haul instruments to the gig.

Riff: A short, catchy phrase that can be repeated as often as necessary.

Solo: In jazz, solos are the improvisational sections played by individual musicians, usually with the rest of the band comping in the background.

Tag: In popular singing, the tag is an extended ending of a song. This ending is often different than the body of the song in form, in chord changes, or rhythmically. Sometimes a tag is simply made up of the last line which is repeated two or three times. Most fake books don't include tags - the tags are put in by the singer or pianist. It's a personal or interpretative thing.

Upbeat: **(1)** The unstressed beat (or beats) in each measure. Traditionally the conductor's baton goes in an upward direction on this beat, thus its name. So if you've got a piece in 4/4 where the beats are counted 1,2,3,4, the typical upbeat is beat #4. **(2)** The upbeat, or any portion of it, can also be a **pickup** - that is, it comes in before the strong rhythmic and melodic beginning of a song phrase.

> Example: The phrase "The <u>Days</u> of Wine and Roses" (Mercer/Mancini) begins its strong rhythmic and melodic line with the lyric "days." The lyric "The" is the pickup. It's also an upbeat.

Vamp: An extended ending to a song, often improvisational, over a short chord progression that is repeated until you run out of musical ideas. Often used when you and the piano player forgot to work out an actual ending to the song. You can vamp while you're trying to decide how to end it.

Tempo Hierarchy (from slowest to fastest)
Largo (broadly)
Lento (very slowly)
Adagio
Andante
Moderato (moderate tempo)
Allegretto
Allegro
Presto
Prestissimo (very quickly)

Tempos That Stand Alone
Accelerando: Gradually going faster.

Fermata: Not a tempo at all, really. A fermata is a pause. The length of this pause depends entirely on how the piece is being interpreted artistically. If you have a fermata in your song, you want to make sure the piano player is watching you and is sober. If you have a fermata in your choral piece, you want to make sure you watch the conductor so you don't end up experiencing the chorister's most dreaded nightmare - singing happily and loudly by yourself.

Ritardando: Gradually slowing down.

Ritenuto: Suddenly slowing down.

Rubato: Elasticizing the tempo, according to your artistic interpretation. In popular music, often used in song introductions or endings. When you sing rubato, you want to keep good eye contact with your piano player, or else you'll both find yourself in different parts of the music at the same time. Never sing rubato if your pianist is mad at you for something. A noted jazz piece using rubato in the introduction is "Lush Life" by Billy Strayhorn.

Tenuto: Sustained.

Theoretical Details

AABA: The form of the song. AABA means that the form is: verse, verse, bridge, verse. When you sit in at a nightclub you might say to the piano player, "I'll sing over the first AABA, then you take the first two A's again for your solo and I'll come back in on the bridge." There are other forms, too, such as **ABA** (verse, bridge, verse), or perhaps the song is simply **AA** (two verses).

Accidental: A sharp, flat, double sharp, double flat, or natural that is notated for a one-time use. (To use sharps, flats, etc. throughout the entire piece without having to notate them each time, you use your key signature.) If an accidental is indicated, it will apply to that same note for the entire measure, even though it is only notated once at the beginning of the measure. It will not apply to the same pitch in different octaves. Accidentals are automatically canceled the minute you hit the next measure. You don't have to notate the cancellation of an accidental unless it occurs in the same measure in which you had the original accidental.

Accidental: Your band plays mainstream jazz and your agent booked you into a country-western honkey tonk. It was a twelve hour drive. There's thirty minutes until you have to go on.

Arpeggio: You sing an arpeggio when you sing up and down the notes of a chord, as opposed to the notes of the scale. An instrument plays an arpeggio when the notes of the chord are played one after another, instead of simultaneously.

Chromatic: This is when you play a scale using all twelve tones; all the half steps contained in an octave. The chromatic scale in C, for instance, would be: C, C#, D, D#, E, F, F#, G, G#, A, A#, B, C. A song passage can be described as chromatic if it uses this scale, even partially.

Diatonic: This is when you play the standard eight notes of a major or minor scale, instead of playing the scale chromatically. In C the diatonic scale is: C,D,E,F,G,A,B,D.

Dominant: The fifth scale degree, or the chord using this fifth note as its root. Usually resolves, often to the tonic, or root. (You notice I say "usually" and "often" because for every rule there are any number of brilliant exceptions.)

Dominant: When the drummer plays too loudly, bringing all the attention to himself, and no one can hear you sing. Tell him to use brushes.

Intonation: Accuracy of pitch production. If someone says your intonation is off, that's a nice way of telling you you're singing flat.

Theory: The study of music in the abstract. Includes the study of harmony, melody, the mathematics of music, the analysis of others' works, scales, modes, counterpoint, form, and all the other components that go to make up what we hear. You have to know theory to do orchestration, to study musicology, to compose, to conduct.

Theory: The idea that if you get a gig, the agent will come.

Things to Pencil Into Your Score:
See the chapters on ensemble singing and the two chapters on dynamics.

Volumes:
See the chapter called "Dynamics: Loud and Soft."

Ways to Impress the Impressionable

Perfect pitch: You are one lucky person. There is tremendous controversy over whether perfect pitch is something you're born with, something you can learn, or something that can be learned if you start out very young. You have perfect pitch if you just know what note it is. (Some people know themselves so well, and have sung so much, that they know how a note *feels* physically when they sing it. Is this perfect pitch? You decide.)

Perfect relative pitch: This you can learn. This is when you are given one note, and you can figure out the rest of the notes from there. You can develop perfect relative pitch by studying ear training, solfege, harmony, and/or just plain singing a lot. The first thing I do when I wake up in the morning is to sing the note A (440 cycles per second). I check myself with an "A" tuning fork which is by my bed at all times. Once I have this "A" in my head, it's there all day, often for days at a time. I can get any note I need from this "A" in my head. Of course I *could* carry a pitch pipe, but that ruins the fun.

Sharp singing #3: Slick, well-rehearsed. Sharp.

Ways to Sound Off key

Flat singing #1: Singing under the pitch
Flat singing #2: You're on pitch, but your voice lacks depth. The tone is flat, not the pitch.
Sharp singing #1: Singing slightly above the pitch.
Sharp singing #2: Your tone has a jarring edge to it.

*If your term is not listed in this Glossary, there's probably a chapter on it instead. Check the Table of Contents.

Notes:

The Glottal Stop

Just in case you were wondering: the glottis is the space between the vocal cords. When you are not making sounds, the glottis is opened - meaning there is a gap between the vocal cords. When you are phonating, or making sound, the cords are rapidly opening and closing. Since the glottis is a variable space, it regulates how much air passes through the vocal cords during phonation. It also affects the pressure, and even the shape of this air. It's active in your production of volume and pitch, and it affects the tone of the voice. For example, lots of air coming through the glottis with the voice at a low volume will result in a "breathy" sounding voice.

You don't have to worry about your glottis. Proper breath support and posture will take care of it.

But you do want to avoid a "glottal stop." This is a condition in which the inhaled breath is "held" before it turns over into an exhale - and during this "hold" the glottis closes. It may only be for a fraction of a second. But the problem is, it causes a kind of "pop" when you then begin your next musical phrase. Sometimes this pop is subtle and does not create too much chaos. Other times it's overt and simply sounds bad - it fragments your otherwise smooth phrasing.

The glottal stop has a feel to it that you can recognize:
- ✓ First of all, if you've held your breath, even for an instant, you know it. It's just a matter of being aware of it.
- ✓ There is also the feeling of the back of the throat closing. Some people describe it as a "locking" feeling in the back of the throat.

It's possible to hold your breathing muscles in abeyance at the top of the inhale and before the exhale, <u>without</u> closing the glottis. While this is not something we try to do, it's not as disruptive as holding the breath and closing the glottis. Try holding your breath to see what it feels like. Do it with and then without the glottal stop. This way you can recognize it if you do it while you're singing or vocalizing.

One of the vocal qualities I stress is fluidity. A singer needs to be able to produce a flowing, smooth, even, fluid sound. The glottal stop, while not a major record-deal breaker, can interrupt the smooth tone you work so hard to create.

It's easy enough to correct. Practice your breathing exercises, making sure there is no "stop," or tightening in the larynx, between your inhale and your exhale. Keep a feeling of the air moving through your instrument freely and without obstruction. Be aware of the sensation of tightening in the neck, and release this tension when it occurs. It's more of an awareness process than a technical problem.

Notes:

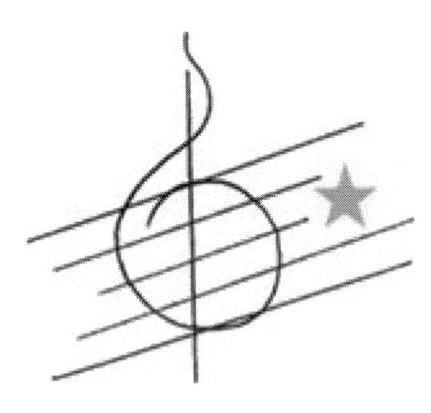

The Larynx

What is it?

Remember people talking about a "voice box" when you were a kid? They were referring to the larynx. In fact, though, it's not one box, it's an intricate set of muscles, nerves, and cartilages located in your neck. This moveable "web" is attached from above to the tongue and the lower jaw, and attached from below to the chest. (The "Adam's apple" is a part of this system.)

What does it do?

- It surrounds the vocal cords and aids in their movement.
- It's also a valve. When it's shut, it blocks the lungs off from the mouth. Thus you can eat without having your tofu end up in your lungs.

What do I do with it?

If you treat it right in a general way, it will take care of producing your sound without you having to worry about it. How do you treat it right?

1) Keep your posture erect (conjure up that string that's attached to the middle of your solar plexus and pulls you up from there), but not stiff. Slouching will impede the ability of your instrument to produce its best sound.

2) Keep your head in alignment with the rest of your body. Don't take this for granted - check in a mirror occasionally as you vocalize or sing. Habits are funny things, because we don't always know we're doing them.

♪ Don't jut your jaw forward during any part of the singing process.

♪ Look up and out, not down. Many singers don't know it, but they look down when they sing. This obstructs the activity of the larynx.

♪ Be careful that your head (or neck) is not extended forward in an "eager" position.

3) This can't be said too many times: your body/instrument must be relaxed. You can't be so relaxed as to be in a coma, but stress points (bulging neck veins on the inhale, gridlocked elbows and knees, shoulders churned up to the ears, a panicked facial expression, stiff lips) must be consciously eliminated. For many of us, this is a lifelong challenge - again, the mirror is your best monitor. (A stiff upper lip is not a good thing.)

4) Some singers unknowingly move the head as they change pitch. This nodding action adds continual blocking and tension in the larynx. Check your mirror and break this habit.

The "Low Larynx" Sensation (aka "Open Throat")

Many singers speak of keeping their larynx low. This is a good thing. It's akin to the feeling of an "open throat." Basically we're talking about a feeling of relaxation or openness in what feels like the very back of the throat - the tongue-root, if you will.

For example: yawn with your mouth closed; as if you're bored stiff but polite. What movement do you feel in the back of your throat? If you feel a kind of lowering of the mechanism, and an open sensation in the throat, this is what is meant by these terms. A "high" or tight larynx is generally undesirable. **A "low" larynx with an open throat usually produces the most resonant sound with the least amount of physical tension.**

Some singers also use the image of the raised soft palate, to open the throat. If this helps you, go for it. Try inhaling with the low larynx, but also adding a feeling slight surprise - raising the eyebrows and almost looking up from under the eyelids. This is very subtle - remember, we don't look down or ruin our posture. You can "feel" the soft palate rise. If this doesn't work for you, the stifled yawn, which lowers the larynx, might also give you the feeling of the raised soft palate. (I personally work with the "low larynx" sensation, and not with the soft palate at all. But each singer is different. I offer these ideas for you to experiment with - find what works for you and discard what doesn't.)

Don't get too bogged down with this. <u>The general feeling is one of an unobstructed breathing mechanism.</u> If you have that, you've got the other elements without even trying.

The "Low Larynx" and Breathing

Here's how it all wraps up. When you inhale, keep the larynx down. This is why we try to inhale through the nose instead of the mouth - it's easier to keep the larynx down, and the throat open. (Why, you are wondering, need we worry about yet this other thing? The answer is basically one of relaxation. If the larynx goes up unnaturally, as happens if we are tense or slouching, we get a higher, more pinched, less resonant sound.) There is some natural raising of the larynx in certain situations, for instance in singing high notes. But you don't consciously raise the larynx. All you need to <u>consciously</u> do is relax, and trust your instrument.

Our intention in this chapter is to get an overview of how the larynx affects the voice. A speech therapist or other specialized health practitioner should be sought out if you develop vocal problems that could be medical in nature.

Notes:

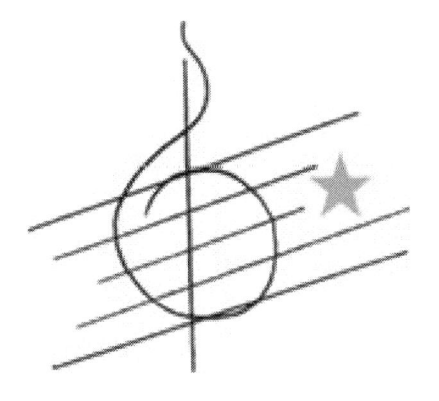

**Legato Singing:
Smooth Moves**

We've gone into depth in other chapters about tone - about achieving a rich, round, resonant tone. Legato singing is about connecting all your sounds. It's about moving smoothly and evenly through the array of lyrics, melodies, and rhythms. This is singing that flows. It's not enough to be able to produce a beautiful tone - it's important to be able to have this tone move fluidly as you sing. As such, legato singing is a dynamic concept. It's about smoothness in motion. Think silk.

You can make artistic choices about the motion and dynamics in your songs that may end up being far removed from legato singing. Certainly a light portamento style with a perfectly even vibrato would sound ludicrous in a post-industrial-grunge heavy metal club. And even within a song in which legato singing is appropriate, you might choose not to use it for the entire song. Strict, classical legato singing in general might not allow room for some of the fabulous and creative dynamics singers are using today.

But it's important to learn legato singing as a basis for a sound technique. I'm going on the assumption that we're aiming here for a beautiful, healthy voice, upon which style and trends can then be imposed. Based on that assumption, the best approach is to learn the basic ground rules first, and then break them. Legato is a singing foundation.

Even if you don't use legato singing to its fullest extent, there will be characteristics of it that you will want to incorporate into your personal, overall sound.

Characteristics of Legato Singing
Here are some of the qualities you'll want to hear in your voice when you practice the exercises at the end of this segment.

   1. Hang on to those vowels.
      Check out the chapter on vowel sounds, and remember that singing can only carry on vowels, not consonants. In singing lyrics, you want to get to

the pure part of each vowel as quickly as possible, stay on it for as long as possible, then clip on the final consonant, if there is one, at the last possible moment. (Also refer to the chapter on the "R" sound.)

As an exercise, take a song you're working on, eliminate all the consonants, and sing the entire song on just the vowel sounds. For example, the lyrical phrase "So close your eyes, for that's a lovely way to be..." from Antonio Carlos Jobim's song *Wave*, would be: "oh oh aw ah, aw aah ah ah ee ay oo ee." You sing the same melody, but just on the vowel sounds.

♪ When you do this, go slowly and give each vowel sound its proper attention - no short cuts or sloppy sounds.

♪ Also, and this is the crux of what we're talking about, make the phrase fluid. Join the various vowel sounds together seamlessly and smoothly.

♪ There's no such thing as doing this little exercise too much! The more you take your songs apart in this way, the smoother and more flowing they will become.

2. Keep your tonal color uniform.
OK, let's get real. The tonal color is going to change as you change registers, as your song goes up or down into a different pitch range, as you make artistic decisions about the emotional interpretation of a phrase. But as we've been talking about all throughout this book, you want to have one basic tone; you want your variations of that tone to match; you want to be able to sing your three octaves without sounding like you have multiple personality disorder.

In legato singing, especially, the tonal color is even and smooth, and if it has to change, it changes subtly and gradually.

3. Although you connect your vowels, tones, and colors throughout a phrase, you're not slurring.
♪ As you sing the scales at the end of this segment, you'll want to find that fine line between stomping and slurring.

♪ In legato singing, you hear each note distinctly - you don't hear microtones as you move from one note to the next, as you would if you were singing an extreme portamento or glide. But neither do you pounce on notes, clomp from note to note, or thud.

♪ Going up and down a scale keeping this kind of balance is an art form.

4. <u>The key word here is "de-stress."</u>
♪ A legato phrase is silky smooth. It's free of marked rhythmic stress.

♪ Any accents or dynamic changes are subtle and gradual. The emphasis is on the melodic line as a whole.

♪ The phrase floats. The song sings itself.

5. <u>Everything ties together: you've got to have mastery of your breathing mechanism in order to sing legato.</u>
Remember in the breathing and related chapters, how we have concentrated on smoothness? In breathing, the expansion and contraction of the muscles must be even, flawless, and seamless. This will provide for even, flawless and seamless sound. ("I <u>knew</u> there was a more important reason for breathing than simply oxygenating the blood," you say.)

Resources
You can practice legato singing on any scale or lyrical song. Use it in conjunction with the chapter on modes - practice modal scales in a legato style, for instance. Use it when you sing arias or ballads. Now this sounds good in the shower.

The **Marchesi** series of exercise books, published by Schirmer's, are excellent for all studies, including legato.

Also from Schirmer's is the **Vaccai** series of books.

These and other study books from the classical genre come in all levels of expertise and for all ranges of voices.

Exercises
Sing the following exercises using the smooth, elastic qualities of legato singing. Transpose each exercise up chromatically, then down, to cover your entire comfortable range. Make up your own series of vowel sounds.

116 Vocal Vibrance — Suzann Kale

Notes:

**Memorizing:
The Challenge of Storage and Retrieval**

There's too much stuff in there already - how can you cram yet one more thing into your head? And why, when you get up on stage, does the head empty itself out suddenly, leaving you with a lyric-less void?

Actually, one of the major causes of stage fright is the feeling of being unprepared. And specifically, the feeling that the lyrics will be the first to go, after which will be your hard-earned confidence.

The good news: Nobody has determined as yet that there is a threshold beyond which things will start spilling out of your ears. Apparently, the amount of stuff you can fit into your brain is limitless. The challenge - how to retrieve it when you need it.

Why memorize in the first place?

Unless you're singing the solo part in a requiem, mass, or oratorio, or unless you're singing in a choir (in which case it's acceptable to hold your music), memorizing is simply a part of learning a song.

But there's more to it than that. You can't really interpret a song and give it your full emotional attention unless you're free from the technical aspects of singing. Once you've memorized a piece, you're free to take it flying, wherever you want to go.

Besides, it would simply look ridiculous if you brought your music up on stage with you.

What to memorize

    1. lyrics and melody

    2. where you will be breathing (especially if there are trouble spots in the song)

3. the song's dynamics (loud and soft, emotional dynamics, accents, rhythmic patterns that might deviate from the written music, etc.)

4. format (where the instrumentalists solo; unusual endings or intros, etc)

5. phrasing

6. in ensemble music:
- ✓ placement of consonants
- ✓ diphthong turnarounds
- ✓ any unusual vowel sounds (pronunciations you don't do automatically)
- ✓ places in the piece where you must be looking at the conductor, and simply cannot look down at the music
- ✓ unusually difficult passages

How to memorize

Here's the storage and retrieval challenge. How to get the stuff into the head and still be able to get it out when the piano player begins the song's introduction. You need to be able to file the stuff away, and remember where you filed it. Easy in, easy out. So let's look at some of the many memorization techniques. See which ones appeal to you.

1. Repetition and drill.
> To many singers, this is the heart and soul of how they memorize. This involves just standing there in front of the piano or with your accompaniment tape, biting the bullet of tedium, and doing it - over and over again. Purchase a pair of earplugs for your spouse.

2. Repetition II: programming the synapses throughout the day.
> Mindless chores can actually be useful - they offer time and opportunity to repeat your song over and over. As you're washing the car, doing the dishes, vacuuming, mowing the lawn, putting away the groceries, standing outside waiting for the dog, standing in the tub waiting for your hair roots to grab color, you are singing this song. If they cart you away, you've gone too far with this. Remember to feed your children.

3. For troublesome lyrics, write or type out the jinxed sections over and over again.
> This works like a charm.

4. Associate lyrics with images.
> The more colorful or sensual the imagery, the stronger the association will be. For instance, you're trying to memorize *Blue Champagne* by Watts, Ryerson and Eaton, and the lyric is: "Blue champagne, purple shadows and

blue champagne, with the echoes that still remain, I keep a blue rendezvous." Conjure up a visual image of a glass of blue champagne - in detail. Know what kind of glass it's in - know what the table looks like that the glass is on. Perhaps it's a tulip glass, half empty, on a small table in a nightclub after hours. You see the purple shadows of the subdued lighting surrounding this table. You actually feel the echoes of the now defunct party. For further reinforcement, add a strong emotion to this image - perhaps in this case one of loneliness. All you need to do to begin this song, is conjure up all this image and its feelings. And you can do it in an instant.

Take the song *Midnight Blue* by Carole Bayer Sager and Melissa Manchester. The lyric is: "Whatever it is, it'll keep till the morning..." Perhaps you can think of something specific from your personal life to associate with that feeling, that lyric. If you can think of a time you were up all night worrying about (insert recent personal "Thing" here) and then in the morning, found that things looked brighter, you will never forget the words to this song.

5. Associating II.

If you don't want to conjure up your own emotional stuff, you can do less mind-blowing associations, such as noticing technical patterns.

I recently was memorizing a song with scat syllables in the introduction, and a second set of scat syllables in the tag. Since the song was being done with another singer, in harmony, these seemingly nonsensical words had to be memorized exactly. The introductory scat was "da ba, da ba." The scat in the tag was "dwee bo, dwee bo." To remember which came first, I simply noted that it was alphabetical.

Memorizing the song *Route 66* by Bobby Troup is always amusing because of the list of cities that comes toward the end of the song. This trips everyone up. The lyrics go "Flagstaff, Arizona, don't forget Winona, Kingman, Barstow, San Bernardino." What one singer did was write these cities down on a piece of paper, like a laundry list. He was able to visualize this list whenever he ran into trouble. Another singer actually purchased a map of the western U.S. and used a yellow highlighter to follow the path Route 66 took through the cities. She did that once, and never had trouble with that song again.

The song *Sister Sadie* by Horace Silver is a seemingly easy song to memorize, except that it's so easy I keep mixing up which verse comes when. So I took just the first lines of each verse - trusting that if I got the first line, the rest of the verse would follow correctly - and memorized the order of the verses that way. For instance, the first verse starts with "Sister Sadie was a mean chick." The second verse starts, "Sister Sadie never worried." The third starts "Sister Sadie was a honey." In my mind, I kept saying "mean chick, never worried, honey". To further associate these phrase beginnings with the correct order, I thought "she starts out mean, then she doesn't worry, but finally she comes around and is a honey. Mean, not worry, then honey." It was easy to think mean, and from there I just kept associating in my own strange and unique - but workable - patterns.

6. Memorizing in a foreign language.

♪ If it's a language you know well, you can use associations and repetitions, as described.

♪ If you don't know the language well, you must get a translation of the piece, and associate in general what the phrases mean, the order of the verses, etc. Know what the song is saying and how it's saying it.

♪ Better still is a rough word by word translation. Write the translated words in pencil above the foreign words on the sheet music. Alternate singing the foreign language with singing the translation.

♪ You can still associate foreign words with sensual imagery, even if it's far-fetched. Certain syllables may remind you of something that you can latch onto.

♪ Speak the foreign lyrics through, without the melody, as if you were reading poetry or a story. Also try speaking the foreign lyrics in rhythm.

7. For complicated or long songs, arias, or jazz vocalese pieces:

a) Start with the first phrase, and go over it until you can repeat it from memory perfectly, five times in a row.

b) Go to the second phrase in the piece, and do the same thing.

c) Now combine the first and second phrases, and work them together until you can do the entire section from memory, perfectly, five times in a row.

d) Go to the third phrase in the piece, and work it by itself until you can do it five times in a row perfectly from memory.

e) Add this third phrase to the first two, and work the entire unit (from the first phrase through the third phrase) until you can do it completely five times.

f) Build the song in this fashion, phrase by phrase, adding each newly memorized phrase to what you've already memorized.

g) If it's a very long piece, you can divide it up into sections - perhaps verses, or whatever division is logical - and build the phrases up one by one

<u>within</u> each section, rather than being overwhelmed by trying to tackle the entire piece as one unit.

8. If you're working on a show with many songs in it, memorize your favorite song last - as a kind of reward.

9. Sing the newly memorized piece in front of others, as practice. Many singers find that the stress of performing produces incredibly frustrating memory loss.

10. Other memorization ideas:
- ✱ Speak the text of the song repeatedly.

- ✱ Speak the text in rhythm.

- ✱ Sing the song in rhythm, repeatedly, but all on one pitch.

- ✱ Sing through the melody on "Lah", repeatedly, with no lyrics.

- ✱ Often the ends of phrases are easier to remember than the beginnings, because they either rhyme, or they just make sense. So pay particular attention to the beginnings of lines and trust that the ends will come to you.

- ✱ Read through the text of the song as if it were a dramatic poetry reading or a story. Know the "storyline."

Saving your voice

This is a whole lot of singing. It would be defeating the purpose to know your piece to the core of your DNA, and not be able to sing it because you've lost your voice from too much practice. Some ideas:

- ♮ You can always do lots of memorization work mentally, in your head. You can repeat a song, music, lyrics and all, just by thinking it. Sure beats the usual mental tape loop of your latest encounter with the office backstabber or the neighbor who yelled at your dog.

- ♮ If it's a strenuous song (perhaps it's very high, or the melody constantly hits on your break notes), try learning it in a more comfortable key - or even down an octave. Put it back in its original key later.

- ♮ Analyze the song technically before you begin memorizing. Know what the composer's ideas are, both musically and lyrically, and know how the composer presents these ideas - how the song works from a logical, technical, or even storytelling point of view.

♮ No need to sing full-voice when learning.

How to cheat
On the other hand, there's no proof that the brain is limitless. I know many singers who will tell you their brains have pretty much had it. If you're drained, fried, frazzled, freaked, exhausted, depleted, or burnt out, or if there's a song you JUST CAN'T GET, even though you've worked it to death, go easy on yourself. Bring a "justincase" up onto the stage with you. A "justincase" is some kind of cheat sheet that is small and easy to see - it's for when you think you know the song but you want something up there with you, "just in case." It can be an index card with the first line of that one forgettable verse. It can be an 8 x 11 sheet of paper that you can put on the floor to glance at, on which you've got key forgettable phrases written in caps in bold black ink. It can even be a tiny word written on the back of your hand (palms sweat in these situations) in pen.

You might find that bringing something up on stage with you gives you the confidence you need to be able to not look at it at all. The mind is a funny thing.

Notes:

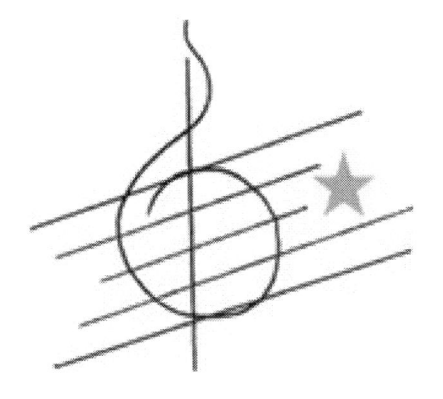

Modes:
How to Develop a Bionic Ear

After you've read the chapters on ear training and scat, you might want to know what modal singing is.

Modes are a certain way of looking at scale patterns. Scales come in almost as many shapes and sounds as imagination permits. In modal theory, there are seven scales, each with its own unique mood.

What do you do with them?
♫ Ear training. A singer who is confident and comfortable with modal scales and arpeggios, as well as modal improvising, is a singer with a bionic ear.

♫ You can "go modal" any time you've got to improvise. And don't be fooled into thinking improvisation is just for jazz. Improvisation occurs in most genres of music. Not all songs render themselves specifically to modal improvisations, but many do. How to tell? After you've learned your modes, you can go through the song analytically and see if it fits into any of the patterns. Or better yet, you can just hear it and know. (It's really not that hard, as you'll see when we describe each mode for you.)

♫ Some singers like to write music as well. Knowledge of modes can spur creativity and open new channels of harmony and melody. I often write a song in a modal key, instead of the usual major or minor, and find that the mood of the mode adds emotional depth to the piece.

♫ Say you're singing a popular song at a restaurant gig. At the end of the song, you and the piano player decide to vamp over the ending. If you can lock into a mode, you can vamp forever and never get stale. Vamp endings work well for many kinds of songs, including ballads, sambas, and bossas.

♫ If the song itself is modal, it will be impossible for you to ever get lost. Harmonically, anyway.

What are the modes?
Ionian, Dorian, Phrygian, Lydian, Mixolydian, Aeolian, and Locrian. Here's a description of each.

1. **IONIAN**

    This is your basic major scale, say from middle C up 8 notes. You can sing this mode right now. You've been singing this mode your whole life. See? You're modal. Most of your warm-up exercises and vocalizations are simply arpeggios or scales in the Ionian mode.

    To play the Ionian mode in any key, just pick your root note (your starting note), and go up the major scale.* So if you want to play the Ionian scale in, say, the key of F, you'd play F, G, A, B-flat, C, D, E, and then F again.

    To hear what the Ionian mode sounds like without worrying about accidentals (sharps or flats), just play eight notes up from C to C on the white keys. It's that easy.

2. **DORIAN**

    Still easy and basic. Dorian is a nice, kind of funky sounding, widely used minor scale. It's my favorite, and a joy to compose with, vamp over, or scat over.

    To play the Dorian mode in any key, all you need to do is flat the third and the seventh of the scale . (In the key of C, for instance, the Dorian scale would be: C, D, E-flat, F, G, A, B-flat, C).

    To hear what the Dorian scale sounds like without worrying about accidentals, just play eight white key notes, starting from D. That's the Dorian sound. (You can learn modes by ear, if you're not a written-notation kind of a singer. Each mode has its own unique sound.)

3. **PHRYGIAN** (pronounced frih'-jee-an)

    A tricky little minor scale, this. Not the easiest to scat over, but worth knowing for its saucy quality. It's not a depressing minor, it's an - eccentric minor. It's not like you just lost your love, it's more like you stayed too late after hours at the club and lost your car.

    To play the Phrygian mode in any key, just start on your root note and flat the second, third, sixth, and seventh as you go up or down the scale. (Or you may prefer to think it this way: half steps between the first and second notes of the scale, and between the fifth and sixth notes of the scale. Everything else, whole steps. In the key of C, for instance, the Phrygian scale would be: C, D-flat, E-flat, F, G, A-flat, B-flat, C.)

    To hear that Phrygian sound without having to count whole and half steps, just play a scale from E to E on your keyboard using just white keys. (Remember, you can do any mode in any key.)

4. **LYDIAN**

Ah, lovely Lydian. Easy, and very major and breezy sounding. To find yourself in a meadow in the country on a pretty spring day, gazing up at the clear blue sky, just program the Lydian mode into your way of thinking.

<u>To play the Lydian mode in any key,</u> play a major scale, but raise the fourth note up half a step. If your root note is C, the notes of the C Lydian scale would be: C, D, E, F-sharp, G, A, B, and C.

<u>To hear</u> that Lydian sound without having to worry about accidentals, just play a scale from F to F on your keyboard with all white keys. Do you hear that raised fourth?

5. **MIXOLYDIAN**

Like the Ionian, I guarantee you've heard the Mixolydian your whole life - perhaps you've just not heard it called by this name. This is the dominant seventh, the five-seven chord, the scale that leaves you hanging if it's not resolved. This is the chase scene. This is the chord that must be resolved. This is the moment before the end. If you play the Mixolydian and then just...stop - it's like holding your breath forever.

<u>To play the Mixolydian mode in any key,</u> all you do is play a major scale and just flat the seventh note. So if you begin on middle C, you play: C, D, E, F, G, A, B-flat, C.

<u>To hear</u> that unresolved Mixolydian sound without worrying about accidentals, play a scale from G to G using all white keys.

6. **AEOLIAN**

We have a scale here about which musicians of both the classical and the jazz persuasions can agree. The Aeolian, a.k.a. the relative minor; the natural minor, is your basic, standard gear minor scale. This is the heart of minor-ness. This is sad. In this one, your love has left you. (In my humble opinion, the Dorian is a street-wise minor, kind of worldly and mischievous. The Aeolian is depressing. The Dorian contains a little night life and neon; the Aeolian goes to therapy in the stark light of day.)

<u>To play the Aeolian mode in any key,</u> you flat the third, sixth, and seventh of the scale. So if you're starting on C, the scale would be: C, D, E-flat, F, G, A-flat, B-flat, C.

<u>To hear</u> the mood of the Aeolian without worrying about which notes to flat, play eight notes from A to A using all white keys.

7. **LOCRIAN**

A minor scale, yes, but Locrian is cool, it's hip. It's the essence of the half-diminished seventh chord, it's been around. Like the Mixolydian, it needs to be resolved. But unlike the Mixolydian, you won't die of asphyxiation if it resolves to something unexpected. You could really score points walking into the club, wearing sunglasses, and casually vocalizing over the Locrian scale. The Locrian aficionado is like an ex-cop: seen it, done it, wore holes in the T-shirt, don't want your kids doing it. But having learned all the angles, the Locrian-ist has become tolerant in a mildly amused way, of musicians who solo over lesser scales.

To play Locrian in any key, put half steps between the first and second notes of the scale, and also between the fourth and fifth notes of the scale. All the other notes have whole steps between them. (What you're doing is flatting the second, third, fifth, sixth, and seventh of the scale.) So if you start on C, the notes would be: C, D-flat, E-flat, F, G-flat, A-flat, B-flat, C.

To hear the Locrian mood without worrying about accidentals, just play the scale from B to B on your keyboard, with white keys.

Examples of each mode:

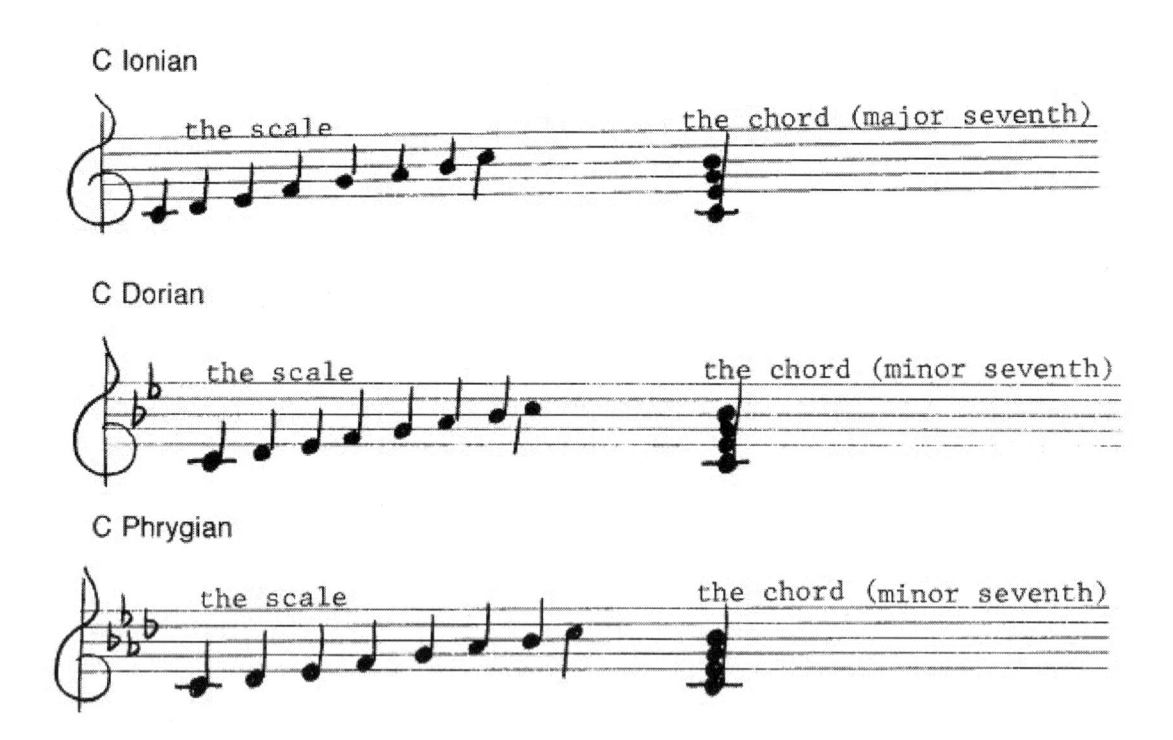

C Ionian

the scale — the chord (major seventh)

C Dorian

the scale — the chord (minor seventh)

C Phrygian

the scale — the chord (minor seventh)

C Lydian — the scale — the chord (major seventh)

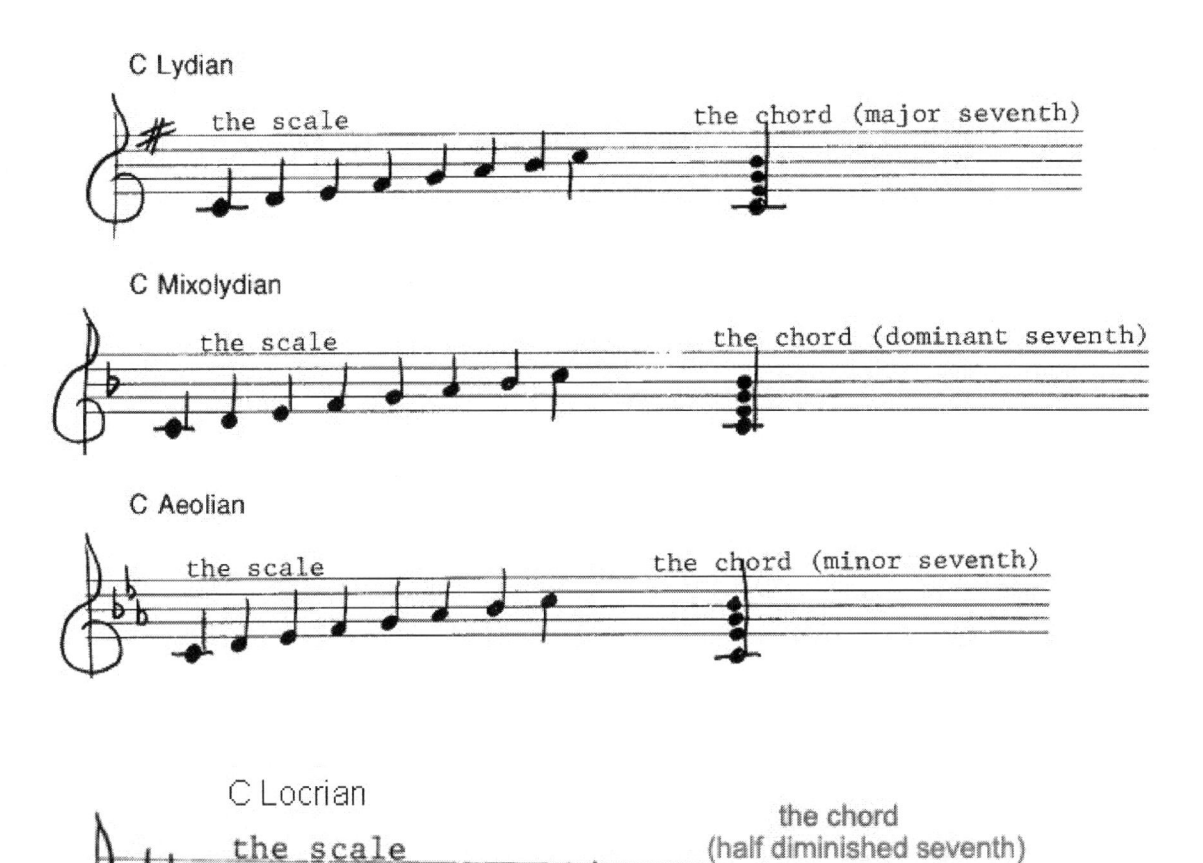

C Mixolydian — the scale — the chord (dominant seventh)

C Aeolian — the scale — the chord (minor seventh)

C Locrian — the scale — the chord (half diminished seventh)

Further resources:

Modal books to check out for more information: *The Source* by Steve Barta, *Flexibility and Improv Patterns* by Matteson and Petersen, *Scales for Jazz Improvisation* and *Jazz Language*, both by Dan Haerle.

Notes:

* *The major scale* means that there are whole steps between each note except between the third and fourth note and between the seventh and eighth notes. Between the 3rd and 4th note there is only a half step; between the 7th and 8th notes there is only a half step.

* *A half-step* means that you go from any note to it's immediate note right above or below it. A whole step means that you go from your note to two notes immediately above or below it. Two half steps make a whole step. Go get that book on music theory we recommended in the chapter on reading music.

Notes:

**Phlegm:
Can't Live With It, Can't Live Without It**

So you've brought one too many pet frogs up to the bandstand with you, and you want to do something about it? Here are some ideas from singers and speakers:

Do:

- One helpful and healthy way to "clear your throat" is to sing staccato scales, exaggerating the quick inward and upward motion of the diaphragm with each note. Sing up, say, the C scale, on the syllable "ha." Do it on one breath but with a push from the diaphragm on each "ha." Or try the "Diaphragm De-Briefer" exercise from Warm-up II. The idea is to <u>shake the phlegm off</u> your vocal cords without grinding or hurting the cords.

- Laughing can also shake off the frogs. Evidently they have no sense of humor.

- Many singers find that if they avoid dairy products, they will avoid phlegm in the first place. For myself, I will cut dairy products out of my diet entirely beginning about three days before a gig.

- Try sucking a lemon.

- For the less adventurous, try adding fresh lemon or lime juice to your plain, tepid water.

- If you're sitting there absolutely dying because you can't stand it any longer, go ahead and clear your throat. But do it gently. Do it softly. Do it minimally. Sometimes a mere glottal stop followed by a quiet "hmmm" sound is all it takes. (See the chapter on glottal stop.)

- Experiment with your beverages. For some, hot tea, plain or with lemon, works well. For others, it doesn't. For some, certain herbal teas help. Coffee will dry most people out and cause vocal problems. For me, it helps get rid of phlegm. Everyone's different.

- Check with your health practitioner and see what remedies she or he can help you with. Singers are very creative people in the phlegm retardant department. There are more remedies than you can imagine. Many use homeopathic remedies, some use prescription remedies, some use herbal tinctures, some acupuncture, some hypnosis.

- Food is a major factor in the phlegm game. In addition to dairy, each singer and public speaker I've spoken to seems to have certain trigger-foods. Be aware of what you eat and when you have phlegm. You might be able to find some astonishing correlations.

- Also be aware of your regular allergies, and how you're dealing with them. Work with your health practitioner to find solutions. Some solutions may be major, such as dusting your house. (Don't let an allergist talk you into giving up your cats. Remember. You can have it all.)

- Vocalize daily. Warm-up before singing. Treat your voice with respect. Read the chapter on "Care of the Instrument."

- Breathe correctly when you sing; watch your posture, especially the alignment of your head and neck.

- Speak softly and beautifully during your work day, especially if you're on the phone all day or teaching. Check out the chapter on the elements of a good speaking voice. Modulating your voice well will keep it from being strained. Strained vocal cords produce more phlegm.

- Drink lots of water during your day, to keep your instrument hydrated.

Don't

- cough or clear your throat a lot, in an attempt to get rid of the phlegm. Habitual throat clearing can hurt your vocal cords. Just listen to it - you're literally grinding your cords together. Put ugly throat clearing noises in the same category as fingernails on blackboards.

- overuse decongestants and antihistamines. They can dry you out. While it's always fun to be able to breathe, you don't want to eliminate all mucus in the process - because then your body will just produce more phlegm to make up for the phlegm you deprived it of. Tricky business, this.

- freak out. Stage fright, nervousness, and panic can cause phlegm for many singers and public speakers. One singer I know has had instances in which she's been entirely phlegm-free for days on end, phlegm-free going to a gig, phlegm-free walking up to the microphone, and then suddenly phlegm-laden the minute she switched the mike to "on." Anything you can do to calm yourself will be helpful. (See the chapter on stage fright.)

- eat your normal half gallon of ice cream just before a gig. It's like a frog mating call.

- start singing first thing in the morning, if you can possibly help it. Most of us tend to be more "phlegmy" with the shock of waking up.

- sing in harmful ways; sing in keys that are wrong for you; sing without first warming up and vocalizing. This kind of trauma hurts the cords, and they respond by coating themselves with more mucus as protection.

- shriek at sports events.

- get into a verbose discourse about what the Q was going to tell Captain Picard about the destiny of the human race on the last episode of Star Trek NextGen, if you're in a noisy nightclub and must yell to be heard.

smoke, breathe in bus fumes, or inhale household cleaners. You think I'm kidding, I'm not kidding. Many singers I know wear protective face masks cleaning out the bathtub.

Notes:

**Pop, Rock, and Belt :
Belting**

What, more controversy? And you thought if you avoided watching the news for awhile your life would settle down. Read on...

Belting - the Traditional Definition
Many singing teachers (I would say "most singing teachers" but the dynamics of this issue are changing as fast as a New York gigasecond) define "belting" as singing forcefully in the chest register and taking that sound up in pitch beyond what would normally be considered comfortable, healthy, or pleasant sounding. It's taking your chest voice up too high. It's staying in chest when switching to a head register would sound less strained. This is the classical perspective on belting.

For most voices to attain their optimal tone throughout their entire range, it is necessary to break from the chest register into the head register at a certain point in the range. This "breaking point, " or "passage," is a naturally occurring point, and is something most singers work on very carefully. (See the chapter on registers.)

Chest register is associated with lower notes, and as singers go up the scale they change to head register in order to avoid strain. Taking the voice up too high in the chest register can sound pinched, stressed, can cause very flat singing, and can damage the voice.

So Why Do It?
Many singers feel that their chest registers are stronger, more powerful, and just plain louder. If they haven't developed their head registers, either from a lack of training or from studying with a voice teacher who is not classically oriented*, they will notice a marked decrease in power when they switch over to head. Therefore they try to stay in chest.

Also, some singers think of head voice as too "classical" sounding - but in fact the head voice is simply a placement and can be made to adapt itself to almost any genre of music.

The Alternative
Beautiful singing requires the development of chest and head, the development of a smooth set of passage notes, and some extra exercises to get the chest and head tones somewhat uniform. This way you can switch gracefully and easily between chest and head, according to the demands of the song.

It takes a lot of work to get both registers oiled up - more vocalizing, more study, more time. But it's worth it. Smooth, expressive singing allows you to utilize your entire range - perhaps three octaves, more or less - with all your notes sounding rich, round, and resonant.

The "Blend Register"
There is another register, which I call the "blend register," which is different from belting. This is a placement I've heard in jazz, blues, and gospel which is a _blend_ of head and chest registers. It's got an edge to it which is appropriate for some songs and some singers. In the wrong hands it can sound thin. But it's got a certain pop or contemporary quality to it that can work well. Many studio singers have developed this register in order to get a certain sound for advertising jingles. And it's got some overtones to it that can cut through a lot of muddy acoustics, in, say, a boomy concert hall.

In the "blend" placement, the chest register is taken higher than in classical placement, but instead of keeping it in "pure chest," a little head tone is added in there. If this is something that appeals to you, you must find a voice teacher who not only specializes in it but also has the health of your voice as a top priority. (Check out the chapter on finding the perfect voice teacher.)

Belt - What the Rebels Say
But back to belt - here's the crux of the problem: There has developed a certain "pop" sound that requires a belt placement in order for it to sound the way whoever the powers-that-be want it to sound. Also, belting is sometimes called for in musical theatre singing.

Many of the voice teachers now are coming up with belting techniques that are apparently safe and aesthetically acceptable. If belt interests you, you might begin at the music store, checking out some of the books, audio tapes, and videos on the subject. Then find a voice teacher who can help you produce this sound without damaging your voice. Many musical theatre professors and teachers at universities are now including belt classes in their curriculum. And a lot of these belt teachers _also_ teach or have been trained in traditional, classical singing.

Avoid Listener Abuse
Classical training is good for singers in all styles. If you study belt, pop, blend, or

chest registers solely, to the exclusion of a strong head voice, you are simply limiting your options.

There are a lot of otherwise good singers out there who sing in chest and simply can't conceive of singing in head. In come the high notes on a song, and there we go, singing flat again. Another abuse of innocent listeners is swooping up to the high note, also in an attempt to avoid switching to head. The swooping is like taking a running start - and in the audience, too, it causes great anxiety: Will she or won't she hit the note?

Even if you are a member of the rebel belt faction, there is no reason not to develop your <u>entire</u> voice - chest, head, and all the break notes in between. You never know when you might need them...

*By "classical" I don't mean unapproachable goddess-type, window shattering operatic - I mean someone who uses both chest and head registers and knows when to break from one to the other. You can have this kind of classical approach and still sound fabulous singing rock!

Notes:

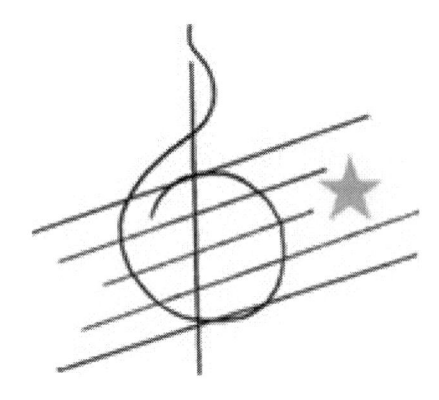

Reading Music: Where to Begin

Most people who don't read music, can't get going on the project because the task seems overwhelming. They see someone writing charts or sight-reading a song and they say, "He must have started when he was two. It would take me seventy-six years of intensive sweating to learn to read music like that. My brain has long ago lost its ability to retain information. My synapses are not what they used to be. I can't find my socks." Not true. I promise.

Let's take this one small step at a time. All you need to do is go to the bookstore or music store, and buy a book. For starters, find one on basic - I mean basic beginning - music theory. You don't need to learn how to read music right away - you just need to know that when you look at a piece of sheet music, there is order in there somewhere and it has the potential to be user-friendly. A book on music theory will get you past any blocks and fears, because you will see that reading music makes sense; it's very logical. Parts of it are purely mathematical. You don't need clairvoyant sight or a Type A personality.

Secondly, you don't have to have a major grand piano in your house in order to learn how to read music. Any keyboard will do (as long as it's in tune). In a pinch, you can give up (insert your particular vice here) and use that money to get a child's keyboard from Toys R Us. Or try the discount superstores: A small electronic keyboard is less expensive than most people think. I'm not talking midi capability here, just a little thing you can drag out of the closet for a few minutes a day to learn on.

So. You've got a book. You've got a keyboard. Your brain will not only hold new information, it will welcome it. Onward and upward.

Music as a second language

Here's the next thing you have to know: Reading music is easy, and learning to do it is actually fun. Remember, you don't have to get good enough to sight-sing at

Carnegie Hall - you can get by with very basic skills, such as how to read notes on the treble clef; how to take a chart and transpose it into your key; how to count out the rhythm of a song.

Here are some of the many books I've found that are non-threatening, non-anxiety provoking, they don't yell at you, and most of them cost under $15.00.

✓ *How to Read Music* by Roger Evans
✓ *Understanding Music Fundamentals* by R. Phyllis Gelineau
✓ *Introduction to Music Fundamentals* by J. Austin Andrews and Jeanne Foster Wardian
✓ *Learn to Read Music* by Howard Shanet (also available through the Aebersold catalogue)
✓ *Music Notation* by Mark McGrain (also available through the Pender's catalogue)

-An alternative idea: Go to the music store and get a child's book on beginning piano. The store clerk, who is often a musician by night, can help you choose a good one. Get a thin, small, softbound book with enormous notes in bold ink, that starts with basic notation and theory. You don't need to be playing "Hits Through the Ages," and you don't need a book that promises to have you impressing your friends - you do need to know how to navigate the staff. Browse. See which books call to you.

♪ Be careful with "overnight" piano playing courses. I'm not saying don't do them, I'm just saying that to really learn music, you need to know music theory and understand the why behind the notation. If you can find a "quick learn" video or course that doesn't by-pass theory, then fine. But if you end up being able to play *Feelings* perfectly in one hour and you still have no earthly idea which way is up, this won't help.

♪ OK, next step. Take the child's piano book, sit down at your keyboard, and go through it, page by page. You'll be amazed at how easy reading music can be. And, like learning a new language, I guarantee that you will be thrilled as these new doors open up for you.

Going the traditional route

You can also learn how to read music quickly and painlessly from a private piano or voice teacher in your town; from an adult informal class or workshop; from a working musician (most working musicians take students to supplement their income); from your mother who always tried to get you to take piano lessons and now you wish you had.

The pros: If you go this route, there is more structure. You can ask questions and actually get answers. The cons: You've got to practice every day, in order to be ready for next week's lesson. The pros: You've got to practice every day, in order to be ready for next week's lesson.

What to do right now, if you don't have time to learn to read music

I've designed **Vocal Vibrance** with all kinds of singers in mind. Many of you read music, many of you are trained musicians. Some of you don't yet read music. Here's what to do if you don't:

1) There is a great deal of material in this book that you can use even without being able to read music. I've described things verbally as much as possible, hopefully without boring those of you who do read. So just go through the book and use what you can.

2) If you are using **Vocal Vibrance** in conjunction with a course or with your private studies, your teacher or coach can go over the sections with you that are notated musically. (If you're not studying with a teacher, ask your choir director or a musical friend to sing the exercises for you.)

3) Obtain some rehearsal tapes. This way you can practice your songs to a solid, professional sounding accompaniment. (See the chapter on rehearsal tapes for ideas on where to get them.)

4) If all else fails, you can take the chapter of **Vocal Vibrance** that you are currently working on, bring it to a local musician in your town, and have her or him put the exercises on tape for you, for a modest fee.

A singer *is* a musician

Please do not be the kind of singer who gives the rest of us a bad name. This is the singer who, when she says she doesn't read music, says it in such a way as to imply that reading music is a randomly distributed DNA pattern: you're either born with it or you're not, and even plastic surgery won't change this genetic trait. This is the singer who goes up on stage to sit in with the band and smiles obliquely when asked what key he does his song in. This singer does not know how to communicate with the instrumentalists on the stage in any way, and has no intention of changing that. This is why so often you hear phrases such as "...musicians and singers..."

A singer **is** a musician. That means you never stop learning. That means that the more you know about all aspects of music, the better a musician you can be. Study music notation. Study music history. Learn about music in other countries and cultures. Go to the opera. Be upset about *Madame Butterfly*. Read Jean-Pierre Rampal's autobiography. Know about Miles Davis. Cry at a concert of Mendelssohn's *Elijah*. Find God in Bach's *B Minor Mass*. Join a controversy about vibrato on the Internet. Have a favorite violinist. Be indignant about the loss of vocal overtones in pop music mixing. Discover a new percussion instrument. Become immersed in knowledge, and you will become a wonderful singer.

Notes:

Registers

**The "Breaking Point"
The Story of Registers, Ranges,
and Bridging the Gap**

A hot topic, and one that's shrouded in gray areas, tributaries and undefined borders. Let's start by staking out boundary lines.

Definitions:
☑ **Register** - A register refers to a particular muscle and vocal adjustment that is an automatic function of the singer's desired range, tone, and volume. Some singers define "register" as where the voice is "placed". For instance, people refer to high or low registers, or to chest or head registers. The vocal cords and muscle adjustments are used differently for the different registers.

   -For many singers, the use of registers comes naturally. These lucky people can float over their entire ranges without a worry or a strained note. <u>For most of us, working with registers is a major part of our daily vocalizing routine.</u>

   -By learning to be in control of the different registers, you can expand your range dramatically, without sacrificing tone or power. Being in control of your registers can also help prevent damage to your vocal cords.

> ♪ **Chest register** (a.k.a. chest voice, first register, monophase register): the lower register. In singing, it feels as if the sound is vibrating off the bones in the front of the chest. In speaking, this is the conversational voice.

> ♪ **Head register** (a.k.a. head voice, second register, middle register, biphase register): the upper register. Singing "in head" feels as if the sound is resonating or vibrating off the bones in the front of the face - some singers specify the bones behind the upper lip, the nose, the forehead, and the sinus cavities.

> ♪ **Falsetto***: a term often used synonymously with the head register.

♪ **High head register** (a.k.a. the super head register): The voice that allows for a very high range. You can hit higher notes in "high head" than you can in "head." Some say it feels as if the sound were floating up through the top of the head. The tone is pure, open, unconstricted, and crystalline.

♪ **Blend register**: It's possible, in the midrange, to blend the chest and head registers somewhat, rather than abruptly changing from one register to the other. Some singers who specialize in pop or Broadway use a blend register in order to get a certain edge to their tone. Some feel it gives them more power in their upper midrange than a pure head voice. When you blend, you often feel as if the sound vibrates off the upper chest and in the nose. It's a nasal focus, but the addition of the chest vibrations gives it more overtones. Thus is does not sound nasal. (See the chapter "Pop and Belt.")

♪ ***For men only**: Many male singers differentiate between their falsetto and their head registers, rather than using the terms interchangeably. In this context, the head voice is a blend register, or middle voice - and the falsetto is the higher register. The falsetto is purer in tone and does not blend with the chest as well as the head voice does. So if we label the registers as "chest, head, and high head" for women, the male equivalent in this context would be "chest, head (or middle), and falsetto."

♪ **Whistle register** (a.k.a. flute register): This controversial register is the next one up in pitch range after the "high head." I would venture to say that most singers cannot use this register and still sound good, but some can - jazz singer Cleo Laine being an example. You get to it by going up through the high head, and then letting the sound float up even higher, aiming it for the top of the head as well as the nose. (Singers have varied imagery that they use, but this imagery works for me.) The sound of the whistle register is thus not as rich as "head," and not as crystalline as "high head," and to some ears has a vibrant but constricted timbre.

♪ **Fry**: While we're talking about extremes here, there is a register that's lower than chest, which has been called "fry." This is not musical and the use of it can damage the voice. Some people "fry" their voices without even knowing it, especially during speech at the ends of phrases. "Fry" is when your voice is so low in pitch that it "breaks up" or pops. Listen to yourself speak - if you hear this register, it would be worthwhile to train yourself not to use it. It's often simply a vocal habit, rather than a major issue.

☑ **Range** - Your range is the actual expanse of notes over which you can sing. It is not the same as the key the song is in. You might say something like, "I have a three octave range," or "My range is from low G to high C." In relation to registers, you might say something like, "My range in my chest register is from low G to the F above middle C; in my head register my range is two octaves, from middle up to high C." (See the chapter called "Expanding Your Range" for more information.)

☑ **Placement** - Placement is the feeling of <u>where,</u> in the body, the sound vibrates. In the chest register, for example, it feels as if the sound is vibrating off the bones of the upper chest; so the placement is said to be in the upper chest. In the head register, the placement is said to be in the head. Placement has a direct effect on the resonance and quality of sound that is produced. (See the chapter on resonance for details.)

☑ **Resonance** - The depth, texture, and color of the voice. It is affected by many factors, including register, and the overtones your voice produces as it vibrates off the bones, soft tissues, and cavities in the body. Resonance is the tone or timbre of the voice. i.e. Singing in "chest" resonates differently than singing in "head." (The "Resonance" chapter has specific exercises.)

☑ **Break** - The notes over which the singer changes register. There are perhaps two or three notes of "break" before the voice is free and clear in the next register. (Also called "passage notes.")

More about the "break"
The "break" is a point in your scale when your voice naturally changes to a different register. As you sing up a scale, for instance, starting in your chest voice, you may notice a few notes of dubious placement as you change to your head voice. If you keep going up the scale, you may again notice some strangely placed notes as you change to high head. Same thing going down. **<u>The notes over which your voice CHANGES from one register to another are the notes where your voice has its "break."</u>**

Who has breaks?
All voices, if the range is big enough. Men have them, women have them. (If you are one of the charmed singers who doesn't have problems with break notes, bless you and move to the next chapter.)

So what's the problem?
The break notes, without training, can sound strained and out of context. In fact, you can damage your voice if, say, you keep singing in a range that constantly hits these break notes. Unless the voice is well trained to handle the

breaks, most singers like to stay away from ranges in which the break notes are used too heavily.

Also, without training, the chest and head registers can sound like two different voices - the chest voice sounding strong and often heavy, and the head voice sounding lighter and more "soprano." (Actually, if you want to yodel, that's all you have to do - change from chest to head very abruptly, and vice versa.)

The ultimate goal is to get the break notes so they sound smooth and relaxed, and the registers so that they blend seamlessly. The break notes serve to join the registers. The smoother the "joint," the smoother your overall sound will be.

Can there be an overlap between chest and head registers in the same range?

Yes. If the range is right, the same note can be sung in both head and chest registers. Take a middle C. Most singers can sing it in either chest or head, and many exercises will take you through techniques to gain that kind of control.

Singing in a particular register affects the tone of the voice, and the ease with which a phrase is sung. A middle C sung by a woman in a chest voice may have more power than the same note sung by the same singer in her head voice. Thus as you become familiar with your voice and your repertoire, you will make decisions about which register you will use and when to break into a different register.

Warning label

- ✓ You can damage your voice if you extend it too high in pitch using your chest register.

- ✓ To care for your voice properly, you need to learn where your break is and then learn how to change from one register to another in a seamless way.

Goals - an overview:

1. To get to the point where you simply smooth over the breaks as you change registers.

2. To make the break notes sound like, and blend in with, the rest of your voice.

3. To make your expanded range smooth and graceful, top to bottom.

Register trouble-shooting

♭ If you're a singer who has been belting, and is not used to singing in head register, don't be alarmed if your head register seems frail and weak at first. This is to be expected. It has to be built up, through these and other exercises - but with careful daily practice, you can make it as powerful and rich as your chest voice. Don't assume you must stay in chest on your high notes in order to match the tones of the rest of your song. You can get the head voice to the point where listeners don't even notice that you've changed over to it. This is true. I promise.

♭ If you're a soprano who is not used to chest voice, same thing. Chest may seem too robust at first, but its tone can be made to match the tones in the rest of your range. Careful one note practices and slow diatonic scales are the best exercises.

♭ If you're a man who seldom uses head voice, you might try developing it. It's a good tool to have, if you need to hit a sustained high note in a song. Instead of stretching for the note, you can just switch to head. Vocalizing over head voice, even if you don't use it in your singing, improves your tone and placement in general.

♭ If you just can't "get" your head register - if you don't hear what it is, and don't know how to produce that sound, try mental imagery. Think: soprano. Think: opera. Think: Goddess. Think: Angelic choir.

> Still can't get it? Try pretending you're an "old lady" at the front door of your son's house. You see the door is slightly opened, but instead of just walking in, you call out "Yoo-hoo..."

♭ Can't "get" your chest register? Begin by speaking the word "hay." Now say the word again, sustaining the vowel sound a little: "Haaaaay." Now, still speaking and still sustaining the vowel, inflect your voice downward as you say the word - as if this were the end of a sentence. Do it again, sustaining the vowel for a slightly longer period of time. By now you're probably singing in chest voice. Many people say that the chest voice is the same as speaking, except that the vowels are elongated.

One singer who had trouble finding her chest register found it helpful to put her hand on her upper chest and try to make her hand vibrate with her voice. By using this image, she was able to get her chest voice. After practicing a few minutes a day for a few days, she was able to stop using the hand monitor.

♭ Once you've found a heretofore uncharted register, be sure to reinforce the feeling of producing that sound by repeating it for five minutes or so. Make notes of what it feels like - what sensations you experience. Record the sound, so you can get it back the next day.

Exercises
1. One Note Changeover

-Begin on a note in the lower part of your head register, but one that you can also reach comfortably in your chest register. A middle C works for many singers. Using the syllable "nah," sustain the note for eight beats, alternating every two beats between chest and head. (If middle C doesn't work for you, try a D or an E-flat - keep experimenting until you find a note that can be sung easily in both registers.)

-When you've finished the eight beats, go up (or down) by half a step and repeat the exercise again. Don't strain. You may only have one or two notes on which this exercise can be done. It's not unusual, however, to have five or six notes which can be sung in both registers.

2. Fly By Changing

-Sing a scale, changing from chest to head at a pre-determined note as you go up the scale, and changing back from head to chest at a pre-determined note as you go down. For instance, you might sing the first four notes of the scale in chest, change to head for the top four notes, then come back down in head and change back to chest on the same "change" note.

-Now do the same scale again, but decide on a different note for your "break." For instance, this time you might sing the first three notes in chest before switching to head.

-As with exercise 1, you'll have to determine for your own voice where to begin your scale. I've got it in C - but if that doesn't work for you, experiment with higher or lower scales until you find one that's comfortable.

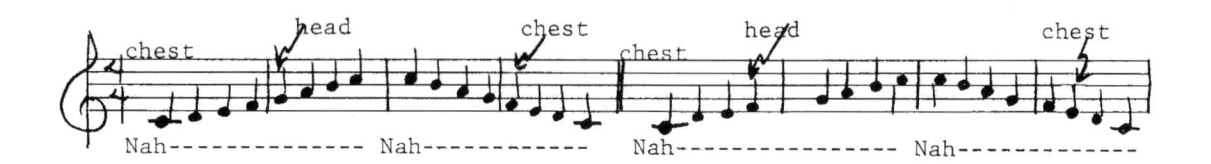

3. Constant Comment

-Sing a four note passage, staying entirely in your chest register. Go up half a step and repeat the passage, still in chest. Keep going up chromatically until you sense discomfort on the horizon. (Don't go so high as to strain your voice.) Go back to your beginning scale and repeat the exercise, this time going down by half steps.

-Now sing a four note passage staying entirely in your head register. Go up half a step and repeat.

-This exercise helps solidify the feeling of being in chest, and the feeling of being in head.

(see top of next page)

Notes:

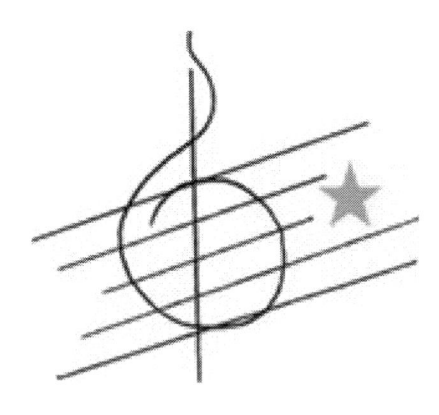

Pre-made Rehearsal Accompaniments

Whether you play piano or not, rehearsal tapes - digital or analog - are a valuable practice resource. These are downloads of the songs you sing, with just the accompaniment on them - no voice. You supply the voice.

If you're practicing a part in an ensemble, you can find downloads that have all the other parts but yours. Most choirs supply singers with these, in the form of CDs or digital downloads.

Here are some of the outlets for rehearsal tapes:

✓ You can get them commercially
✓
- ♪ through specialized catalogues such as Music Minus One

- ♪ Jamey Aebersold

- ♪ Pender's Music Company

- ♪ Sher Music Company

- ♪ ChartsForChurches.com and Partpredominant.com

(If you're a classical singer, "Music Minus One" has a lot of classical accompaniments for you, in a variety of ranges. Jamey Aebersold is mostly jazz, but you'd be amazed at how many Broadway and pop standards are available through the jazz outlets.)

- ✓ Your online sheet music store may be another source.
   Sometimes you have to just browse.

- ✓ If you sing original material or songs you can't find on accompaniment tapes, ask a local musician to put the piano part on tape for you. The fee is usually modest. To find a pianist, go to people's gigs, or put a notice on the university's music department bulletin board.

- ✓ Another reason to have your accompaniments custom made is if you sing in an unusual range, and the keys chosen for commercial tapes are not right for you

- ✓ If you play piano, you're golden. Make your own tapes and build a library of accompaniments to all the songs in your repertoire. The tapes don't have to be studio quality. You can even record acoustically in your living room.

- ✓ Singers who are taking private voice lessons can tape their lessons. Some teachers who also play piano will tape the piano part of your song for you, as part of your lesson.

Notes:

Resonance, Placement, and Tone

Basic to a gorgeous voice is control over the resonating system. Knowledge of this system, control of placement, and a mastery of breathing and vowel sounds will guarantee you a voice that will turn heads, knock socks off, and smooth your way over many a musical rough edge.

The Resonating System

This is what brings your voice to life, acoustically. Your phonating system - the vocal cords and larynx - produce the original sound. But the original sound, by itself, is thin and lifeless. It has to be amplified and enriched in order to be anywhere near aesthetic. This is done in-house, with what's called your "resonating system."

The resonating system determines how the original sound reverberates within your body. Anything the sound can vibrate with or bounce off of, is part of this system of components. This is what gives your voice its overtones, timbre, depth, personality, and carrying power.

The tangible components of the resonating system include:
♪ Your body. This is the "housing" for your sound, so to speak - like the wood and shape of a guitar "house" the sound made by the guitar strings.

-Major body part components include the "mask" or front of the face (the nose, sinus cavities, mouth, and the bones and skin of your face), the pharynx (the soft throat tissues), the larynx (see the chapter on the larynx), the trachea (windpipe), and the upper chest.

♪ Your articulating system - the jaw, teeth, tongue, lips, and mouth - which help shape the sound.

Ethereal aspects of the resonating system include:
♪ Placement (where and how the sound vibrates within its "housing")

♪ And that most elusive variable of all - tone.

Tone

Tone is the quality of the sound you produce. It's the most noticeable thing about a voice. You hear people speak of a nasal tone, a rich tone, a thin tone, a breathy tone, a soothing tone, a hollow tone, a mellifluous tone, and many other subjective descriptions. You can manipulate your tone to get it just the way you want it.

There does seem to be a certain part of a person's vocal timbre that is like a signature, or thumb-print - a base color that makes it uniquely recognizable. And although that one-of-a-kind timbre may always remain, that doesn't mean you can't work with your total sound - changing it, modifying it, enriching it, and coloring it to suit your needs.

For singing and speaking, the best way to begin work on tone is to define for yourself what you want. Go for a basic, optimal tone that is textured and resonant, smooth and full of overtones. Make it free of breathiness, boominess, or shrillness. Yes. This could be you.

From this basic voice, you can then deviate when you need to, for special effects - you may want a touch of breathiness as part of a torch song dynamic, for example. You may decide to add a slight nasal quality to your lower chest tones, to brighten them up.

It's a matter of learning what it feels like to make certain sounds. You've got to tune into yourself, listen to yourself, and be aware of how you produce the myriad of tones and overtones you hear coming through your voice.

For starters, here are some easy exercises:
- ✓ Listen to singers or speakers whose tone you admire. Saturate yourself with their sound, until it becomes a part of you.

- ✓ Work with a good tape recorder, fine tuning the sounds you produce, listening, adjusting, until you get the tone you want.

- ✓ When you hear yourself making sounds you like, be sure to capture them on tape. Reinforce them by re-playing that tape repeatedly. Try to broaden the range of the preferred tone by applying it to different sounds and different situations.

- ✓ Watch for and eliminate tension in your throat, neck, and jaw. Tension is a powerful tone-mangler.

Resonance

Defined by Webster's as "the intensification and enriching of a musical tone by supplementary vibration that is either sympathetically or mechanically induced..."

Resonance is how and where the sound you produce resonates, or vibrates, in your body/instrument. Resonance is determined by placement. Piano strings resonate off the shape, size, and quality of the wood housing. A grand piano produces different tones than an upright. A piano with dried wood resonates differently than a piano with more moisture in the wood. Voices in a church resonate differently than voices in a small, carpeted room. Your voice resonating off the bones in your nose will sound differently than your voice resonating off a larger part of your face and chest.

Sound must resonate; vibrate; bounce off things - in order to become textured.

Placement

Placement is <u>where</u> the sound vibrates to produce overtones. Although placement technically involves many intricate muscular movements, most singers use mental imagery to learn, develop, and use placement. You can bounce your sound off any part of your body, by using mental imagery. And the amazing thing is, the imagery actually produces different measurable tones and overtones. The mind is where placement happens.

Singers say things like: "The sound feels like it's vibrating off the mask part of my face," or "I'm aiming the sound up and out," or "I'm using my chest voice." Or you may hear things like "I'm placing the sound in my forehead between my eyes." And even stranger things can be heard in the halls of music schools, such as "I'm placing the sound in my foot." "I'm using a placement centered in the middle of my back." "I'm aiming for my adenoids." "My sound comes up from the ground, through my spine, and out the top of my head."

Here are some commonly used images that usually achieve a desired placement:

- <u>Your basic tone, through all your registers, should be</u>
    - rich (full of overtones)
    - round (free of breathiness)
    - "open" - that is, not constricted or strained

- <u>When placed in the head</u> you generally want the sound to vibrate off the "mask" part of your face - that is the area from the nose down to the top lip, and in to the roof of the mouth and the sinus cavities. The sound should be bright and "forward," but not nasal or thin.

- <u>When placed in the chest</u> you generally want the sound to vibrate off the upper bones of the chest. You should also feel it on the roof of the mouth. The sound should be bright and rich, but not boomy or dark.

- <u>When singing in the high head register</u> you generally want the sound to vibrate off the upper part of the forehead. The sound should be pure and round, never strained.

-Check out the chapter on registers for more details and images.

Other Factors Influencing Tone
Each of the following aspects of voice need to be studied in order to possess the skills it takes to produce your desired sound:
- Breathing
- Articulation and vowel sounds
- Use of the jaw, relaxation of the tongue
- Pitch
- Use of registers
- Relaxation and care of the instrument as a whole
- Volume
- Vibrato
- The acoustics of the room, or the sound system

PLACEMENT EXERCISES

NOTE 1: Start each exercise in your mid-range, then take it up chromatically. Go back to the mid-range and take it down chromatically. Don't go higher or lower than is comfortable.

NOTE 2: Tone is intricately interwoven with how you pronounce your vowels. Be sure to review the chapter on vowel sounds.

1. Hum Up, "Nah" Down
- On a five note major scale (or, if you want to add ear training, try a minor scale or a whole tone scale), hum up the first four notes, drop the jaw and sing "nah" on the fifth note. Hold that note until you get a rich, round, forward-sounding tone, then go back down the scale to the root note on the "ah" sound. This is done in a legato style, with one note seamlessly blending (but not slurring) into the next.

-When you hum up the scale, feel a slight vibration in the lower nose and/or upper lip.

-When you break into the "ah" sound at the top, drop the jaw so the sound can come out. Dropping the jaw will bring the sound out of the nose and down to the roof of the mouth.

-If the sound is falling back into your throat (a throaty sound) when you sing "ah," try smiling slightly. The slight smile should bring the sound out of your throat and forward into the mask.

Nnnn------------ah------------

OR

Mmmm-------------ah-----------

2. "Ee" Up, "Ah" Down

-Same as above, but go up the scale on "ee" instead of on a hum. -Feel the "ee" vibrate in the area between the base of the nose and the top of the teeth.

-When you change to "ah," drop the jaw, as before, and feel the sound drop slightly to the roof the mouth. (In the lower register, don't drop the jaw quite as much as you do in the upper registers, or you'll lose that "mask" placement and get instead a throaty sound. "Mask" is good; "throaty" is bad.)

-Sing "ah," but think "ee".

-The "ah" should be open and unconstricted. The throat should be "open" (relaxed), allowing for the sound to flow freely out.

Eeeee-------------ah-------------

3. The Teasing Child

NOTE: This exercise is to be used to correct a "boomy" or throaty quality that may be showing up in the lower register. <u>If your lower register is already bright and round, don't do this exercise.</u>

-Conjure up that favorite of children's taunts. Unlike the previous exercises which were on a round "nah" sound, this exercise is on "naa," as in "nag."

-Feel the sound vibrating off the area from the nose to the top teeth.

-Although you would never use this tone in a song, you can use the exercise to learn the feeling, or placement, of a bright sound on a low note.

Then when you transfer that skill to song singing, you can brighten up low notes to the degree necessary for a pleasant sound.

Na na na na na

4. Experiments in Mental Imagery
☼ Sing "nah" (as in "far") on a note in your mid-range.

☼ Aim the sound for the mask, make sure the throat is open (sense the soft palate being lifted), and the jaw dropped (slight smile if necessary). Go for your optimal, basic, rich, round tone.

☼ Now experiment (taking breaths when necessary):
- Aim this sound into your nose.
- Put in back. Now aim it into your throat.
- Put it back in the mask. Now try bouncing it off the upper bones of the ribcage.
- Put it back. How about the forehead?
- Put it back. Can you vibrate the sound off the wall in front of you?
- Put it back. Now try this: can you sound brassy, like a horn?
- Can you sound pure and crystalline, like a flute?
- Give an imitation of "an opera singer."
- Now pretend you're singing Gregorian chant.
- Imitate your favorite singer.
- Make up your own images.

☼ Make a note of the different sounds and sensations you get as you change placements. This will help you know and remember your optimal tone, and it will also help if you need to adjust your tone for a special effect.

☼ Use your imagination. Play with placement. Know your instrument. Know how it feels to produce certain sounds. Hear the different overtones, colors, textures, nuances.

5. Changing Registers I
- Start on a note in your chest register, perhaps a G below middle C, or whatever is comfortable for you. Sing "nah."

-Now glide up an octave, changing to your head register in the process. (Glide = one continuous sound rather than individual notes.)

-When you hit the top note, say, a G above middle C, you should be in your head register.

-Take a breath if you need to, and reverse the process, going from head down to chest as you return to your original note.

-Do this twice.

-Repeat the exercise going up the scale chromatically as high or as low as is comfortable. (Don't strain to reach notes in a particular register.)

-Do this exercise on each of the vowel sounds.

-Use a mirror to keep your face free of contortion. (Contortion causes tension and weakens the sound.)

-**NOTE**: **As you change registers. make sure the quality of the sound remains the same.** The registers, by nature, have different tones, but you want to match the tones of the two placements as closely as you can. Then, when you are singing a song in which you must change registers, you can keep a somewhat uniform tone. (See the chapter on registers for details and more exercises.)

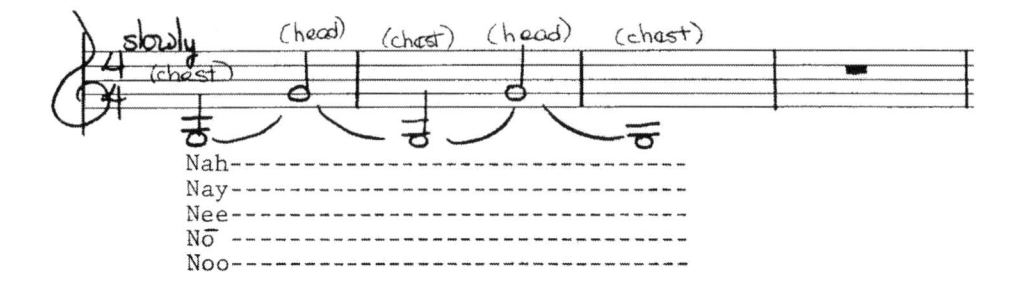

[Musical notation: slowly, 4/4 time, alternating (chest) and (head) notes with syllables Nah, Nay, Nee, No, Noo]

6. The Roller Coaster (Speakers' Version of #1, 'Hum Up, "Nah" Down')
NOTE: The singing exercises are ideal for speakers, too. However, here is a version of Exercise #1 that does not require specific pitch.

- Begin with the sound of either "nn" or "mm."

- Starting in the lower middle part of your speaking voice, slide up to the upper middle range of your speaking voice.

- At the top (don't go too high), drop the jaw and let out the "ah" sound.

- Slide on "ah" back down to your starting point.

- You should feel vibrations in the upper part of your chest on both the hum and the "ah." In addition, you should feel vibrations as described in Exercise #1.

- Your "ah" sound should be open, relaxed, round, and rich. Not pushed or strained. Keep the volume soft to moderate.

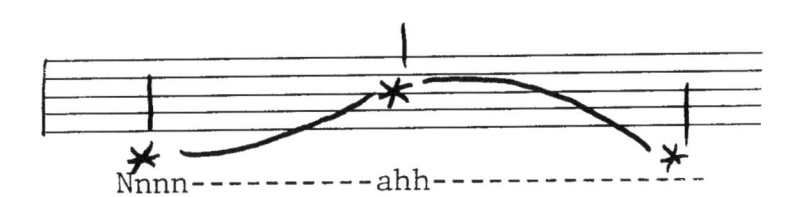

Nnnn---------ahh--------------

Notes:

The "R" Sound

The English language can made to sound quite lovely, with one exception: the "r" sound. This horrific auditory intrusion sounds even more gruesome when it comes at the end of a word. It's not so bad when speaking - but when singing, you've got to be always alert. Otherwise the "R Squad" will get you.

Why is the "r" sound more venomous when singing than speaking? Because in singing we are elongating our sounds, we hold them, we do things with them. When we speak, we say what we have to say fairly quickly and we are done with it. Nothing is "held."

What can you legally hold?

When singing, we use the vowel sounds - that's how we project the voice. The melody, the lyrics, everything floats on the vowel sounds. Consonants are quickly stuck in there in order to make understandable words, but it's the vowel sounds we work on when we work on tone.

You can hold a vowel sound as long as you can sustain your breath. Sing "nah" on any comfortable note, and hold it for eight beats. Sing "nee" and hold it. "Noh." No problem.

Now sing "t". It doesn't sustain for very long. Try singing "p". Or "b". You just can't hold them.

Granted, there are consonants like "s", "f", "l", "m", "n", and even "h" and "v" to a certain extent if you try very hard, that you can sustain. But none equals the true ugliness of the "r" sound, which is unfortunately, sustainable.

What will the Squad get you for?

Try singing the lyric "whirl" on a comfortable note, and sustaining it for 8 beats. Listen carefully to yourself. On what sound are you sustaining this lyric? If you hear an "r" sound for more than half a beat at the tail end of the word, you're going to get a serious moving violation from the "R Squad."

What to do if you get a ticket
Here's what to do: Sing the lyric "whirl" again on 8 beats, but stick the final "rl" sound in there just before you're about to stop singing. The "rl" gets clipped in quickly at the very end of the word. You sustain the lyric on the "uh" sound of "**whirl**." So it's:
whuh -uh ---------- uh-----------rl. (Not: whir---r- -r ---------r ----- r- -l.)

Similarly, if you sing the lyric "**dare**," you'll want to sing: daa -a -a- -re. (Not: dar---r----r----r----re.)

The lyric "**heart**" is sung:
hah- ah----------ah---- ah ------rt. (Not har- -r------ r----- r- -rt.)

"**Bird**" would be:
buh----uh- uh -------- rd. (Not bir- -r -----r   r------d.) And so on.

How to practice
Singing into a tape recorder - so you can get the raw ugly truth - is the best way to hear if you're gnarling your words with incorrect "r" sounds. You can also get feedback from friends and if you're taking voice lessons, you should already be cured of this affliction. Singing "r" correctly is not technically difficult. It's more a matter of remembering to do it.

Take a song you know that has some phrases in which the last lyric ends on an "r" sound. Something that must be sustained. *On a Clear Day* by Lerner and Lane is a good example. Tape it and see if you're holding the lyrics "clear" and "are" from the first 8 measures, correctly.

It should be: "On a clee---ee---ee---r day, rise and look around you, and you'll see who you ah---ah---ah---r." (Not: "On a clear--r--r--r--r day, rise and look around you, and you'll see who you are--r--r--r--r.")

Notes:

A Scat for All Genres

This is for you, no matter what genre of music you sing.

Ear Training and Confidence Boosting
First of all, if you're working on ear training, scat can be a marvelous tool. Scat teaches the singer to really hear - scales, modes, intervals, rhythms, patterns. And scat teaches you to sing what you hear. This is ear training at its finest.

Secondly, if you've got a confidence problem or you get attacks of stage fright, learning to scat can be a lifesaver. The confidence it builds is immeasurable. If you can scat - even a little bit - you feel you can handle anything that comes up.

Life as Improv Class
I mean, couldn't life itself be thought of as a giant improvisation class? Couldn't art be thought of as abstracted bits of our life experience, transformed into understandable segments by filtering them through our instruments? (Well, perhaps not completely understandable...)

We don't go through our days with pre-written scripts in our hands. You don't know exactly what you'll be saying on the telephone five minutes from now. Central Casting sends actors to be in your life's movie without always auditioning them first. You find yourself doing gigs in new nightclubs all the time - with all kinds of surprises and plot twists in store. Your personal movie script and the accompanying soundtrack is being written <u>as you're doing it.</u> You get a feel for something, you know what the spirit of the thing is, and you trust that the rest will flow. That's improvisation.

Scat singing is improvising; it's writing your own musical score, right up there on the bandstand. It's composing. It's making things up as you go along. It's nothing more than we do every day in our own lives.

Even if you've never scatted before, you've got the skills. And even if you don't intend to scat within the musical style you sing, having some experience in scat singing is a brilliant way to boost your confidence; to know that no matter what comes up, you can turn it into beautiful music.

You can do vocal improvisation in any genre of music. Lots of improvisation goes on in pop, gospel, soul, fusion, rock, Latin. Baroque music was more improvisational than most people realize.

If you're just adding a spontaneous series of legato background "oo"s, you're improvising. Improvising doesn't have to be complicated. It's not the exclusive property of bebop. When you practice improvisation at home, you can by all means practice it over whatever genre of music you sing.

Accompaniment Tapes

The main "aid" you'll need in practicing scat singing is someone, or something, to play the piano for you. Many singers who don't play piano use rehearsal tapes. If you play piano, you may still want to record your own accompaniments, to free yourself up to concentrate fully on the scatting. For more details on where to get these tapes, see the chapter called "Reading Music."

How to Begin

So let's start with easy improvising. Get a song you know well, and sing it with your accompaniment tape. Now take it through a second time, this time on "oo" (no lyrics), playing with the melody. You can stick as close to the melody as you feel you need to to keep your place. Just take liberties here and there, enjoy it, take it up an octave, down an octave, embellish notes, change phrasing, change endings of phrases, change the rhythms.

You always keep your "inner ear" open to the melody and the chord changes of the song as it's written, while your voice is actually singing "around" that written melody; doing creative things with it. Play with the concept this way just to get acquainted with the "feel" of it.

How Not To Get Lost

Many singers who begin their scat experience ask the question: How do you keep from ending up at the dead end of some dark musical alley, with the harmony police on your tail, guns drawn, and no hope of escape besides death or off-key singing? Especially if you're scatting up a storm; if you're really taking the piece "outside," which means way far away from the main melody. Here are some of the ways singers stay out of that alley:

1. No matter what you're doing improvisationally, an inner part of you is always humming the written melody, or "head." That way you always know where you are in the music.

2. You know the piece so well that getting lost is not an issue.

3. Some singers keep the rhythm in their head, instead of the melody.

4. Some singers actually count in their head, as they're singing. They may be counting measures, or if it's within a phrase they may even be counting beats. Another rhythmic indicator of where you are in the music can come from the drummer. Some singers always have an ear tuned to the bass drum, especially if they know the drummer well, and know how he or she plays.

5. If you've got the ear, you can tune in to the piano and/or bass, and take your musical cues from them. One singer said he never begins a scat phrase without taking a few seconds to scope out the piano's voicings. So he lets the piano begin each phrase, he gets his melodic bearings, then he comes in. Remember, in scatting, you can come in whenever you want to. The bass is an excellent indicator of where you are musically, because the bass often plays the roots of the chords. It's a matter of tuning your ear to whatever helps you, as if your ears were antennae.

6. Some singers stay quite close to the melody during their entire scat. It's a safe way to begin, you can't get lost, and you can always get a little braver each time you do the song. Then one day, there you are, on the "outside," scatting up an electrical storm. People will be asking <u>you</u> how you keep from getting lost.

You're In the Alley, Trying to Escape Over a Barbed Wire Fence:
If you're in the middle of a scat and suddenly find yourself in deep trouble, here are some alternatives to quitting music, leaving town in the dark of night, and selling gerbil food for a living. See which works for you:

1) Hold your note - now, cooly and easily, take that note down a half step. If you're still in the wrong key, go back to the note and go up half a step. One or the other will get you back into the correct key. (Keep your wits about you, though, you've got to do this fairly quickly, and even then it can only be done if the song stays with the same chords long enough.)

2) Pause for a few seconds, listen to the piano, and regain your bearings.

Then begin scatting again. This is the easiest and most graceful form of recovery.

3) If worse comes to worse, just stop singing. (In scat, you can stop whenever you darn well please.) It's better than ripping the seat of your velvet gig pants on the barbed wire.

4) Another graceful resuscitation technique: Go back to the written melody (still using "oo" or your scat syllables) until you get yourself straightened out.

5) Say to the horn player, "Take it, Gerry."

6) Whatever happens, don't let the terror show on your face. If you seriously panic, if you lose control and let it show, the scat squad will shoot. No matter how horrible you sound, how idiotic your scat syllables are, you must keep your cool. You are, after all, a performer. You needn't bare your soul to the audience. Smile, pretend you meant to do that, put that confident look on your face that you practiced in front of the mirror before you went for your head shots, and freak out later in private.

How Not To End Up in the Alley in the First Place:
Here's how to learn to scat:

1. Remember the purpose of scat:
Why are you doing this? The purpose of scat is to express more of the song, and more of what's in your soul relating to that song than is possible through the confines of the written melody. It's to amplify the meaning behind the song, as you see it through your personal vision. The purpose is not to torture yourself (or your listeners). A simply done scat that is meaningful is a much better scat than a manic but emotionless race up and down scales. So - if you've got music in your soul, you've got all you need. The technical will come with time and practice.

2. Listen to the jazz masters.
The best "scat school" is sitting in your living room with Ella Fitzgerald and Miles Davis as your teachers.

-Listen. Analyze. Enjoy. Get a feel, through listening, of various ways of phrasing; of scat syllables that work well rhythmically; of ways to add variety.

-Find a scat or instrumental solo that excites you, and memorize it. This is standard procedure in jazz studies.

-If you have the skills, take a solo you love and transcribe it. Then learn it from the written transcription. (*Downbeat Magazine* publishes transcriptions already written out.)

-Learn, say, a Miles solo or a Charlie Parker solo, and write your own lyrics to it.

-Who are the masters? Jon Hendricks, Mark Murphy, Eddie Jefferson, King Pleasure, Ella Fitzgerald, Sarah Vaughan, Betty Carter, Mel Torme, Urszula Dudziak, Louis Armstrong, Annie Ross, Jackie Paris and Ann-Marie Moss, Kurt Elling, Leon Thomas, Joe Carroll, Cab Calloway, Anita O'Day, Carmen McRae, and many more. (Some of these singers, such as Eddie Jefferson and King Pleasure, specialize in "vocalese" as opposed to strict, on-the-spot-"scat" - meaning that they would often take instrumental solos and put lyrics to them. The group Lambert, Hendricks, and Ross took vocalese to its pinnacle of excitement and dazzle, with Manhattan Transfer and Rare Silk being some of many examples of contemporary descendants.) Listening to any of these people scat is the best way to learn scat singing yourself. If you're a serious jazz singer, it's just plain illegal to walk around saying "Who's Betty Carter?"

3. Practice improvising over everything you hear.
In the car listening to the radio, in the elevator listening to elevator music, in the supermarket listening to cereal-purchasing-mood-music, in your office listening to classical music, in your living room listening to the blues - play with what you are hearing. Work it. See how far you can stray from the melody and rhythm while still staying within the chord changes. The point is to develop your ear for hearing the chord changes, and your creative mind for playing with these changes.

4. Start easy.
Just go one step at a time.

-Take a song you have an accompaniment tape for, and begin by singing the melody. Now take it through a second time, on scat syllables or on "oo"s and "ah"s, just altering the melody a little bit. Take it through again, this time altering some of the rhythms. Each time you go through the song, take it a little more "out." This repetition will also get you tuned into the chord changes of the piece - so you will be able to take more chances and try more interesting approaches without getting lost.

-Get a tape, or have one made, of a standard blues progression in a key you like. This tape should have no melody - it's just the rhythm section "comping," or playing the background chords. This tape should repeat the 12-bar form as many times as possible. Ten times through, say, will allow you to keep practicing without having to stop and rewind the tape. (If you get momentum going, you don't want to stop and rewind.)

Now, work with this tape. Begin by scatting a simple blues melody to the changes. The second time through, keep your main melody in mind, but alter it a little. The third time through, keep the spirit of your main melody in mind, but go farther out melodically and rhythmically. You can use "oo" as your scat syllable, you use "la la la," or you can go for the hot stuff - "bwee ba da shwee ah ba."

Speaking of blues, there's no such thing as too much of it. Knowing the blues inside and out, learning the solos of the great blues artists, will make you into a fine scat singer. The blues progression (I, IV, 1,1, IV,IV, 1,1, V, IV, I, V^7) is almost like a universal cosmic language - everyone knows it. My bet is that when they finally land on Neptune, there will be a jazz band there, playing in a funky converted spaceship, and the thing that breaks the language barrier is the special intergalactic code known as the blues progression.

You can sit in at any nightclub, tell the band to play a blues in your favorite key, count out the tempo, and then scat to it, and this would be perfectly acceptable behavior. We will discuss modes and other scales later, but if modal singing seems too overwhelming to you, forget it. If you know the blues, you know all you need to know.

5. Determine your personal level of obsessiveness (Practice scales and arpeggios)

Of course if you <u>want</u> to go farther, this is the next step. But wait - it's OK - it's not like your mom used to make you do. Why? Because, no matter what genre of music you're singing, jazz rules can apply. Meaning that there is a jazz mindset that transcends regular rules - and there never really were any jazz rules in the first place. Musicians have historically made them up as they went along. We're talking about 21st century creativity. So go for it. Because we've got modes. We've got altered chords. We've got substitutions. We've got thirteenths. We've got pious sounding raised fourths and funky sounding sharp ninths. We've got tritones and if we want to, we hold on a passing tone. My dear, we've got things your mother never knew about. Our things are fun.

> ♮ If you know music theory (and if you don't, there are videos and tapes available to take you through these scales and arpeggios), then get your ear trained. Practice all your modal scales. Be able to sing any one of them; be able to hear which mode another soloist is in. Be able to sing and hear the subtle difference between an Aeolian minor and a Dorian minor. Do the modes not only as scales, but also as arpeggios. Knowing your modes cold will assure you of fabulous solo technique.

> ♮ What are modes? A mode is a way of defining a scale pattern. You know there are major and minor scales and chords, and you can probably hear whether a song is in major or minor. Modes are more detailed ways of expressing these kinds of moods. Just as you can learn to hear major and minor, you can learn to hear and sing modes. (Check

out the chapter on modes for details.)

♮ Sing up and down other scales such as the harmonic minor, the pentatonic scale, the blues scale, the melodic minor, the whole tone scale, the chromatic scale. You can learn these scales from any resource book, such as **The Hierarchy of Music and Complete Scale Anthology** by Tib Van Dyke, **120 Blues Choruses** by Dan Higgins, or **Scales for Jazz Improvisation** by Dan Haerle. Emile DeCosmo has a series available through Aebersold called **The Polytonal Series** which has a special book for each scale, from the augmented 11th scale to the Arabian scale. OK, it's a lot of work and you can scat brilliantly without knowing a thousand scales. Only you can decide for yourself how compulsive you want to be about this.

How to practice scales and modes:

Idea #1) During your daily vocalizing session, why not "go modal" occasionally? We tend to vocalize only over major scales, triads, and arpeggios. If you're going to go up and down scales every day, why not go up and down a minor scale once in a while? If you're doing arpeggios to warm up your voice, why not go up and down a diminished chord? A half diminished chord?

Idea #2) Let's take the plain old major scale in C, and see how we can breath life into it.

-First, sing the scale up and down in 4/4, just as you might do when warming up.

-Now do the same scale, but change the rhythm to 3/4.

-Go back to 4/4, but swing the beat.

Nah-------------------- Nah--------------------

-Do it again with the swing beat, but do it on simple scat syllables such as "shwah, bah, dah, bah, dah," instead of the standard warm-up syllables.

Schwah-bah-dah-bah-dah-bah-dah-bah Dah-bah-doe-bee-do-ah-do-ah

-Now keep the swing, but start embellishing notes as you go up and down the scale. Come at a note from a half step above, for example, or a half-step below.

Do-wah bah dah bah dah do wah dah dee-ah bah
Do wah dah dee-ah dah do bah dah bwee oh

-Now do the scale, but skip every other note, to make an arpeggio of sorts.

[musical notation with lyrics:]
Lah bah dah bah Lah bah dah bah Lah bah dah bah dah bah doe
Lah bah dah bah Lah bah dah bah Lah bah dah bah dah dwee oh

-Add your own alterations. For instance, you could do the scale, alternating skipping notes and singing the passing tones. It would look like this:

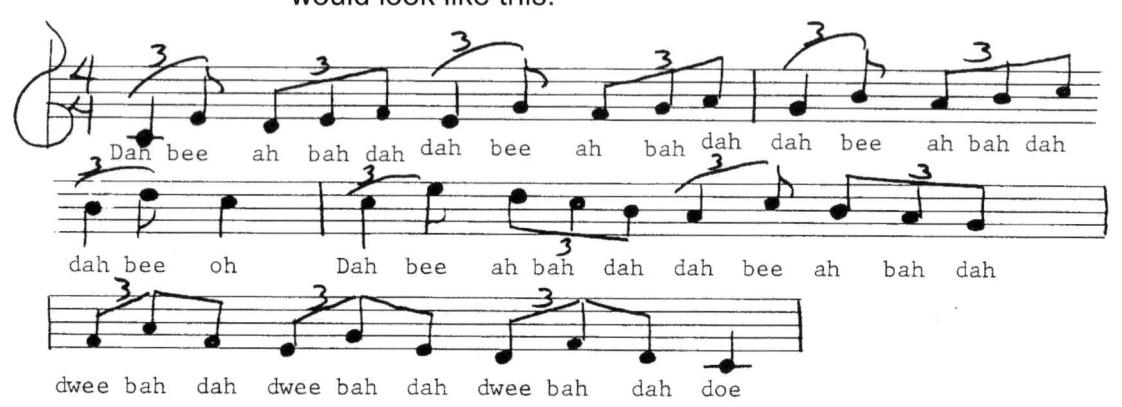

[musical notation with lyrics:]
Dah bee ah bah dah dah bee ah bah dah dah bee ah bah dah
dah bee oh Dah bee ah bah dah dah bee ah bah dah
dwee bah dah dwee bah dah dwee bah dah doe

Other Practice Ideas

Take a song or song segment you want to scat to. Determine what scales or modes are involved. Even if you can't name the scale or mode, perhaps you can just hear it, which is fine. Now go up and down the particular scale pattern you are hearing. Then put your accompaniment tape on, and apply some of what you've practiced to the actual song.

-For instance. You're singing Jobim's *Corcovado* in C. At the end of the song, you decide to repeat the lyric "Oh my love" over and over, improvising over the alternating tag chords of C and B-flat. You determine that this tag alternates between C Ionian and B-flat Lydian (or you don't determine that at all, you just hear something and you can relate to what you hear).

-You know the C Ionian mode, it's the basic C major scale. The B-flat Lydian is a plain old B-flat major scale, with the fourth note raised by half a step. Now turn off the tape recorder and practice singing up and down the two scales: C major and B-flat Lydian.

-Now take the same scales, sing up them and then down them, but vary your rhythm. Spice it up a little.

-OK, take the same scales, vary your rhythm, and instead of just going up and then down the scales, try going up for, say, 5 notes and then down for 4 notes, up for another 5 notes, down for 4. For instance:

C Ionian

Nah - - - - -

B-flat Lydian

Nah - - - - -

-The next step is to think up your own little melodies that might sound good on this tag. For instance:

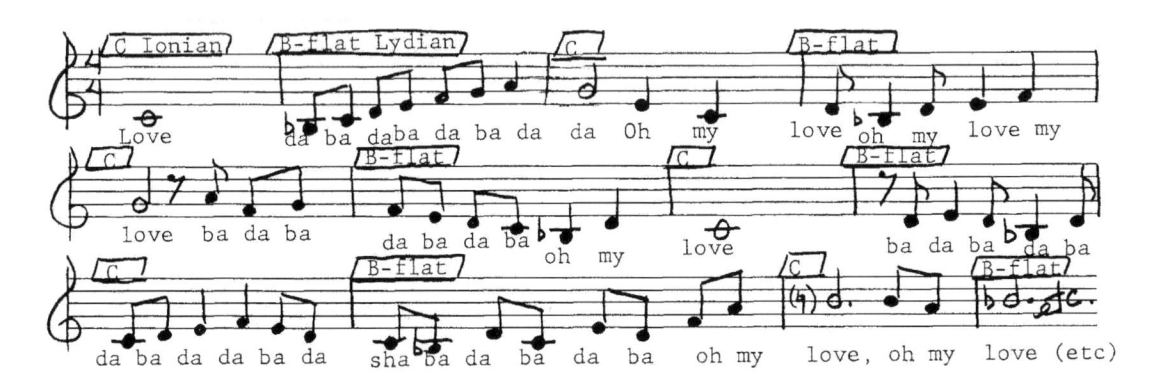

[C Ionian] [B-flat Lydian] [C] [B-flat]
Love da ba daba da ba da da Oh my love oh my love my

[C] [B-flat] [C] [B-flat]
love ba da ba da ba da ba oh my love ba da ba da ba

[C] [B-flat] [C] [B-flat]
da ba da da ba da sha ba da ba da ba oh my love, oh my love (etc)

-You see what we're doing? You know the scales, you just figure out different ways of expressing them.

-Once you know your parameters (the notes of the scale you're in), the scat possibilities are limitless.

Other Resources:

Vocal Improv in the Be Bop Idiom by Bob Stoloff
Vocal Improvisation - An Instrumental Approach by Patty Coker and David Baker (comes with cassette)
The Singer's Jam Session by Patty Coker (comes with cassettes)
Anyone Can Improvise (video) by Jamey Aebersold (perfect for beginners)

Stay With the Spirit

When you scat, just as when you solo on any instrument, you want to keep the spirit of the main motif in mind. The freedom to improvise does not give you the freedom to go haywire in all directions. Each song has a mood - you as a soloist are given the freedom to interpret that mood through your unique instrument, through your own filter of experience and musical skill.

How to stay true to the mood:
- Some soloists keep the title of the piece in mind. If you're soloing over "Betrayal of My Soul" by trumpeter Terence Blanchard, you've got to remember that that's what this song is about. Within that memory you can express it your own way when you solo, but you can't start thinking about the Joffrey Ballet. You've got to keep thinking about how you feel about soul betrayals.

- Remember that your solos are artistic, emotional, and spiritual reflections of what you want to say. They are not forums to show off your technical expertise. Legal offenders are those who forget about the spirit of the piece and instead speed through scales to show off. This kind of playing drives listeners nuts and gives jazz a bad name, yet there is a lot of it out there. The soloist gets off on his own pyrotechnics, and everyone else is feeling cheated. I call that autoeroto-soloing.

- You can stray as far from the piece as you want to rhythmically and melodically, you _can_ shoot up and down scales, you should have pyrotechnical abilities, you can thrill people in any way you want - as long as you stay within the emotional or spiritual context of the original motif.

Notes:

Singer's Formant

If you've been to the opera, you've heard it. It's that particular vibrant ringing quality that certain singers are able to incorporate into their sound. It's that bell-like part of the vocal timbre that allows the voice to carry. When you sing it or hear it, you know it.

> Perhaps you've wondered how it is that a soloist on a huge stage in an enormous concert hall with no microphone can be heard over an entire orchestra. This is the singer's formant - that concentrated band of frequencies within the overall tone of the voice that creates a unique ring; a particular "aliveness."
>
> Formant can be heard in all styles - blues, musical theatre, big band jazz. It's not the property of opera, although opera may be the best place to experience it. Called "squillo" by Italian singers, it's a vocal quality, not a genre of music.
>
> The term is not yet in most dictionaries or music books. The Swedish scientist Johan Sundberg, author of **The Science of the Singing Voice** and contributor to major publications, including *Scientific American*, has studied this quality extensively. According to research, the frequency for the singer's formant is in the 2 KHz to 4KHz range (2000 Hz to 4000 Hz), with male voices at the lower end of this frequency band and the women's voices at the higher end. This is fairly piercing. But because this piercing quality is only a part of the overall resonance, it does not, in the hands of a skilled singer, make for a shrill voice.
>
> Every sound has its fundamental frequency and then its harmonic overtones. The singer's formant is a certain part of the harmonic overtone of the voice that is emphasized more than other overtones.

Do I need this in my life?

Although producing this sound directly into your microphone in an intimate little nightclub might empty the place out rather quickly, if you sing Broadway, classical, opera, or jazz, or if you do large concerts, singer's formant is a fabulous tool to have. And it feels great to be able to produce it. Developing this quality is one of many ways of using the full potential of your vocal instrument.

And I must tell you, singing it feels good. Have you ever vocalized when you felt really rested, your voice was open and strong, you were miraculously free of allergies, your acoustics were unobstructed, and your entire range floated out easily - and you just heard this certain ringing quality as you sung out on your higher notes? If so, then you have it.

A more resonant voice
Another reason to develop singer's formant is that it can make your voice more resonant. With formant, your sound is brighter and therefore capable of louder sounds - without belting or actually shrieking. The voice can be treated gently. This applies to the lower registers as well as to the higher.

How to make your soft volumes "carry"
Singer's formant is not a volume, and is not a function of "loud and soft." You can use formant in either loud or soft singing. In fact, it's fabulous in your pianissimo tones because you can sing those soft volumes and still have the sound carry. It carries on the formant. Let's go back to the opera. Have you ever marveled at how the singers' voices can be heard all the way to the back of the theatre, still unmiked, even when they're singing soft passages? It's the formant that delivers that sound.

How to get it
Singer's formant, like vibrato, is not something you can specifically learn. It's something you discover. The best way to discover it for your own voice is to listen to other singers who have it. When you do hit on it yourself, take note of what it feels like, what the physical sensations are, what it sounds like in your head. Then reproduce those sensations. Eventually you will work with it enough to get it under your control.

To get a taste for what it feels like, go back to Warm-up I and practice the "Ghost" and the "Siren" exercises. Try to create a consistent hollow, or ringing overtone.

Singer's formant is a component of a beautifully developed voice. Work on your breathing and vowel sounds, work for purity of tone, and you will discover it. Teachers who specialize in the bel canto style of singing, and of course in opera, are equipped to help you with this.

How to make your piano strings hum

Have you ever vocalized, and then stopped singing only to hear the piano strings humming? Try it with a piano or a guitar. Sing up and down scales in your higher register. Use your supported breath and your pure, consistently placed vowel sounds. See if you can get that certain "ring" into your voice that will cause those strings to hum. You see? It's not that hard.

Notes:

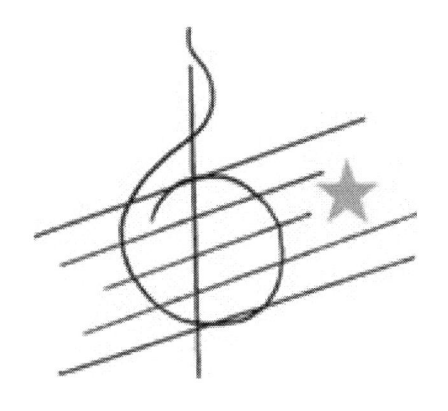

Song Singing:

Repertoire, Upkeep, and Automatic Pilot

1. Choosing a song

♪There's a lot. of music. out there. The best way to sift through it all is to know yourself, know your musical soul, and let the right songs come to you. You may hear something on the radio and just know that you must obtain the sheet music for it. You may go to the opera and realize that a particular aria, one that you had overlooked before, must become part of your repertoire.

♪Then there's style. If you know your musical soul, you can take almost anything and make it your own. As the song flows through you, things happen to it dynamically, rhythmically, emotionally, and the song is changed. It becomes your song.

♪Still, the choices must be narrowed down. Ironically, one way to sift through what's out there is to be open to everything, and alert to where your intuition tells you to go.

♪In choosing a song, remember that other genres can inspire things within your own chosen niche. There's a lot of cross-pollination in music. Some of the jazz repertoire comes from Broadway. Folk songs are routinely covered as pop songs. Oldies are a staple of the wedding repertoire. Opera singers sometimes include contemporary songs in their commercial concerts. Classical music has been funked up. Aaron Copeland turned western music into brilliant symphonies. There's nothing you can't use, and no reason to become inbred.

♪Most singers enter this earth plane already knowing with a passion what kind of music they must have in their lives. I imagine singers emerging directly from the womb saying things like "East coast jazz, mama, not west coast." But to keep your repertoire alive, you've got to try all kinds of music, all styles of songs. You can only be enriched by singing Italian arias - even if you're a blues singer. It's excellent ear training to sing jazz - even if rock is your genre. Cross over. Listen to music of other cultures. Part of the process of making your musical voice exciting and unique is experimenting.

2. Choosing a song that keeps you alive

☼ The very worst thing a singer can be, worse even than an "R" sound offender, is boring and predictable. Lots of singers are technically and artistically brilliant - but their licks are always the same, their particular song ending vamps are used over and over, their phrasing never changes. It's one thing to have a recognizable style, timbre, or signature sound - it's another thing to do it so much your listeners just start tuning out. Exposing yourself to other corners of the world will keep your ideas fresh - even if your niche is small. You've got to know who's hot in Finland, just to keep your antennae functional. You may not travel a lot, but your ears and mind can. Being worldly will help you stay dynamic.

☼ The other aspect of choosing a song is to make sure it's one that moves you. A song that "clicks" for you emotionally and technically can really make a difference in the kind of spirit you put into it - and then how it's received by your audience. You may be doing restaurant gigs, but that doesn't mean you have to use the same old restaurant repertoire everyone else uses. Okay, so you have the chart for Feelings just in case it's requested, but if everyone's eating and chatting, you may as well opt for your pop version of the Sesame Street theme. Even if someone does want to hear Melancholy Baby, you can do it with your own passion, your own aliveness, an unusual time signature, perhaps, or a twist in phrasing.

☼ If you find yourself falling asleep on the bandstand, it's time to make a new plan. Search out songs that are vehicles for the best aspects of your voice. Make the effort to find that out-of-print album that had a song on it that just blew you away. Take the time to seek out lyrics to songs that mean something special to you.

-One singer I know was driving in her car with the radio on, and Ruby, My Dear by Thelonious Monk was being played. This particular version had lyrics. The singer, who loves Monk, pulled her car over to the side of the road, grabbed a lipliner pencil and gum wrapper, and wrote down the lyrics. Ruby, My Dear is now in her repertoire and she sounds fantastic.

-I was at a concert recently and one of the singers was very good. His voice was pleasant and his material was fine. Then for his last number he did a blues - it was an original - and suddenly the place caught fire. You could almost see the smoke coming through the microphone. People were yelling and screaming, they were so thrilled. He had suddenly gone from good to spine tingling. And the only difference was the shift in choice of songs to something that came from the level of his bone marrow.

3. Organizing a repertoire

♪ Many singers keep looseleaf notebooks - each notebook containing sheet music, lead sheets, and/or charts for a different genre of song.

- For example: One singer I know has a notebook full of original songs, including separate sheets for bass, piano, drums and vocal harmony. It's all alphabetical. She has a second notebook filled with material that would be suitable for weddings and general parties. This one is alphabetical, but she re-organizes it just before each gig and puts it in the order in which she will be singing. Then she has a third notebook containing material suitable for restaurant gigs. This notebook has charts for her pianist, and lyric "cheat sheets" for herself, and she keeps it in the order in which she usually sings the songs at the restaurant.

♪ If you sing in restaurants, clubs, at parties, and at weddings, you must make up a "set list" - a list of songs you will sing in the order that they will be sung. Give a copy of this set list to each musician.

♪ Some singers have so much material that they must keep it shelved at home or office, and then fill up notebooks as the appropriate engagement presents itself.

♪ Keeping your music organized and ready to use is a big deal - non-singers don't realize just how left-brained us singers really are. I won't tell if you don't.

♪ In using your sheet music or charts when rehearsing or practicing, always use pencil to make notes on the music. In your music, you'll be notating format changes, chord substitutions, notes to yourself, breath marks, key changes, etc. As you keep singing over the years, you'll be surprised how many times you will decide to change the format or the key of a song.

♪ If it's your band, it's your responsibility to have charts for the accompanists. ("Charts" - see glossary.)

♪ If you don't write charts, you can use standard sheet music purchased from a music store - if it's in your key. If the store-bought sheet music is not in your key, you'll have to do a chart - because you'll have to transpose the song to your key. (A local musician or voice teacher can do charts for you for a fee, if need be.)

♪ You're safer at an audition, for example, having your own chart to hand to the pianist, rather than trusting that a pianist you don't know will have your song in your key with your format. (The exception might be an audition with a classical piece in an accepted version from a major publisher - the pianist probably has the same version. Or if you sing standard jazz classics in the original keys, most of the musicians will already know the songs by heart.)

4. Practicing Your Songs
a) Find your key

- ✓ To find your key, sing the song in the original key, and when you hit a section that's too high, you know you've got to lower the key. Or, if you're singing in the original key and hit a section that's too low, you've got to raise the key. Usually you should raise or lower the key by half steps, trying the song again each time. If the original key is grossly wrong for you, start by putting it up or down perhaps a fourth - and then move it by half-steps to make the final adjustments.

- ✓ To really test your "key" acumen, I challenge you to find out what key you choose to sing Antonio Carlos Jobim's *Wave*. If you can find your key for that song, you can skip the rest of this section. (*Wave* has almost a two octave range with both high and low tessitura.)

- ✓ NOTE: The key of a song is not the same as the song's range, or its tessitura. The key refers to how the song is harmonically based. The range refers to how broad a series of notes the song encompasses; how high and low it goes. The tessitura is how concentrated the very high or very low sections are - a song with a high tessitura, for example, is a song that's constantly hitting your high notes.

  - ✓ You can have a song in the key of A with a range of four notes. You can have a song in the key of A with a range of four notes that are too high for you. A song in the key of A can have a range of four notes that are too low for you. You can have a song in the key of A with a two octave range, but a midrange tessitura. The point is, you can't just go by what key a song is in. (On a more comforting note, many pop and jazz singers have keys that they do prefer, regardless of range, and much of their repertoire is in those keys. That's because in popular music, when a song is in a certain key, it often hovers closely to the root, or the key note.)

✓ A song is in a good key for you if:
    *it feels right
    *you don't have to strain
    *you don't get tense
    *your tone is gorgeous
    *you can easily add dynamics.
    *But don't get too comfortable. If the song is drab or tonally flat, you might try raising the key by half a step to add some life to it.

b) Learn the song. Learn the exact melody the way the composer wrote it, and learn the original rhythmic components. This way you won't inadvertently fall into some other singer's phrasing or interpretation. Later, when you add your own dynamics, you can make your own choices about style and interpretation, knowing that you won't be overtly derivative. (Of course if you're in a choir, singing backup vocals, or doing studio work, you're interpretive choices are limited.)

-Then get a rehearsal tape - check out the chapter on rehearsal tapes for sources.

c) Next, make preliminary decisions about your own dynamics and where you will breathe.

- Many singers write breath marks onto the sheet music when they are learning a song. These are pencil notations reminding you where to breathe. A breath mark looks like a large apostrophe.

- In addition to breathing where it is comfortable physically, you also want to breathe where it makes sense lyrically. For instance, you don't want to breathe in the middle of a phrase or thought, and would never think of taking a breath in the middle of a word, even if the word is held for two measures.

- It's usually safe to breathe where you see a comma or a period in the lyrics. You'll also want to breathe before a large interval jump or before a difficult passage - but again, only where it is lyrically aesthetic.

- Refer to the chapter on Dynamics, both the "Loud and Soft" segment and the "Energy and Emotion" segment. Add refined dynamics to the song at this point. And don't angst out about this - you can always change your dynamics, either during practice sessions or right there up on the bandstand if you get struck by some sort of inspiration.

♒ Take the time to decide how the song builds, where it builds, how you will get emotionally and technically to that point, and how you will resolve the song.

d) Memorize the song.

See the chapter on memorizing.

e) Now it's time to de-bug the piece. Take apart the phrases or passages that are giving you trouble. Work with them. Make up specific exercises to smooth out the rough spots.

♮ Example: Suppose you've got a good key for your song, but the ending is high - not so high as to want to lower the key, but high enough to produce fear. So - make up exercises to combat any thin or nasal sounds that frighten you. Go back to the chapter on resonance. Take the melody line from the song and do it on "ah" as an exercise. Do it over your whole range. Try other exercises to get your tone and placement right. Then go back to the song and apply that same refined tone to the song.

♮ Or suppose there is a section where you simply can't get enough breath, and there is no logical place to breathe to correct the problem. Again, take the segment apart. Do breathing exercises and try the segment again. Or perhaps you can put in a rest where there was not one written in, and use that rest to take an extra breath.

♮ Maybe there is a section where you just aren't getting the rhythm correctly. Take it apart and make up exercises. You could do the song very slowly, on one vowel sound, tapping out the rhythm gently with your hand. Or you might practice with a metronome. Then put the song back together again, and see if you can get that rhythm right.

♮ There is no part of your song that is unimportant. The tiniest trouble spot must be rehearsed and corrected.

♮ When you make up exercises to go with or correct the difficult passages in the song, do these exercises in all keys, not just the key your song is in. This is a confidence booster.

f) A fun thing to do with songs is to go through the entire piece on just the vowel sounds. Take out all the consonants. This makes you aware of how resonant and round you really can make your sound. Remember, the voice can only make music on vowel sounds, so by perfecting the vowel sounds in the song, you are rounding out the overall tone of your voice. (A detailed description of this exercise is in the chapter on vowel sounds.) When you're happy with your tone, then put the consonants back in - remembering and reproducing the beauty you had when it was just vowel sounds.

g) Now you can start practicing the song with a microphone if you'll be using one. But don't discontinue practicing acoustically.

h) The next step is to practice the song over and over again, so you can sing it backwards if you were in a coma. Know every nook and cranny of the piece, including breathing and dynamics. Over-learn it. There should be not one nuance, one breath spot, not one 16th note rest, not one small crescendo that is not a part of you. You'll be amazed at how your confidence will soar and you'll be able to let go and fly with a song if you know it this well.

5. And on to automatic pilot

✱ Now the magic starts. Because now the technical aspects of the song will come to you automatically. You've got the piece memorized, you've got your dynamics in, your breathing comes at just the right points, your tone is smooth, your vibrato is just the way you want it. Now you can let go and really feel what the song means to you. You can make the song yours. At this point, no one can sing it like you do. No one else can bring the perspective to the song that you can. You are one with it. It flows through you. Even if it's *Melancholy Baby*, you have brought the song to life.

Notes:

Speaking

Elements of A Good Speaking Voice

Who doesn't adore a luscious speaking voice? A voice that's full of depth and rich with overtones is a priceless asset. And the best way to acquire this asset is to learn how to sing. You don't have to sing at the Met - but if you go through the moves, learn about pitch, resonance, tone, vowel sounds, and rhythm, you're going to be a great speaker.

In general, these are the elements you want to transfer from your singing experience over to your speaking.

1. Fluidity

- ♯ Your speaking voice needs to flow smoothly and easily.

- ♯ Go for a minimal number of "um"s, tics, quirks, and repetitions. Most of this is habit, which can be broken by taping your speeches and being aware of these qualities.

- ♯ Another way to get fluid is to slow down. Most people talk too fast, and as a result end up with a voice that's saying words faster than the words can come through the mind. Thus we hear a lot of "um"s, as the mind tries to catch up.

- ♯ The chapter on "Legato Singing" is an excellent workout for speakers who want to get smooth.

- ♯ A fluid voice is also a result of confidence. Check out the chapter on stage fright.

2. Correct Pitch

- ♯ If you are speaking in a range that is either too high or too low, you will not only strain your voice, but you can make listeners uncomfortable.

♯ Your pitch is correct if your voice sounds round and resonant; bright but not shrill; rich but not boomy.

♯ Your pitch can be wrong if you are experiencing sore throats or hoarseness. (Sore throats should also be checked out with your health practitioner.)

♯ If your pitch is too high or too low, a voice teacher or speech pathologist can help you correct it.

3. Tone

♯ You want a basic tone that is full and vibrant.

♯ Here especially, singing practice is invaluable. Check out the chapters on vowel sounds, the articulators, and resonance. A knowledgeable singing voice can easily be translated into a fully tonal speaking voice.

4. Placement

♯ Again, go for the song singing. You'll learn more about placement from music than from anywhere else.

♯ Work through the chapters on expanding your range, and on registers.

5. Rate of Speech

♯ Tape yourself speaking. If you were listening to yourself, would you ask yourself to slow down? Most problems occur when people speak too fast, causing slurring of words and blurring of ideas.

♯ You want a basic voice that is smooth and slow. You can get this by just being aware of it.

6. Volume

♯ You want to avoid both mumbling and shouting. Being aware of your volume is usually all it takes to adjust it.

♯ Check out the chapter on "Dynamics: Loud and Soft." The exercises are useful for speakers as well as singers.

7. Relaxation
- It's amazing how many vocal problems will just "go away" once you get your instrument relaxed and in shape. Stress shows not only in forehead worry lines, but also in a person's vocal timbre and rate of speech.

8. Breath Support
- If you speak in front of large groups - say you're a professor or corporate trainer - you need to go through the chapter on breathing, and learn how to breathe like a singer.

- A working knowledge of breathing to sing is useful, even if you use a microphone or address small groups.

9. Sincerity
- You've got to believe what you're saying - unless you're a brilliant actor, we'll know if you don't. No place to hide, babe. It comes right through.

- You may have given this speech or lecture a thousand times, but we've got to think it's your first time.

- Some voiceover actors I know will refuse jobs if the commercial is selling a product that the actor personally finds offensive. One actress I know refused a job advertising a so-called "gentlemen's" club. Another will not do voiceovers for fur or meat.

10. Inflections and "Musical" Patterns
- Here's another reason for the speaker to learn how to sing. If you've got control of your range, if you can go up and down scales with fluidity and a uniform tone, your speaking voice can be...mellifluous.

- Speak into a tape recorder, and listen for repetitive inflections - or, not enough inflection. Make sure your musical patterns are varied slightly. Speakers who continually pound out the same patterns and inflections lose their listeners.

11. Regional Accents are fine, as long as
- they don't distract from your message;

♯ they don't mutilate individual words to the point of incomprehension.

♯ Unless you're a voiceover actor - or perhaps a stage or screen actor - the old rule that you have to have "no accent" no longer applies. If you've got an accent you don't want, acting classes are your best route.

12. Variety
♯ Just don't bore people to death. You can keep from doing this by adding variety to volume, inflections, rate of speech, pauses, and tone.

Notes:

Stage Fright and Bubonic Plague: A Comparative Study

You're chanting "om" and your kneecaps are still jiggling. You've done your pre-performance visualization exercises and still your eyeballs are popping in and out like hot mud bubbles at Yellowstone Park. What's going on? As you stagger to the stage, gasping asthmatically for air, wondering about life after death, and hoping you're merely drooling and not bleeding from your ears, know one thing: you're not alone.

In fact, this condition is normal. Almost everyone gets it.

Symptoms of stage fright are similar to those of the black death: knocking knees, shaking hands, constricted throat, difficulty swallowing, stomach distress, cardiac arrhythmia, sweating, chills, leg cramps, vomiting, partial amnesia, shallow breathing, facial tics, dizziness, hives, and/or temporary paralysis of an essential body part - i.e. if a pianist, then the fingers freeze up; if a singer, then the throat closes completely, etc. (With luck, you're a singer and you simply have minor edema.)

The most common things heard backstage before performances are:
"How did I get myself into this?"

"I promise, God, if You get me through this I'll never (insert vice here) again."

"After this, I'm going to a rest home and I'm not coming out."

"Why wasn't I content selling firewood?"

"I must be out of my mind."

"I can always relocate and change my identity."

Yes, it is contagious. If the rest of your band has it, you can catch it - it travels through eye contact and etheric aura. But there are cures. And if the cures don't work, there's still no cause for major alarm: It eventually goes away by itself.

1. The best way to get rid of stage fright is to perform and audition a lot.

♪ Join a performance workshop or audition class.

♪ Sing at parties. Really.

♪ Force your friends to listen to you, even if you must resort to blackmail.

♪ Go on as many auditions as you can, even if it's for things you'd never actually do in a million years - auditioning itself is priceless experience.

♪ Organize your own workshops with other singers or speakers.

♪ Join Toastmasters.

♪ Offer to lecture at networking functions.

♪ Sing at "open mikes."

♪ Read your poetry at coffee houses, even though you're ten generations older than anyone else.

♪ Audition live for agents, in addition to giving them your demo tape.

♪ Do all of the above, but do it for pay (if they pay). The added stress of actually having to be good is a helpful perk.

♪ Volunteer to sing once a week at a hospital, nursing home, or rehab center.

♪ Volunteer to read to children once a week at the public library.

♪ Volunteer at your local radio reading service, or at Recording for the Blind.

2. Be completely prepared with your song(s) or speech.
In fact, be over prepared. Know your material backwards. Know it in your sleep. Practice it so much your dog knows it and your spouse has had permanent earplug implants. If you've practiced a song ten times a day for two weeks straight and you're so sick of it you want to hurl yourself off a tall building, then practice it ten times a day for another two weeks. (If you're a classical singer, you are familiar with the routine of practicing a piece for perhaps a year before performing it!)

3. Vocalize daily.
Keep your instrument tuned up and dependable, and watch your confidence soar. Half an hour a day of vocalizing will truly help. This is <u>in addition to</u> your song or speech practicing mentioned above.

4. Figure out what's really behind the stage fright.
- ♪ It could be the usual need to be revered and lauded. Or loved and applauded. Or just liked.

- ♪ Or it could be the need to be able to go up on stage without dragging an oxygen tank behind you. Or perhaps your thumb is tired from constantly hovering in anticipation over the "send" button of your cell phone on which 911 has been permanently keyed in.

- ♪ The other thought that feeds stage fright is the idea that somehow your whole life depends on this one gig; that you will never get another chance at this; that nothing else in the world matters. This is called "catastrophic thinking." It is not realistic. If you find yourself thinking the following things, you are indulging in catastrophic thinking. Catch yourself. Don't think like that:

    - 💣 This is my one big chance;

    - 💣 Everything I've ever worked for in my entire life will become utter unrecognizable rubble if I forget my lyrics;

    - 💣 The Mr. H. from Hotshot Talent Agency is out in the audience. If I am not as good as Joan Sutherland He will never come back again and I will be blacklisted forever;

    - 💣 The Ms. Hotshot from the newspaper is out there. Her review will determine my worthiness as a human being taking up space and valuable foodstuffs from the planet;

    - 💣 If I bomb, it's back to selling lizards at the pet store. Actually, they are kind of cute;

    - 💣 How do you walk, anyway?

5. Thoughts you *can* think:
- My goal is to share my music with the audience; to brighten their day. (As opposed to: My goal is to be rich and famous.)

- My goal is to get the information in this business presentation across to my clients. (As opposed to: My goal is to make everyone love me.)

- It's OK to make mistakes. Walter Cronkite makes mistakes. Mistakes are human. (As opposed to: One slip up, and I'll kill myself.)

- I'll do the best I can, and whatever happens I can learn from the experience. (As opposed to: I'll settle for simply not making a complete fool out of myself.)

- I enjoy singing - or - I enjoy public speaking. (As opposed to: Tomorrow I'm going for career counseling.)

6. Clothing
For a performance or audition, don't wear anything new. Wear something you know well and are physically and mentally comfortable in.

JUST BEFORE GOING ON STAGE, TRY:
- a slight yawn (this opens up the back of the throat)

- loosening up the body with a few shoulder rolls, or shaking out your legs and arms

- a deep breath

- a smile (It's amazing how a smile can relax your whole body.)

ON STAGE:
- Remember to breathe. And keep breathing through the entire performance.

- Let your fears come out. To heck with them. If your knees are knocking, let them knock. Go with it. If your voice sounds tense, just keep on singing and breathing. Once onstage, knocks and death rattles usually go away within a few minutes. Relax into it. Smile if it's appropriate.

Remember, you're doing this because for some reason at some point in time, you wanted to. This is not lethal injection. This is fun.

☺ Fighting tension will make it worse. Just ignore it.

☺ If you're auditioning, imagine that the producer has a hyena on his head.

☺ If you're auditioning, you usually don't want to make eye contact during your song. Do you really want to try to decipher what the producer's grimace `means`? There's no way you can ever know if the producer has heartburn or simply dislikes your shoes. Or perhaps she's one of those people whose mouth turns downward when they smile. Why get into it?

REGULAR DISCIPLINES TO CONSIDER:

 ⚱ Daily vocalizing, as mentioned possibly five hundred times in this book. - Daily exercise (Check with your health practitioner.). Remember, your entire body is your instrument. The better shape it's in, the better sounding your instrument can be.

 ⚱ Regular relaxation techniques. Each person will respond differently to different techniques. For myself, when someone starts, say, a guided imagery routine by telling me I'm walking peacefully along a beautiful warm beach at sunrise, I get nervous. (Many singers report sunrise to be a somewhat startling experience.) You have to find what works for you. This can run the gamut from meditation and prayer to massage, sweat lodges, visualization, breath work, dance, sports, affirmations, yoga, and yes, guided imagery. (If they say, "You are in the middle of Times Square at 2 a.m...." I actually do start to feel relaxed. What can I tell you?)

 ⚱ Doing volunteer service work on a regular basis can get you out of yourself and into thinking about other people. Sometimes we just focus on ourselves too much. Helping others with their problems can help us remember that stage fright is a very small thing compared to the larger epidemics that are out there.

Notes:

Toning: It Just Feels Good

Sound can be soothing. And as such, it can be healing. The voice is an instrument with capabilities that can calm the mind. This is the essence behind the concept of toning.

Toning is using the voice in such a way as to heal whatever it is you need to heal. Music therapy is a valid, scientifically based, much-used aspect of this concept. People have historically turned to music for comfort, peace, well-being, and spiritual connection. We turn to music, too, for inspiration, for beauty, to praise God, as prayer, and for self-expression.

There are as many specific ways to tone as there are unique individuals with unique needs. One singer says when she sings scales in a legato style, it makes her feel calm and relaxed. Some studies have concluded that listening to Mozart has a direct effect on mental acuity. I find that when I'm stressed all I have to do is put on a classic Miles Davis ballad, and the stress melts away. Another singer I know finds that chanting - repeating a soothing musical phrase over and over - helps him let go of the cares of the day. Putting on a tape of beautiful operatic arias sung by the great sopranos is how another friend transforms her moods.

Toning as a part of living

Imagine filling your home with harp and flute duets, instead of the constant heavy handed, violent drone of the television set. Imagine what it might do for the overall health and well-being of the people in a home that was alive with the lush sounds of string quartets and violin concertos, or the richness of the great symphonies.

Sound is vibration. It resonates off people and things around it. It bounces around. It affects.

You *can* try this at home

Toning is being able to create your own music, your own sounds, that help you achieve your needs and balances. It can be as simple as finding one note that sets up a certain pleasant resonance with you, and then singing that note.

To try it, find a single pitch that is comfortable for your voice and pleasant to your ear. Choose a vowel sound that pleases you, and sing it on your chosen note, holding this for the length of one breath. Then take another breath, and repeat the process. Don't worry about vocal technique. You simply want to listen to your own voice and let it calm you. Do this for a few minutes, and see how you feel afterwards.

The word "tone" refers to the color, the quality, the character, the texture of a sound. As you work with your voice and experiment with different sounds and ways of producing those sounds, you can find the tones that you want to incorporate into your voice. This applies to speaking as well as singing.

The "new age" that began 1300 years ago

From a western perspective, the use of voice for therapeutic purposes has been used as far back as ancient times, but was noticeably prevalent with the blossoming of plainsong, beginning in the eighth century. Plainsong, or plainchant, is a kind of unison, a-rhythmic, unaccompanied chanting that was used by the churches. Gregorian chant is its famous derivative, and today albums of chanting and sacred a capella music are best sellers. (Modal singing, which is covered in another chapter and with a completely different slant, began with plainsong as well, and the harmonic patterns that developed were called "church modes.")

It just feels good...

One singer said she loves to sing because she simply loves the sound of her own voice. She didn't mean this in an egotistical way - she loves the way her voice makes her feel. She says it balances and pleases her on every level: physical, emotional, mental, artistic, and spiritual.

Resources

If toning interests you, here are some books to check out:

Sacred Sounds by Ted Andrews
The Infinite Variety of Music by Leonard Bernstein
Copland on Music by Aaron Copland
Sounding the Inner Landscape: Music as Medicine by Kay Gardner

Healing Sounds by Jonathan Goldman
Toning: the Creative Power of the Voice by Laurel Elizabeth Keyes

Notes:

Vibrato:

If You're Calm, You Will Oscillate

What is vibrato?
Vibrato is a smooth and even oscillation in sound. Although it pulsates around the central pitch of each note, it is never so pronounced as to alter the pitch.

Vibrato must be a natural product of singing correctly (singing correctly would include proper breathing, a relaxed body, an open throat, good posture, rich resonance with correctly articulated vowels). It shouldn't be forced. An easy, natural vibrato adds to the depth and tone of the voice.

Each person's vibrato will be different. When you vocalize, you want to find your own personal vibrato - you don't want to copy someone else's. Your own vibrato adds to the uniqueness and beauty of your individual voice.

A vibrato has a pulse, or beat. If done correctly, this pulse will be even and fluid - that is, the pulse will remain constant even while you're changing tempos, changing dynamics, or making interval jumps. This pulse will remain the same even while you're changing registers, even while you're singing on your break notes.

The rule, then, is that the pulse of the vibrato must be constant, no matter what you're doing with your song. Since that's the rule, let's also break it: You can change the sound of your vibrato for certain effects. These effects might include pop singing, where you might choose to use little to no vibrato until you get to the ends of phrases. It might include rock singing where you choose not to use vibrato at all. It might include choral singing where you might choose, depending on the instructions given by your choral director, to use a lighter vibrato than you'd use when singing solo.

Treacherous vibrato pitfalls
1. The tremble trap
Vibrato is not the same as tremolo. Tremolo, in the context of singing, means the voice just shakes. Shaking is not musical. If your voice trembles, there may be an underlying problem. Perhaps it's fatigue. If the trembling is persistent and accompanied by hoarseness, you may want to check with your health practitioner. The term "tremolo" is also

used by some to describe a vibrato that is simply too fast.

2. The wobble trap
Wobbling is when the vibrato is too slow. Wobbling is off-key. It sounds funny. People use it for comic effects to imitate bad singing. Some people call it an "old lady voice," although people of all ages, if not trained properly, can fall into this wobble-trap.

How do I develop a natural, beautiful vibrato?

- The main thing is to let it happen. You can't <u>make</u> it happen.

- Practice singing one vowel on one note and holding it for eight beats, with a slight crescendo over the phrase.

    - When you do this, make sure you're breathing correctly. For a vowel sound, start with "nah" because of its open feeling.

    - Relax your body. Concentrate on beauty, richness of tone, depth of timbre.

- The vibrato will happen. It's one of those strange things that happens when you don't try too hard, and doesn't happen - or sounds awful - if you get too focused about it.

- There should be no movement in the jaw or throat in an attempt to get a vibrato going. You can't shake anything to make it happen. In fact, it's the opposite - if you're calm, you will oscillate.

Exercise 1:
Sing the following, and just let the sound flow out naturally. Don't try to use vibrato, just concentrate on your breathing and tone. Once the vibrato starts, let it float out on the resonance of your voice.

How do I get control over my vibrato - for different needs or effects?

-Sing a lot. Use your vibrato in its natural form. Get used to it. Know your voice.

-Then, practice singing a phrase with different levels of vibrato.

Exercise 2:

Sing the first line of *Somewhere Over the Rainbow*...
1. with your natural, even, constant vibrato
2. with no vibrato
3. with vibrato added onto the last note of the phrase.

-Even in your car or shower, you can practice scales or phrases from songs: Do each scale with vibrato, without vibrato, and with vibrato just on the end of the phrase.

-You will probably find that on quick phrases or fast tempos, you don't use vibrato at all. That's fine, and even preferable, as long as it sounds natural.

Vibrato troubleshooting

If you wobble, your vibrato is too "large," the pitch fluctuates too much and the oscillations are too slow. If you find no one will sit next to you in choir, and you haven't had onions or garlic in days, you might be wobbling. You've heard the expression, "vibrato so large you could drive a truck through it"? This is not a good thing.

♪ To correct a vibrato that is too large, try going back to your basic breathing techniques. Make sure you're breathing is "connected" - that you really can feel the exhale coming directly from the lower abdomen and diaphragm. Concentrate on getting energy into your breathing. Pull your posture up.

♪ Be careful who you listen to. If you're listening to singers who use huge vibrato, you may have a tendency to copy them without even realizing it.

♪ Listen to singers whose vibrato is smooth, even, natural, and in whom the vibrato does not draw attention to itself. You might not be able to copy them, but listen a lot, and let the beauty of their voices become a part of the way you think when you think music.

♪ If you're still having problems, try working on your ear training. (See the chapter on ear training.) Some people who are having pitch problems, mask the pitch problem with a large vibrato. This is done without even realizing that you're doing it.

♪ Are you in good shape physically? Sometimes vibrato problems can stem from not having enough energy. Are you getting enough exercise? Do you put vitality into your body and voice? Pull yourself together, babe.

♪ Are you tense? This could be the culprit. Buy a book on relaxation techniques. Some singers use exercise, prayer, or meditation.

You are trembling if your vibrato is too "tight" - meaning the oscillations are too quick. This is not aesthetically pleasing, and may sound dated and self-conscious. You don't want to draw attention to your vibrato, but rather to the message or lyricism of the song.

♪ Tension is an enormous "tightener." Most trembling vibrato is a result of tension. And this is not just your usual floating anxieties, fears, dreads, and re-livings of traumas. This is simple physical tension - this is when your knees are locked and you don't even know it, or when you unconsciously raise your shoulders. Other things you can stop doing right now, as opposed to after years of therapy, include tensing up the neck, tightening the jaw or tongue, or singing with your hands clasped behind your back.

♪ It's true you can't be entirely relaxed without being dead, but these simple physical things can be corrected just by being aware of them. Work with a mirror if that helps.

♪ Try going back to your basic breathing exercises and see if working through that doesn't make for a more natural sounding vibrato.

♪ Sometimes when a singer "pushes too hard" the vibrato gets trembly as a result. Work on making your breathing more natural, less forced. -Try listening to classical singers, opera, and Broadway. And stop listening to that 60's folk music!

And the controversy begins
It's been referred to on the Internet as "The Vibrato Wars," and it has been said they "get mighty ugly." Just know that if your voice teacher or choir director starts talking about these issues, (1)he or she will be highly emotional, so you might want to walk on eggs, and (2)for every voice teacher and choir director who says one thing, there

will be an equally excellent teacher or choir director who says the opposite. Here are the points of controversy:

- ✓ Many singers and teachers say vibrato cannot be taught - many say it can. -Some say vibrato is an adornment. Some say it is a natural part of the voice, not an adornment.

- ✓ Some say vibrato is used, however unconsciously, to cover up pitch problems. Others say no, that singing or playing an instrument on pitch with no vibrato is practically impossible anyway. (And there is a whole corresponding pitch issue that is equally as emotional.)

- ✓ Some claim that eliminating vibrato from the voice can damage the voice. Some say that's not true.

- ✓ You cannot change the pulse, or tempo, of your vibrato without damaging your voice. Versus - you can change the pulse of your vibrato.

- ✓ It is not exactly known where vibrato comes from within the body, although many people have definite opinions. Most agree that the body should not move - there should be no movement in the jaw or throat. Some point to one or another famous singer whose throat does move and say, "See?" All agree, however, that any movement must be extremely small.

Here's all you have to know:
- ♮ If what you're doing produces strain, pain, or hoarseness of any kind, then it's wrong.

- ♮ If you develop tension anywhere in the body while concentrating on vibrato, then what you're doing is wrong.

- ♮ If your throat is open, your breath is supported, and your body is energized but relaxed, you're on the right track.

- ♮ Tape yourself, so you can hear what's going on.

Exercise 3:
1) Sing the following scale, transposing up half a step with each new repetition. As you sing, think that your voice is fluid and smooth, and allow the vibrato to oscillate evenly, over your pitch changes. Go back to your midrange, and do the scale again, transposing down half a step with each new repetition. Don't forget to support the breath.

2) Do the entire exercise again, at a quicker tempo - still keeping your vibrato pulsing evenly and naturally. Then do the exercise at a slower tempo, with

the same natural vibrato.

3) Your vibrato will ideally pulsate at the same natural tempo, no matter how fast or slow you take the scale. There will be no interruption of the vibrato's oscillation, even as you change pitch.

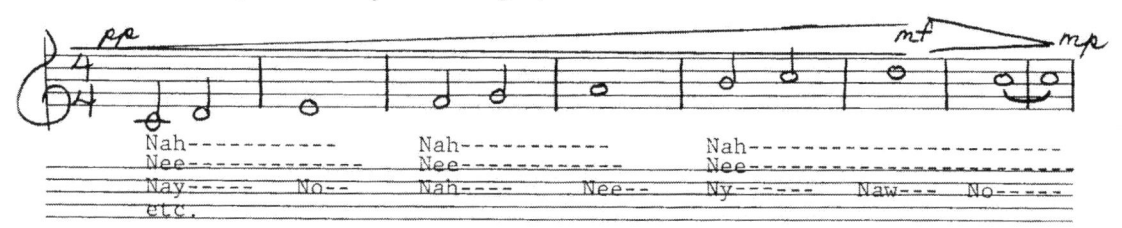

Nah----------- Nah----------- Nah-----------------
Nee----------- Nee----------- Nee-----------------
Nay----- No-- Nah---- Nee-- Ny------ Naw--- No-----
etc.

Notes:

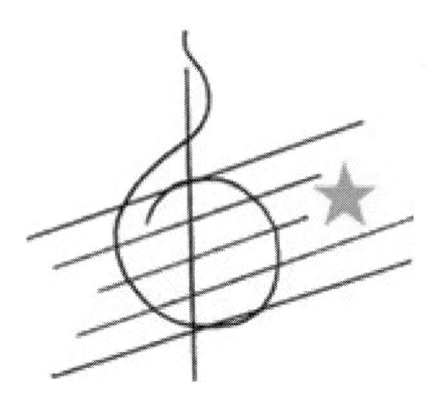

Vocal Cords

Vocal cords (not "chords"!) are like two strong, thick rubber bands. Made of muscle and ligament, they stretch horizontally across the inside wall of the larynx, and are attached in the front and the back. They are about 30mm (1/2 inch) long for men and 20mm long for women. Moveable cartilages in the larynx, which are attached to the cords, aid in their movement. When we phonate (produce sound), we push air over the cords (this is one reason why a trained, controlled breathing mechanism is so important), causing them to vibrate rapidly. As the air moves over these vibrating cords, it is converted into specific sounds. The resulting sound waves resonate in the various parts of the body and are heard as your voice.

In singing higher notes, the cords vibrate at a faster rate. Also, the space between the cords gets smaller. This sets up a kind of "block" to the airflow, causing the higher pitched sound. In singing lower notes, the cords vibrate more slowly and there is more space between them.

The space between the vocal cords is called the "glottis." When we are not phonating, the glottis is opened. This is what allows the breath to pass in and out noiselessly and freely.

We mention vocal cords so that you know what's going on in your instrument. You don't have to "do anything." Just treat your cords with respect. Send them love and gratitude, and don't smoke cigarettes.

(See the chapters on "Care of the Instrument," "Voice and Age," and "Phlegm" for more detailed care information.)

Notes:

Vocalizing: How to Vocalize

What exactly is vocalizing, and how does it differ from rehearsing; from warming-up; from practicing songs?

Vocalizing is a daily process - a workout, so to speak - in which you want to accomplish two main things:

1. Maintain your voice (practice things you know or have learned, keep your tone the way you want it, keep your breathing mechanism in shape, and keep your vocal habits strong and healthy)

2. Keep progressing in your vocal development (learn new things, fine-tune other things)

Aside from these requirements, vocalizing is a personal process. No two people will have the same instrument with which to work; the same goals for that instrument; the same time constraints. You'll want to design a daily routine that is unique to your needs.

Warm-ups
Most singers begin their vocalizing with a warm-up - just as an athlete would begin with a warm-up. The purpose is the same: to avoid injury by beginning slowly; to warm up the muscles; to "remind" your instrument about placement, tone, and fluidity; to loosen and de-stress all your body parts; and to feel the connection between the breathing and the production of sound.

Maintenance and New Learning
After the warm-up, the vocalizing can take any turn you need it to take. You can work on new vocal techniques - for instance, you might be working on trills, a process that requires daily practice. You might be working on pitch precision in large, quick interval jumps. You might be working on the blending of head and chest tones, or on weak spots in your range. Or you might be trying to get your sight

singing up to a higher level, or your ear training. These vocal challenges never end - so don't worry about running out of things to work on.

Songs

At this point, many singers like to proceed to the actual songs they are working on.

These fall in the following categories:
1. songs you have in your repertoire that you want to maintain
2. songs you are in the process of learning or memorizing
3. songs you have learned, but need polishing
4. songs you are toying with

Depending on how large your repertoire is, how much time you have to practice and what your musical demands are, the time you allocate to each of these song upkeep categories will vary.

Vocalizing Ideas

♪ There are lots of ideas in the various **Vocal Vibrance** chapters that you might want to consider including in your daily routine. And there are also three sections of warm-ups to check out.

♪ Ask your singer friends what their favorite exercises are, and share yours with them as well.

♪ Go back over your music textbooks.

♪ Create your own exercises. Whatever you're having trouble with in a song, that's what you want to make an exercise out of. For instance, if you find yourself singing flat, make up some interval jump exercises and work on them over the part of your range that is giving you problems. If you find you can't remember the melody of a certain part of your song, take that phrase from the song and sing it on "nah," beginning on a note in your midrange and repeating it over and over again, going up by half-steps with each repetition. Then go back to your midrange and do the melodic phrase going down into your lower register. For any problem area, you can create an exercise that will solve it.

Keep It Fresh

♫ Because your needs will be changing over time, you'll want to keep your vocalizing regime up to date. As new vocal challenges present themselves, include responses to those challenges in your workout.

♪ Don't get stuck in a rut of doing the same exercises every day forever.

♪ Keep an ear out for new ways to practice; new ideas to incorporate into your vocal habits. Perhaps you vocalize with a friend one day, and learn new exercises from her. Perhaps you get a new book on vocal technique with new, more challenging exercises. Or maybe you take an acting class and decide to incorporate some actors' vocal exercises into your singing practice.

Posture and Relaxation

- ✓ While you're vocalizing, it's important to keep your body balanced and - except for the muscles and mechanisms you use for breathing - relaxed.

- ✓ Stand. (Everyone wants to vocalize in the car. Except for articulator warm-up exercises and facial relaxation techniques, I've got to break the bad news to you - don't do it in the car. You're bent in the middle with a seatbelt over your chest. It won't work, it won't work.)

- ✓ Check in the mirror: is your posture good? Remember the old thing you learned as a kid about feeling as if there is a string pulling you up? This actually works. Pretend the string is connected to a point in the middle of your chest (not your head, as we were told as kids, since having the string in your head can create neck tension), and is gently directing your body upward.

- ✓ Your head should be up - not forward. Your gaze should be straight out in front of you - not down.

- ✓ Arms often seem to be in the way. People don't know what to do with them. Be careful you don't lock your hands behind your back, wring your hands in front of you, make fists at your sides, or lock your elbows at your sides. The arms should be loose and at your sides, with the elbows bent ever so slightly to prevent them from locking. Have you ever seen a ballet dancer walk?

- ✓ Standing with one foot slightly in front of the other will prevent knees from locking.

- ✓ Don't be a toothpaste tube. Make sure your shoulders are relaxed and down. As you vocalize, keep checking your shoulders to make sure they don't creep up! This is the well-known but dreaded toothpaste tube syndrome.

✓ Your mind should be completely focused on the purity of your tone and the beauty of your music.

"Oh sure," you're thinking, "as well as the three million other things such as jaw position, vowel sounds, not locking my elbows, not to mention fluid interval jumps, remembering the lyrics to my song, and toothpaste tube syndrome."

True, but at some point, and with enough practice, all the technical things will become automatic - leaving you with the luxury of being able to put your entire focus on the artistic interpretation and emotionality of the sound.

Rehearsing
Rehearsing is done separately from vocalizing. Your vocalizing time should be private, or with a coach. And remember - you never want to go to rehearsal without having vocalized that day.

Vocalizing: Some Case Histories
Here are a few hypothetical case histories which might give you ideas in planning your own vocalizing regimen.

Solange is a jazz singer who plays in clubs on the weekends. She has had many years of private voice training, and now vocalizes daily by herself. When she feels she needs it, she sees a voice coach. This is her daily routine:

- ♯ She warms up with 5 minutes of shoulder rolls, neck rolls, articulator warm-up exercises, and arm circles,

- ♯ then does about 5 minutes of placement exercises.

- ♯ She takes a 5 minute break.

- ♯ Next she does scales in her midrange, then some staccato diaphragm exercises. (See Warm-up III.) This takes 6 or 7 minutes.

- ♯ By now she feels good. She goes back to the scales, beginning again in her midrange but this time going up to the top of her high register, coming back down and going down to the bottom of her lower register. She is working on expanding her range, and spends about 7 minutes here.

♯ She takes another break, during which she listens to some Miles Davis trumpet solos.

♯ Now she puts on an accompaniment tape and practices her scat singing for 10 minutes.

♯ Out come the songs she'll be doing for her next gig. She goes over 5 songs quickly - she knows them, but doesn't want to go all week without singing them. (Each day she does 5 different songs, so by the end of the week she has kept up a large part of her repertoire.)

♯ Now she drags out the new material she is learning. She's currently working on 3 new songs, each in a different stage of development.

♯ Her whole vocalizing routine lasts between 1 and 1 1/2 hours, including breaks.

♯ When she has the time, she divides this routine into two segments of about 45 minutes each - one in the afternoon, one in the early evening. She finds this places less stress on her voice than one session of 1 1/2 hours.

Robert has had classical training, and gets gigs singing at formal weddings, doing the tenor solos at classical concerts around town, and small parts in the lyric opera company. He sings regularly with the opera chorus and with a small, elite madrigal group. Although he sings professionally, he sees his coach at least once a month. This is his daily vocalizing routine:

⌒ He begins his warm-ups with various breathing exercises. 10 minutes.

⌒ He continues with 10 minutes of non-melodic vocal warm-ups, such as the "Ghost" and "Siren" (see Warm-up I). (Instrumental musicians in the halls of famous music schools have been seen shaking their heads in bewilderment, mumbling "Singers...", upon hearing some of the strange noises that come out of singers' practice rooms.)

⌒ He then goes into tone and placement exercises which he does in his midrange for about 15 minutes.

⌒ 10 minute break.

⌒ Scales. All kinds of scales, on all kinds of syllables. 5-note scales, 9-note scales, even 8-note scales!

⌒ Arpeggios. All kinds of arpeggios, covering his entire range. (He has waited until this far into his workout to go for his very high and very low notes.) -Another break, during which he listens to some of his favorite singers.

- Agility exercises. He wants to get more fluid and more precise in the very fast passages that some of his upcoming songs contain.

- Robert is working on a difficult aria for an upcoming audition. He now turns to this aria and works on it for 20 to 30 minutes, taking short breaks the whole time.

- He ends his routine with a piece he will be performing for a wedding in the near future. He already knows the piece and wants to end his vocalizing on an "up" note.

Amber is an actor who just landed a role in an upcoming musical. She has had voice training throughout her career, but hasn't vocalized in a few weeks. The last play she was in was not a musical. She will be going to a voice teacher twice a week until the show opens. On a daily basis, by herself, this is how she vocalizes:

♪ 5 minutes of breathing exercises

♪ 5 minutes of articulator warm-ups

♪ 5 minutes of bizarre sounds from acting class

♪ 10 minutes of placement exercises

♪ a 2 minute break

♪ 10 minutes of scales and agility exercises

♪ 5 minutes of exercises her voice teacher designed for her to strengthen her chest register, and 2 minutes of exercises to aid in matching the tones of her head and chest registers

♪ 2 minute break

♪ Now she works on 3 songs for the show.

Mike is actually a speaker. He is a professor, and regularly gives lectures to large groups of people. If the group is very large, he uses a microphone - otherwise not.

♫ He begins with the Lip Trill and Tongue Trill from Warm-up I. After doing these on no pitch, he then does them gliding up and down notes in a comfortable register. He then continues with the Ghost, Siren, and Rubber Lips (also from Warm-up I).

♫ The Diaphragm De-briefer from Warm-up II gets his blood moving and shakes the phlegm off his vocal cords.

♫ Next he goes up and down scales. He doesn't have a piano, so he uses a pitch pipe to get his starting notes. Since he's not a singer, he uses the singing segments as warm-ups, and is not overly concerned with some of the details professional singers must deal with. (Translation: He sings flat but figures hey, who's there to sue him.)

♫ He finishes with exercises from the chapter "Dynamics: Loud and Soft."

♫ Total playing time, about 20 minutes.

Karen has had voice training and sings a lot, mainly popular songs for parties, receptions, and in restaurants. Her main problem is time. She works a day job, but needs to keep her vocal instrument in tune and healthy.

♪ In the morning, she leaves hair conditioner on her head for about 2 minutes. During this time she does non-vocal breathing exercises (inhales and exhales from the lower abdomen, looking into her full-length mirror to check for posture, check her rib cage expansion, etc.).

♪ Waiting for the coffee water to boil she feeds the cats and does the "Diaphragm Energizer" from Warm-up I.

♪ In her car on the way to work she does the Lip Trill and Tongue Trill from Warm- Up I. She carries glass cleaner and paper towels in her car to then get the spit off the windshield.

♪ At home at 5:30 she heads right for the piano, before other distractions take her time and energy.

♪ She begins with a combination of warm-ups and placement exercises. (The "Hum Up, 'Nah' Down" exercise from the chapter on Resonance, Placement and Tone is her staple.)

♪ Next she does staccato diaphragm exercises (the "Diaphragm Debriefer" from Warm-up II is one she likes).

♪ Then she does scales, working on her legato sound.

♪ She finds arpeggios perfect for working on expanding her range, because she can cover large interval jumps in a single bound.

♪ She finishes with some songs.

Panic Attack: Who's Got Time to Do This?
Ideas from singers:

- Skip the television at night. Nix it. Unplug it and put it in a closet. Lock the closet.

- Hit the piano the minute you get home from work at 5:30. Stand there until 6:00, inspired or uninspired.

- Re-evaluate how you spend your time, as opposed to what your goals are. If you have time to vocalize but instead choose to re-arrange the furniture, you might explore the possibility of a discrepancy existing between your goals and the actions you are taking to accomplish those goals.

- Are you fragmented, depleted, drained, exhausted, and fried? Actually, sometimes an uninterrupted daily focus on singing and vocal exercises can help you re-focus; smooth out some of the rough edges. Often, singers will become so absorbed in the vocalizing that time ceases to exist - an hour flies by in what seems like minutes. This kind of intense focus can take our minds off daily problems, at least for that time. If an hour goes by and you're thinking of nothing but beautiful tone and flowing arpeggios, it's like a gift you are giving yourself: the gift of pure focus; the gift of letting go of anxiety for a time; the gift of beauty and personal development.

Frazzle Attack: Who's Got the Space?

- One singer who has neighbors who don't like to hear her vocalizing, goes to her waitress job early in the evenings and vocalizes at the restaurant before it opens. There is a piano where she works - but if there weren't she could always bring a pitch pipe. (I mean, you could get discovered...)

- A singer I know has the problem of the piano being in the middle of her busy house. There is not a time of the day or night when she could have the privacy she needs to stand there and make strange noises, especially since her kids are teenagers and think she is eccentric to be vocalizing in the first place. What she did was convert a small laundry room into a practice room. Other ideas might be to practice in your bedroom, or, funds and time permitting, to rent out a professional rehearsal space two or three times a week. Be resourceful - there is always a way out of the no-privacy-dilemma, even if it is singing in the living room and ignoring the laughing teenagers.

Lurking in on singing discussions on the Internet has revealed other creative solutions to the "where can I do it?" problem:

- ✓ One singer whose day job is at a bank, stays at work after the bank closes and vocalizes in the vault.

- ✓ Another singer, who lives in an apartment building filled with hostile people, has hung layers of heavy blankets on the walls of his music room. This has dampened the sound enough so that he doesn't get noise complaints and hate mail anymore.

- ✓ One singer, who travels and must vocalize in hotel rooms, sometimes sings into a towel.

- ✓ Some apartment dwelling singers are reluctant to vocalize, not because the neighbors are complaining, but because they simply feel self- conscious, knowing everyone can hear them. There's no way around this one except to realize that even though neighbors can hear you, most of them are not sitting there listening with rapt attention. The sound of someone vocalizing, or practicing piano, or violin, or whatever, is simply one of the many sounds of the cities. You'll blend right in. If you can't lose the self-consciousness, go ahead and feel embarrassed - but vocalize anyway.

Notes:

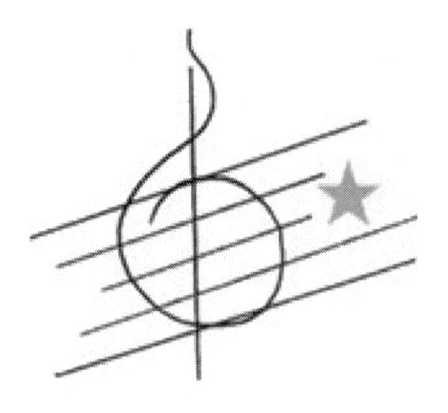

The Joy of Nonlinear Time

Contrary to popular opinion, I would like to suggest that the passing of time is not by itself a causal element of decay. A catalyst for change, surely. This is good news, because change is dynamic. And within this dynamic motion is the potential for anything - including the qualities that are the foundations of a beautiful voice - growth and expansion, fluidity, vitality, and a quality I like to call aliveness.

I personally feel, in my late 40's, that my voice is better than it was at 30, better by far than at 20. I can listen to tapes from twenty years ago, and compare them to recent tapes - and know that "time" has improved my voice. This is not sloshingly positive goo - it's real; I can hear it. Many singers experience the same thing. I'm talking about richness of tone, control and precision, agility, depth of emotion, and a confidence that can only come from experience. I'm talking about a voice that stays elastic, a mind that gets more creative with the passing of time.

To Expand or to Contract

As we go about experiencing our life situations, we can use them to expand ourselves - to broaden our range of choices, to grow, read, go out at night and hear live music, go to the theatre and ballet, take courses, join groups. Or we can react to life's experiences with contraction - by pulling in, allowing fear into our thinking, sitting in front of the television.

This is all about personal choice - it's not about how old you are.

And Now for the "Experts"

Another way to beg off is to believe what someone else tells you, when your inner voice is telling you something else.

There are those in certain professions who will tell you that technically the voice deteriorates with age, as does the body. Certainly at some point we do fall apart - after all, nobody makes it out of this particular gig alive.

But I have seen first-hand, and have talked to many singers about this, that up until we pretty much lose it completely, our voices can not only sound good as we age, they can get better. Not only can our voices get richer and more agile, but the way we interpret the songs we sing can only get more textured, more sophisticated, more worldly - with time. Nuances, things we know, feelings we've felt, complex emotional situations we've come through - become an intricate part of the way we interpret a song.

There are things a 50 year old singer can share with an audience that a 20 year old simply can't know. Jazz musicians know this, as do blues artists. How can you sing the blues, if you don't know anything about them? (And "experience" doesn't have to be horrible in order to sing well, either. The old cliché of the suffering artist is not a rule - it's yet another thing you can buy into or not, depending on your needs. There is joy as an option. Singing is a sharing of knowledge - even *My Favorite Things* from **The Sound of Music** requires life experience to be able to put depth into the interpretation.)

OK, reality check. Perhaps you can't become an opera star at the age of 75. But I personally know people in their 70's who have beautiful singing voices by anyone's standards, except possibly the Met's.

Be wary of nay-sayers. If you want to sing, at any age, don't let some party-pooper talk you out of it.

The choice to choose
The first thing we can do - and if you're 20, don't stop reading this chapter because at some point you're going to be 70, too - is make choices about how we will live our lives in order that our voices will be constantly getting more beautiful. Here are some of those choices:

> 1. The choice not to smoke. (If you're young and smoking, you may still sound good. But it will probably catch up with you one day, and your voice will be shot.)
>
> 2. The choice to avoid whiskey. Not being a scientist I don't know what it is about whiskey, as opposed to other liquid vices - but I have noticed that whiskey, specifically, can damage the voice.
>
> 3. The choice to vocalize every day. You know? I mean, this is it. Do it, or don't sing.
>
> 4. The choice to keep singing for other people. You can lose the confidence it takes to sound good, if you don't sing in front of others. Go out and put on a show at a retirement home. Do it for free if you have to, just to

keep singing. Put on a children's show at a hospital. Sing at open mikes or piano bars. Get gigs, even if you're 50 and you've never gigged before. Organize benefits for causes you believe in, and charge admission - you and our singing friends can provide the entertainment, and you can give the money to your cause. Get together with musical friends once a week and sing in your home. Join the church or civic choir. Sit in at a friendly jazz club, or sing with the band after hours. Mingle, baby, mingle.

5. <u>The choice to keep studying voice.</u> Even successful opera singers keep studying. Broadway stars go to vocal coaches regularly. Study at a local community college. Take private singing lessons. Sign up at a music school. If money is a problem, go to the library and get books and tapes on singing and practice at home by yourself.

6. <u>The choice to keep your body (which is your instrument) in as good a shape as is possible.</u> Work with your health practitioner to develop some kind of movement program that keeps you as fit as you can be within whatever physical environs you are working. I'm not talking about jogging in the freezing rain twice a day. I'm just talking about keeping the blood in some kind of motion, rather than having it freeze in a couch-sitting position with the potato-chip-filled hand half-way to the mouth. I'm talking about staying supple. It doesn't have to be a big deal.

7. <u>The choice to practice good posture and healthful speaking habits</u> as you go about your day. Perhaps "old" is not an age, but a posture. I've seen 25 year olds slump, mumble, and drag themselves around in an exhausted stupor. These people, bless their hearts, are old. (Although it's nothing that can't be reversed - and I'm not talking about illness or emotional problems - I'm talking about plain old slouching for no reason.) Conversely, a young person will sit up straight, stand and move in a balanced and energetic way, speak with clarity and compassion, and have been alive for 70 years.

8. <u>The choice to keep your mind supple.</u> Become devoted to knowledge, books, stimulating conversations. Read with passion about music and singers, the technical aspects of music, the history of music, biographies of contrarians, new musical trends. Another way to stay mentally supple is to keep learning new songs, think up different endings to songs you already do, try songs in different keys, memorize new lyrics. Keep those synapses flowing. Sometimes I get to a point where I think my mind won't hold any more stuff - but then more stuff gets in there, and apparently stays. I don't think there's a cap on how much can fit into our heads.

9. <u>The choice to keep the spirit within reach.</u> Where does music come from, anyway? What is it? Is there something that touches you spiritually about music; about singing? If so, don't let go of the pursuit of that elusive goal. Your spirit, your soul, is what makes your voice unique and gives it such a special beauty. That's what makes singing so joyful - sharing that part of your soul with others who would be receptive to it.

10. <u>The choice to eat only life-affirming foods.</u>

11. <u>Make sure that your voice teacher has your vocal health as a top priority.</u> You can damage your voice in any number of ways, including singing in chest register in too high a range, straining for high or low notes, breathing wrong, forcing a vibrato, singing with stress in your neck or throat. If you regularly leave your voice lessons with a sore throat, this is a warning sign that something is amiss. Talk to your voice teacher about it, and if necessary, find a new voice teacher.

12. <u>Pamper your voice as if it were a priceless treasure.</u> If you must use your voice a lot in your day job - perhaps you teach or talk on the phone a lot - do whatever you need to do to avoid vocal burnout, One grade school dance teacher I know uses a small, portable microphone system which saves her from having to yell all day long. Aerobic instructors often use these microphone systems rather than shrieking. If you talk on the phone a lot, try to talk softly and drink lots of water (no ice).

Notes:

Vowel Sounds:
Their Importance, Their Pronunciations
("The Rain in Spain...")

Goals:
1. To let the vowel sounds carry the melody of the song.

2. To enunciate each vowel clearly in order to achieve a rich, round, open sound.

3. To glide from one vowel sound to another seamlessly. The resonance as a whole must be even; the tone uniform.

4. If you want a luscious voice, obsess about vowel sounds.

Importance of Vowels

It actually does matter how you pronounce "the rain in Spain." Correct use of vowel sounds can make your voice sound gorgeous. Mutilating your vowel sounds has all sorts of nasty consequences, like dampening your tone, ruining your placement, and thinning out your resonance. (You were worried about thinning hair - that's nothing compared to thinning resonance.)

Try singing a short melodic phrase on the sound "ah" or "oh". No big deal, right? Now try singing the same thing through on the sound "t" or "b". You just can't sing a song on a consonant. Consonants are necessary in order to make actual words, and make the lyrics understandable. But a melody can't float on one. A melody can only be carried on vowel sounds.

Jaws II (Jaws I is in the "Articulator" chapter.)

It's easy to experience vowel sounds and tone being directly related to one another. Here's an experiment: Try singing a simple melody on "ah" with your jaw almost closed, like a ventriloquist. Now try singing the same melody on "ah" with your jaw dropped; that is, your mouth opened. Really opened. (Try fitting two fingers in your mouth sideways.) Did you hear the difference in tone? The mouth has to be opened for the sound to get out. Even if you are a master at diaphragmatic breathing, the sound still can't get out if you won't open your mouth.

Watch a singer whose tone is rich and round. Watch an opera singer. Watch a gospel singer. Everyone opens their mouth. (The image, however, is that of a relaxed, dropped jaw, rather than that of sitting in the dentist's chair gagging.)

Fear of Gaping
I've noticed that one of the biggest obstacles people have to producing a rich tone is also one of the easiest to correct technically - but not the easiest to get people to do. That, of course, is dropping the jaw. Don't forget, it feels like your jaw is dropped a lot more than it is. A mirror is a good way to check yourself.

"Ah" as a Reference Point
Many singers say that if they can get their "ah" sound happening, the rest of their voice falls right into place - tone, placement, resonance, the works. Some singers begin their daily vocalizing with work on the "ah" sound, just to get that reference point. It is considered the most difficult vowel to do - and yet once you have it, you've got a sound you can always work with. Here's a place to begin:

    a. Look in the mirror. Smile slightly. Sing "nah" as in "father" on a note in your midrange. Drop your jaw. Stick two fingers in your mouth sideways. (You don't need to throw up. What you want here is the sensation of how low the jaw can be dropped. Check the mirror, too, to see how low the jaw is dropped with two fingers crammed in there. This is a good thing.)

    b. As you sing lyrics and form the different vowel sounds, your jaw will be opened more or less than it is now, on "ah." But you want to keep this two- finger "ah" sound as a reference point.

    c. Lyrics in all languages have an abundance of that "ah" sound. It's a gorgeous sound and can be used, with the lowered jaw, as a standard by which you can judge the resonance of the other, less gorgeous, vowel sounds. When you sing a song, be aware of all the "ah"s in the lyrics and get the jaw opened for all of them. "Far," "farther," "father," "bother," "what," etc., are all words that easily allow for a dropped jaw. Even words like "love," "above," "sorry," that are not exactly "ah" sounds, can still benefit from thinking of the "ah" sound.

    d. Look through the lyrics of songs that you sing. See where you can really get that jaw dropped.

As you work with the "ah" sound, you will want to fine-tune your jaw to get just the sound you want. If indeed the jaw is dropped too much (yes, it can happen), the "ah" sound can fall back into the throat, giving you a "throaty" tone. If the jaw isn't dropped enough, the "ah" sound can be too thin. You may also notice that your jaw will be dropped to different degrees depending on the pitch. I find that midrange, my jaw is dropped the most, and in lower tones it's dropped the least. (Drop your jaw too much in your lower range, and you'll get a boomy or foggy quality.)

Haul your pitch pipe in front of a mirror, and experiment. Make notations to yourself of your optimal sounds and how they relate to the way you use your jaw.

The Jaw on Other Vowel Sounds

1) Try singing "The rain in Spain" with your jaw nearly closed.

2) Now try singing "The rain in Spain" with your jaw nicely opened, as in Julie Andrews.

3) Even on an "ay" sound, you can still get that mouth opened. Doesn't it sound better?

3) Try singing "ih" as in "with", and then "eh" as in "when", on a note in your midrange. Again, do it with jaw nearly closed, then repeat it with the jaw more dropped.

The Jaw on a Long Ee

But how, you are saying, can the jaw be dropped when you're singing "ee"?

a. Again, sing a note on "ee" in your midrange, with your jaw almost closed.

b. Now, sing the same thing, but drop the jaw. You can't drop it as much as you can on "ah", but you can drop it more than we do when we speak.

c. Although "ee" is a front-resonating vowel, you can still get a rich tonality on it. Experiment with jaw and placement, and get the richest "ee" sound you can - one that will blend nicely with the "ah" sound you've been working on.

d. Some singers use the mental image of singing "ee" but thinking "ah." This can round out the "ee" sound quite a bit.

The Diphthongs

No, it's not a type of bikini worn on the beaches of Copacabana. A diphthong is a sound - actually it's a vowel sound that is really two sounds. This presents some tactical problems for singers - so here are some guidelines:

1. Although a diphthong is two sounds, you only want to carry your melody on one of those two sounds. Usually it's the first.

2. Say or sing: "ay" as in "may"
    "oh" as in "so"
    "i" as in "find"
    "yu" as in "few"
    "ow" as in "now"
    "oi" as in "choice"
Can you hear the two sounds?

3. "Ay" is two sounds: it's "eh", with an "ee" clipped on to the end.

    "Oh" is "o" as in "dog", with an "oo" at the end - two sounds there, also.

    "I" (as in find) is an "ah" with an "ee" tagged onto the end.

    "Yu" is a quick "ee" with an "oo" at the end.

    "Ow" is "ah" with a quick "oo" at the end of the sound.

    "Oi" is "aw" with a final, quick "ee."

4. When you sing, <u>carry the melody on the **first part** of each diphthong.</u> Then clip the second part of the diphthong on at the very end, just before going on to the next word. The exception is "yu" as in "few," in which you sing on the second part of the sound, or "oo."

5. Listen to the great singers singing Italian arias. You'll hear all the vowel sounds and diphthongs just as they should be. You will of course modify the sounds to suit the style of music you choose. But a rich, round, lush <u>tone</u> is appropriate to almost any style of music, from opera to folk to jazz to pop to torch to Broadway to choral singing to novelty songs.

Experiment

Pick a comfortable note in your midrange, and sing the following lyrics, holding each for, say, 8 moderate beats.

"Brave" should be sung:
Breh------------------------------eeve.   (Not "bray----ay---ay----ee----ee----eeve")
1   2   3   4   5   6   7   8   1   2   3   4   5   6   7   8

"Going" should be sung:
Go--------------------------------oo-ing. (Not "goh------oh--------oo--------oo------oo-ing")
1   2   3   4   5   6   7   8   1   2   3   4   5   6   7   8

"Shine" should be sung:
Shah------------------------------een.   (Not "shah----ah----ee------ee-------ee-----een")
1   2   3   4   5   6   7   8   1   2   3   4   5   6   7   8

"You" should be sung:
Yee-oo--------oo--------------oo--------oo. (Not "yee----ee------ee------oo---------oo------oo")
1   2   3   4   5   6   7   8   1   2   3   4   5   6   7   8

"Found" should be sung:
Fah-------------------------------oond.   (Not "fah------ah------oo--------oo---------oond")
1   2   3   4   5   6   7   8   1   2   3   4   5   6   7   8

"Boys" should be sung:
Baw-------------------------------eez.   (Not "baw------aw------ee-----ee-------eez")
1   2   3   4   5   6   7   8   1   2   3   4   5   6   7   8

Guide to All the Vowel Sounds: Shades of Differences*
Vowel sounds are divided into four groups, based on where they resonate in the body/instrument.

-Group #1: The Back Vowels
- "ah" as in "father"
- "o" as in "dog", "fog," "Bob"
- "aw" as in "ball," "call," "fawn"
- "oh" as in "over," "so," "grow"
- "oo" as in "book," "took"
- "oo" as in "fool," "soon," "moon"

-Group #2: The Middle Vowels
- "u" as in "burn," "turn"
- "uh" as in "sun," "the," "fun"

-Group #3: The Front Vowels
- "ee" as in "beep"
- "ih" as in "with," "miffed," "skinny," "bit"
- "eh" as in "when," "Ben," "mend," "glen"
- "a" as in "pair," "hair," "air"
- "aah" as in "hat," "mat," "stand," "band"

-Group #4: The Diphthongs (combinations)
- "ay" as in "may" - sing on "eh" from Group 3
- "i" as in "find" - sing on "ah" from Group 1
- "oh" as in "glow" - sing on "o" from Group 1
- "yu" as in "few" - sing on "oo" from Group 1
- "ow" as in "now" - sing on "ah" from Group 1
- "oi" as in "choice" - sing on "aw" from Group 1

* I have made up my own "phonetics" here, knowing that many people are not familiar with the traditional phonetic symbols. If you know phonetics, write in your own symbols where they would be helpful to you.

Vowel Modification

Just when you thought you had this, here's a new twist. Although the goal is to keep your vowel sounds as pure as possible, all the time, there are exceptions t this rule.

Some voice instructors allow for what is called "vowel modification." On very high or low notes, for example, you may want to deviate from the pure vowel sound and go into a slightly modified version of it, in order to keep the timbre of your voice from getting pinched or stressed-sounding. We're going for an even, seamless tone. If you're singing the lyric "may" in a particularly high part of your range, for example, you might get a better tone by singing "meh" (which allows for a fuller timbre) and just thinking "may." If you think "may" and sing "meh," the audience will hear the "may." It's uncanny.

Exercises

NOTE 1: On all these exercises, begin on a note in your midrange. I have used middle C, but you may wish to start higher or lower. Sing the phrase as indicated, then take the whole phrase up chromatically, as high as you can comfortably go. Then go back to your midrange and start again, this time taking the phrases down chromatically. Don't try to reach very high or very low notes. Keep the range in your comfort zone. If you don't read music or don't know how to proceed chromatically, have your voice instructor or a friend show you how.

NOTE 2: Play with the exercises. Change the order of the vowel sounds - or practice the exercises using different beginning consonants.

NOTE 3: In addition to keeping the vowel sounds pure, don't forget to breathe properly (see chapter on breathing); and don't forget about placement. Placement and vowel sounds are inextricably woven together - a pure vowel sound properly sung is, by definition, placed properly. (See "Resonance, Placement, and Tone".)

1. One At a Time

INSTRUCTION: As you sing, keep the vowel sounds pure; keep the phrasing smooth and even. Remember that when you sing diphthongs, sing on the first part of the sound, then clip the end of the sound on just as you finish the syllable. Sing your entire range on "Mah," then start from the beginning and sing through your range on "May," and so on.

and so on, up as high as is comfortable, then work down.

Mah--------- Mah--------- Mah ------ Mah-------
May--------- May--------- May ------ May-------
Mee--------- Mee--------- Mee ------ Mee ------
Mi---------- Mi---------- Mi -------- Mi --------
Moh--------- Moh--------- Moh ------- Moh ------
Moo--------- Moo -------- Moo ------- Moo ------

2. Vowel Fever

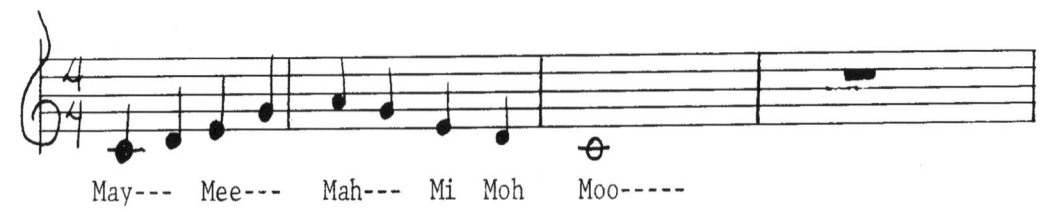

May--- Mee--- Mah--- Mi Moh Moo-----

INSTRUCTION: Keep the vowel sounds pure, the jaw dropped, the phrasing smooth and even.

3. From Ah to Ee

INSTRUCTION: Glide from "ah" to "ee" with as little jaw movement as possible. (But keep your body relaxed.) Feel the subtle shift in your resonating areas as the vowel sound changes back and forth. Keep the sound smooth and graceful.

Ah-----ee   Ah----ee   Ah----ee   Ah-----ee   and so on

4. From Ah to Anything

INSTRUCTION: Glide from "ah" to the next sound indicated, still with as little jaw movement as possible. You think "ah," no matter what vowel you're actually singing.

Ah - -oh   Ah - - - ay   Ah - - - - i   Ah - - - - - oo

5. Carousel Vowels

INSTRUCTION: Sing smooth, even phrases as you gracefully change vowel sounds. Keep the vowels pure and the sound seamless.

May---   Mee--   Mi----   Mah---   Moh---   Moo----   Mow---

6. Song without Consonants

-Take a song you know, and sing it, but leave out the consonants. Sing on just the vowel sounds.

    i.e. "Row row row your boat" becomes "oh, oh, oh, aw, oh"
"Somewhere over the rainbow" becomes "ah, eh, oh, uh, ah, ay, oh"

-Let each sound blend into the next, with the jaw fairly steady (and opened), and the tone consistent, except for the slight changes that must occur to enunciate.

-Make it smooth, seamless, and richly resonant.

-Keep the jaw open, and don't let it move too much. If it must move, just the lower jaw moves downward - <u>the head does not move at all.</u>

-Then sneak the consonants back in, keeping the mental image of the smoothness you had singing on the vowels only.

Notes:

Warm-up I

These exercises can be used:
1. as the basic beginning to your extended vocal work-out
2. alone as your sole warm-up, if you're in a hurry
3. as "on the run" exercises - in the shower, waiting for the rice to boil, etc.

Benefits:
a) warms up the vocal apparatus
b) relaxes and loosens up the body
c) aids in "reminding" the body/instrument about placement

1. The Diaphragm Energizer
This warms up, strengthens, and revitalizes the diaphragm and the muscles supporting the lower rib cage. It's a great one to have as a staple in your exercise repertoire. Basically, it's a breath in, then a hissing sound on the exhale.

    a-If you need to, first review the chapter on breathing.

    b-Place one hand <u>lightly</u> on one side of your lower rib cage and the other hand (lightly) on the point in the center of your solar plexus where your diaphragm is attached.

        ✓ Check out the diaphragm chapter if you can't find this spot.

        ✓ The reason you place a hand on the side of your lower rib cage and the other hand on the diaphragm is to monitor these muscles; to make sure they move smoothly and evenly. There should be no sudden or choppy movements. (Your hands should not "push" or "help" anything - they're just impartial observers.)

    c-Now inhale by gently expanding your ribs out to your sides and your diaphragm out in front of you in one smooth movement.

        ✓ Some singers say they feel as if the lower ribs expand outward all the way around their body, even in their backs.

- ✓ **This rib expansion is outward. It is never upward.** Raising the ribs and trying to hold them up will cause tension, fatigue, and flat singing. Try it both ways, so you can feel the difference.

- ✓ This muscular expansion will naturally draw the air in through your nose. (If you have hay fever, you have permission to inhale through the mouth.) Some singers say they feel as if the air "falls into" the lungs - they don't "draw" it in.

- ✓ Your upper chest should not noticeably move. (Although there's no point in being militaristic about keeping the upper chest immobile.)

- ✓ Make sure there is no tension in your neck, jaw, chest, arms, or knees.

d-At the top of the inhale, gently and evenly push the air out by "contracting," or pulling in your diaphragm. Exhale on an "s" sound, through your mouth. (It's a hissing sound.) *See item "h"*

- ✓ The hand on your diaphragm should be moving inward. (Again, don't use the hand to push the diaphragm - rather, use the hand just to monitor.)

- ✓ There should be no stop whatsoever as you turn over from inhale to exhale. If you catch yourself stopping there, or holding your breath even for an instant, stop and begin the exercise again. You can be militaristic on this point.

e-Listen to that "s" sound you are making. <u>The hissing should be soft but perfectly even. This hissing lets you audibly monitor the smoothness and control of the muscles on the exhale.</u>

f-Keep the diaphragm contraction smooth and even throughout the entire exhale.

g-When the diaphragm has pushed out as much air as it comfortably can, let the ribs then slowly contract to push out more air.

- ✓ Keep the rib action smooth and even.

- ✓ Stop <u>before</u> you run out of air. Be graceful. Don't end up gasping. This is not a fainting contest.

h-(If you're using the Modified Breathing Version, your diaphragm, <u>and rips will contract together,</u> evenly. But the hissing sound should still be your indication as to how evenly this contraction - this muscular movement - is.)

2. Lip Trill
1- Inhale gently as before.
2- On the exhale, make a trilling sound with the lips. (Sounds like a horse.)
3- Listen for a smooth and even sound.
4- Do this with no pitch. Just the noise of the lips.
5- Trouble doing this often means that you need more work on breathing.

3. Tongue Trill
1) Inhale gently as above.

2) On the exhale, make a trilling sound with the tongue. (Like a cat purring.)

3) No pitch.

4) Again, difficulty doing this can often indicate the need for more breathing exercises.

5) Some people have trouble with the Lip Trill and Tongue Trill because the noises are so strange that they are self-conscious. In singing, we do a lot of embarrassing things. This is just for starters. Might as well forget the baggage of worrying about how you look or what kind of alien noises you are making. This will pave the way for even more bizarre things to come.

4. Yawn
♪ This loosens up the back of the throat.

5. Ghost
1. Inhale gently.

2. On the exhale, round your lips into an "o" shape and, on a hollow "oo" sound, slide up and down your mid-range, like a child making ghost noises.

3. The slide is non-melodic. It's a glide. Think of the noises you made on

Halloween.

4. Keep the volume soft but the tone pure. Don't strain. Have fun with it.

5. The gliding should go smoothly up and down your register. Don't rush it.

6. This is also a great exercise for smoothing out the "break notes" between your chest and head registers. (For more on that, see the chapter on registers.)

7. Stop to breathe whenever you need to, rather than sounding strained by trying to continue the sound even after you've long since run out of air.

6. Siren

a) Inhale gently.

b) On the exhale, slide up and down your mid-range on an "ah" sound. Pretend you're a kid imitating a fire engine.

c) This "ah" sound should be pure; the jaw should be dropped. See the chapter on vowel sounds if you're unsure about pronunciation. Do this into a mirror to check your jaw. If your jaw tries to creep closed during the exercise, you'll distort your sound. The jaw is very sneaky - it does try.

d) Vary the pitch, but keep the sliding smooth and even. Keep your volume soft and your tone pure. Check to make sure there is no tension in upper chest, jaw, neck, arms, or knees.

e) No need to rush through the gliding. Take it slow, and savor the smooth, fluid flow of the sound. Stop and breathe whenever you need to.

7. Rubber Lips

1) If you need to, first review the chapter on correct pronunciation of vowel sounds.

2) Inhale gently.

3) On the exhale, speak the following syllables:
 MAY - MEE - MAH - MOH - MOO

4) Start slowly, making sure that "MAY" and "MOH" get equal attention on both sides of the diphthong (i.e. "MAY"= MA-EE, and "MOH= MO-OO).

5) Build up to a faster speed while still being true to the vowel sounds. (If you're slurring, you're going too fast.)

6) If you have time, do the exercise beginning with different consonants: i.e. NAY - NEE - NAH - NOH - NOO; LAY - LEE - LAH - LOH -LOO; PAY - PEE - PAH - POH- POO; BAY - BEE - BAH - BOH- BOO; etc.

8. Advanced Rubber Lips
♪ Do Rubber Lips on a comfortable note in your midrange, rather than speaking it. With each repetition, go up half a step. When you've reached your highest comfortable note, go back to your midrange and do the exercise going down chromatically with each repetition.

You've now got yourself a nice, workable, quick, effective warm-up. I hope you enjoy it.

Notes:

Warm-up II

The Warm-up II exercises can be used:
1. instead of Warm-up I
2. as a slightly more advanced version of Warm-up I
3. alone as your sole warm-up
4. as the beginning of a more extended vocalizing regimen

Benefits:
a) you've got to warm up the vocal apparatus before working on your songs
b) relaxes the body/instrument and, if done correctly, loosens you up
c) reminds the body/instrument about breathing, placement, and tone

1. Breathalyzer

What we're doing is simply practicing inhaling and exhaling. You might want to review the chapter on breathing before beginning. We're not producing sound on this exercise, we're just isolating and strengthening the muscles.

1. Gently place your hands on the sides of your ribs, as monitors - or, stand in front of a full-length mirror.

2. Keep the inhale gentle but full (although not overstuffed), the exhale relaxed but definitive.

3. The cycles of inhale/exhale should be smooth, fluid, circular. You want to feel your body as this magnificent, controlled, strong breathing mechanism. You want to feel a direct link between the movements of your abdominal muscles and the intake and expelling of air.

4. Remember, the process of rib and diaphragm expansion naturally draws

the air in. There should be no feeling of forcefulness. Some singers say they feel as if the air <u>falls into</u> their lungs as the ribs and diaphragm expand.

5. <u>The ribs expand to the sides. Never upward. An upward expansion will cause fatigue and flat singing.</u>

6. On the exhale, there is a feeling of concentrated contraction in the lower abdomen, but it should not cause tension in other parts of your body.

7. Check in the mirror to make sure
   ✓ there is no tension in your neck or face.
   ✓ your posture is erect, but not stiff (shoulders should be down and relaxed, arms loosely at your sides, elbows slightly bent to prevent locking, one foot slightly in front of the other to prevent knees from locking)

8. Do a mental "body scan" to make sure there is no tension elsewhere in the body/instrument.

9. At the end of each inhale/exhale cycle, gently and smoothly begin the next. There should be no starts and stops. Every motion flows gracefully into the next motion - like a dance. Never hold your breath, not even for an instant.

10. To avoid passing out, do this exercise for only a few minutes at a time. Take a break, then do another couple of minutes. This is a perfect thing to do during many of our daily "waits" - waiting for the tea to steep, waiting for the elevator to arrive, waiting for the computer to boot up. (You can't do it waiting for the light to turn green, though, because you want to be standing.)

2. Diaphragm De-Briefer and Pitch Precision Wake-up Call

♪ Now you need a piano or other reference instrument (a pitch pipe is fine).

♪ Begin in your midrange, say middle C.

♪ Sing the following arpeggio (or make up your own melodic pattern) on one breath, making each note staccato (short - see glossary).

♪ I have found that this exercise works best if I:

   ▫ keep the sound light, not heavy

♪ slightly exaggerate the "y" on "yah" and the "h"s on the "hah" syllables

♪ You can monitor yourself in a mirror or with your hands placed lightly on your ribcage. Some singers like to put one hand on a rib and one hand on the diaphragm.

♪ Even though you do the arpeggio on one breath, you should feel a slight quick tightening of the diaphragm on each note.

♪ This quick, light, almost sharp in and up movement of the diaphragm is the energy behind the staccato sound. You should feel a definite connection between the sound coming out and the motion of the diaphragm on each note. It should feel like the sound is directly produced by the motion of the diaphragm.

♪ Even though this is staccato, the tone you produce should be even. The interval jumps should be precise. (It's hard - you've got to hit the exact pitch with no time to waver. In other words, **the moment sound comes out of your mouth, it has to be on the pitch.** This exercise humbles the most stout-hearted.)

♪ Again, make sure there is no tension or movement elsewhere in your body. -After the arpeggio, go up a half-step and do another arpeggio on a new breath.

♪ Take the exercise up by half-steps, as high as is comfortable. Then go back to your midrange and begin again, this time doing each arpeggio a half step lower. Go down as low as is comfortable.

♪ I recommend recording this exercise and playing back each arpeggio - that's your best check to make sure your pitch is precise on the interval jumps. If you hear yourself go off pitch, even a little, go back and re-do that particular arpeggio. If you're in a hurry it's better to do one or two arpeggios and get them exact, rather than cover your entire range sloppily.

Alternate version:

[Musical notation with lyrics: Yah hah hah hah hah hah hah / Yah hah hah hah hah hah hah]

3. Legato Diaphragm

- ♪ The same arpeggio is used in this exercise as is used in #2, except that this time we do it legato (smoothly) instead of staccato.

- ♪ This time we don't feel the quick upward movement of the diaphragm on each note. Rather, we feel a smooth, flowing contraction of the diaphragm and ribcage on the exhale. This contraction continues evenly through the entire phrase. It should be one even movement.

- ♪ The sound produced should be smooth, the tone even, the interval jumps precise. Although the melody should be smooth, as opposed to the staccato sound from exercise #2, it's not a glide. Each note is articulated, though connected. (Glides were used in Warm-up I. Glides are basically pitchless; they slide. This exercise is not pitchless; the notes must be defined.)

- ♪ This is a great exercise to do in front of a mirror, mainly because it's one of the few exercises we actually look good doing. But also you can check to make sure:

    ✓ that your head does not move, or nod, as you change notes

    ✓ that your body is relaxed (except for the abdominal area)

    ✓ that your neck (or anything else) does not tense up on the inhale (Necks tend to tense up if you take in too much air. If you see the old veins bulging, stop and begin again.).

♪ Unlike some of the UFO-mating call sounds we make on some of the other vocal exercises, this is an exercise on which we can really sound gorgeous. Go for it. Smile slightly. Imagine an audience of appreciative well-wishers. Relax that furrowed brow. Enjoy the seamless beauty of your own voice.

Note: The apostrophes you see indicate where to breathe.

4. Placement Waker-Upper

a) This is a great one for most singers and speakers - but I have noticed that there are some who don't need or don't benefit from it. (As always, you need to tailor these exercises to suit your own personal needs.) If you find that this exercise makes your tone too nasal, or more "bright" than you want, just skip it.

b) For most people, this exercise will place your sound forward, and give you a nice, round, bright tone to take with you into your song singing.

c) Begin on a comfortable note in your midrange. Hum on "mmm," then change to "nnn," then drop the jaw to "ah." The sound continues uninterrupted through these three articulation changes.

d) When the jaw drops to "ah," you should be able to fit at least two fingers in it. If you can't, you haven't dropped the jaw enough.

e) You should feel a buzzing in the middle of your nose on "mmm" (you can even put a finger on the bridge of your nose and feel it vibrate); buzzing still on "nnn"; then a sudden absence of nasal buzzing on "ah." When the jaw drops for "ah," you still _think_ "mmm" and "nnn." Although you're _thinking_ nasal, you're singing "ah." Your jaw is dropped, causing the sound to actually drop from the nose and vibrate instead off the roof of your mouth.

f) The resulting "ah" sound should not be nasal in tone. Rather it should be rich and full, and forward. (This is a good "correction" exercise for people whose sound sometimes falls back into their throat, or who feel that their sound is too foggy or breathy.)

g) I know this whole thing sounds dangerously "nasal," but done correctly it's a mainstay of many good singers.

h) How do you know if you're doing it right? Second only to a voice teacher who is your best ear, you should feel and hear a beautiful tone on the "ah" sound. (Tape recorders on this particular exercise can be misleading, unless you've got a really good quality recorder.) It should be light and unobstructed, round and resonant.

[Musical notation: Mmm----nnn--------ah (repeated four times in different keys)]

5. Waiting for the Agent to Call

While you're burning your awareness into the telephone waiting for your agent to call, stand there and do the **Lip Trill**, **Tongue Trill**, **Ghost**, and **Siren** from "Warm-up I". If she actually does call, you can answer the phone in your now confident, ready to gig, most toneful voice.

Notes:

Warm-up III

These exercises can be used:
1. after you've become sick to death of Warm-ups I and II
2. alone as your sole warm-up (these are more advanced than I and II)
3. as the beginning to a more extended vocal work-out.

Benefits:
a) Better than a cup of coffee
b) Warms and loosens the vocal apparatus
c) Just as you wouldn't do aerobics without warming up, so you don't want to sing without a warm-up. It's just not healthy.

1. Count Breathing

→ Inhale to the count of 4. (You can use a metronome if you prefer, setting it to about 108.)

→ Exhale to the count of 4.

→ Inhale to the count of 4.

→ Exhale to the count of 6.

→ Inhale to 4.

→ Exhale to 8.

→ Inhale to 4; exhale to 10.

→ Inhale to 4; exhale to 12.

→ Keep going. Stop before losing consciousness.

NOTES:

♪ On this exercise, there are no pauses. If that metronome is going, every beat is accounted for. (i.e. Don't stop after your exhales. It's 4 in 4 out; 4 in 6 out, etc. with no missed or added beats.)

♪ You will notice that <u>you must consciously accommodate the intake and outflow of air TO the time you have to inhale and exhale.</u> This is a fabulous exercise in breath control!

♪ When you sing a song, you don't always have the same amount of time to take a breath. And singing each phrase in the song requires a different rate of diaphragmatic contraction in order to complete the phrase with enough air.

♪ This exercise requires you to learn to <u>gage</u> how much air you can take in in a specified period of time, and how much air you can afford to let out to evenly cover a predetermined length of time.

♪ Remember the primary rule, though: **EVERYTHING MUST BE FLOWING, SMOOTH, AND EVEN**. You can't gasp air in in 1 count and hold it for 3, waiting to exhale. You must bring the air in EVENLY over the 4 beats. And on the exhale, the air must be allowed to leave EVENLY over the specified number of beats. You can't be exhaling on, say, 10 beats, and find after 8 beats you've got no air left. You've got to gage how fast you can exhale in order to have the same breath control on beat 10 as you had on beat 1.

♪ As the months go by, see how far you can go with this exercise. Can you inhale to 4 and exhale evenly to 20? To 36?

2. Hum Up, "Nah" Down
This is a fabulous exercise for placement and tone. You'll find it in the resonance chapter - it's the first exercise in that section. For many singers, this is a mainstay of their warm-up diet.

3. Legato Vowels
Sing the following exercise as beautifully and smoothly as you can. Pretend the syllables mean something and there are people listening.

✓ Sing it slowly, giving each vowel sound its proper pronunciation.

✓ Keep your vibrato, if you are using it, completely <u>even in its pulsation</u> throughout the entire phrase.

✓ Keep your tone consistent, even as you change vowel sounds. Flow gently through the phrase.

✓ Don't let your jaw clamp up as you near the end of the phrase - keep the jaw open the entire time sound is coming out of your mouth. (Check in a mirror to MAKE SURE THE JAW DOES NOT CLOSE TOWARD THE ENDS OF PHRASES.)

✓ Don't let the breath and the sound "trail off" at the ends of phrases.

✓ Begin in your midrange. Take the phrase up by half-steps at each repetition, working your mid and then your upper registers. Then go back to your midrange and do it again. Now take the phrase down by half-steps at each repetition, working your lower register.

[Musical notation: Three staves with the syllables "Mee May Mah Moh Moo" written below each, followed by "etc"]

4. Breathe or Die

〰 Sing the following passage legato, on one breath.

〰 Remember to pay attention to vowel pronunciations.

〰 Also remember to keep your tone smooth and even throughout the entire phrase.

〰 Again, don't allow the jaw to close toward the end of the phrase. Keep it open until the sound stops! I've noticed many singing students whose jaw has a mind of its own - the landing gear comes out half-way through each phrase in this exercise, and the jaw begins its descent. It lands against the upper jaw, clenched happily and safely, slightly before the end of the musical phrase, providing a nicely stifled sound. The best defense: work with a mirror.

- Begin the phrase on a note in your midrange. Transpose up, then down, as described in exercise #2.

- This is also a good exercise for smoothing out the "break notes" between your registers. (See the chapter on registers if you need more information on "break notes".)

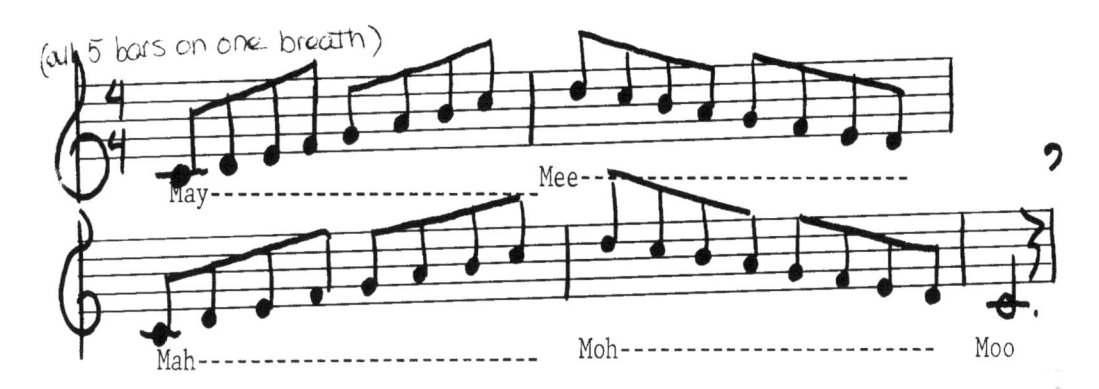

(all 5 bars on one breath)

May-------- Mee--

Mah-------- Moh-------- Moo

5. Flight of Fancy in "4"

* This is for agility and precision.

* Sing the following phrase as quickly as you can without slurring, without distorting your vowel sounds, and without going off pitch. You may want to start slowly, for accuracy, and then day by day go a little faster. Keep track of your progress.

* Begin in your midrange, and transpose up, then down by half-steps as described in exercise #2.

* Make up your own syllables, such as "Nah, ay...etc." or Noh, oo..."

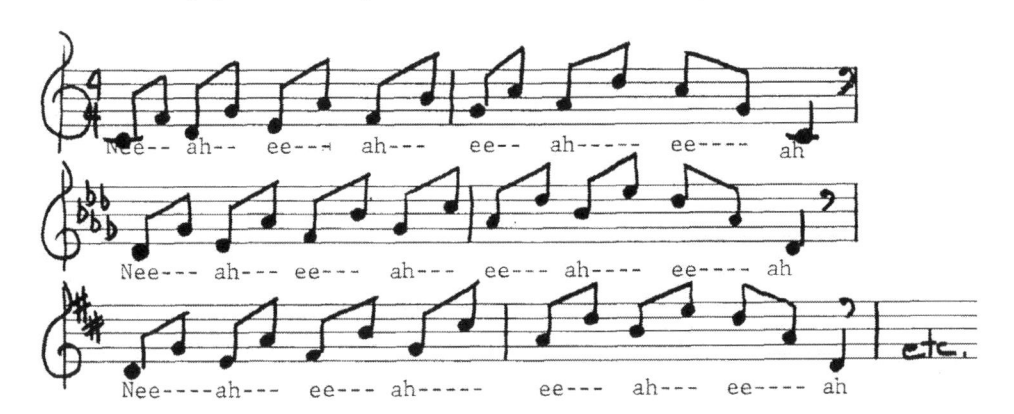

Nee-- ah-- ee--- ah--- ee-- ah----- ee---- ah

Nee--- ah--- ee--- ah--- ee--- ah---- ee---- ah

Nee----ah--- ee--- ah----- ee--- ah--- ee---- ah   etc.

6. Flight of Fancy in "3"

Same instructions as the previous exercise. This just works your voice a little differently. **Breathe only where you see the breath marks.** (NOTE: This exercise is called Flight of Fancy in "3" because it has a "3" <u>feel</u>. It's actually in 6/8.)

[Musical notation: Two lines of music in 6/8 time with syllables "Nee---- ah---- ee---- ah---- ee---- ah---- ee---- ah"]

7. Creative Flights of Fancy

Try composing your own agility exercises. Make up a complicated little phrase, like the ones in #4 and #5 of this warm-up, put your own syllables or even lyrics to it, and treat it as an exercise. Begin at a point in your midrange and repeat it, changing keys chromatically with each repetition. As with the exercises here, always strive for accuracy of pitch, an even tone, and pure vowel sounds. Start slow, and build your speed with patience.

Notes:

Made in United States
Orlando, FL
23 November 2021